THE MUSIC OF MANAGEMENT

To Seth on bass, Barry on sax, Mark on piano and Cheryl on point

The Music of Management
Applying Organization Theory

DENNIS R. YOUNG
Case Western Reserve University, USA

ASHGATE

Published by
Ashgate Publishing Limited
Gower House
Croft Road
Aldershot
Hants GU11 3HR
England

Ashgate Publishing Company
Suite 420
101 Cherry Street
Burlington, VT 05401-4405
USA

Ashgate website: http://www.ashgate.com

British Library Cataloguing in Publication Data
Young, Dennis R., 1943-
    The music of management : applying organization theory
    1. Organizational effectiveness 2. Industrial management
    I. Title
    658.4'02

Library of Congress Cataloging-in-Publication Data
Young, Dennis R., 1943-
    The music of management : applying organization theory / Dennis R. Young.
        p. cm.
    In the title the initial M's in music and management appear as musical eighth notes.
    Includes bibliographical references and index.
        Contents: Prelude -- First movement: coordination -- Second movement: motivation -- Third movement: finding and maintaining a niche -- Fourth movement: innovation and change -- Finale: achieving and maintaining excellence -- Coda.
    ISBN 0-7546-4134-1
        1.Management. 2. Organization. 3. Employee motivation. 4. Organizational change. 5. Organizational effectiveness. I. Title.

    HD31.Y625 2004
    658--dc22

                                                                                    2004046329
    ISBN 0 7546 4134 1

Printed and bound in Great Britain by MPG Books Ltd, Bodmin, Cornwall

Contents

List of Tables   *vi*
Acknowledgments   *vii*

1   Prelude   1

2   First Movement: Coordination   9

3   Second Movement: Motivation   37

4   Third Movement: Finding and Maintaining a Niche   67

5   Fourth Movement: Innovation and Change   93

6   Finale: Attaining Excellence   123

7   Coda   157

Bibliography   *159*
Index   *167*

List of Tables

1.1	Ensemble Attributes and Coordination	30
1.2	Coordination Strategies	31
2.1	Ensemble Attributes and Motivation	58
2.2	Motivation Strategies	60
3.1	Ensemble Attributes and Niche-finding	84
3.2	Niche-finding Strategies	87
4.1	Ensemble Attributes and Innovation	117
4.2	Innovation Strategies	119
5.1	Ensemble Attributes and Seeking Excellence	146
5.2	Strategies for Seeking Excellence	148

Acknowledgments

This book has been in gestation for a very long time, hence there are many people to thank who have given me feedback and encouragement over three decades. It is likely that the vagaries of memory have caused me to leave out some below who deserve my sincere thanks and appreciation. If you read this and remember helping me, please let me know and I'll include you in the second edition! The affiliations listed below are not all current, but they reflect where people were at the time they helped me.

In Stony Brook, New York where these musings began, I thank my former colleagues Joan Weinstein and Richard Silkman for their comments and suggestions, and Tom Sexton who indulged me and accompanied my ukulele playing at student parties. In the Three Village School District where my children went to school, I thank Frank Vaccaro and Donald Palmer of the Music Department for meeting and discussing musical concepts and ideas with me.

I want also to thank Richard Nelson of Columbia University and Harry Newstone, whom I met at the University of Kent at Canterbury during my sabbatical in 1981, for their feedback and suggestions. Also, thanks to Paul Judy of the Symphony Orchestra Institute for his comments, and especially Erin Lehman and Richard Hackman of Harvard University who have shared their materials with me.

Special thanks go to Peter F. Drucker for his comments and words of encouragement, and to Lance Buhl for his extensive feedback and moral support of this project. I'm especially indebted to Gary Ciepluk of the Music Department of Case Western Reserve University for reviewing the manuscript and allowing my students and me to observe his student ensembles and discuss their experiences with him. I am also particularly indebted to David Cerone and Frank Caputo of the Cleveland Institute of Music, Tom Morris of the Cleveland Orchestra, and Harriet Fader of the Diabetes Association of Greater Cleveland, for their reading and comments on an earlier draft manuscript.

I wish also to thank the students in my classes in organization theory at the Mandel School of Applied Social Sciences at Case Western Reserve University for putting up with my musings about organizations and music, and to the University at Stony Brook and to Case Western Reserve University for sabbaticals during which I could work on this project. Thanks also to Brendan George and Mary Savigar of Ashgate Publishing for their guidance in the final stages of this book, to David Billis, Mary Tschirhart and Melissa Stone for reviewing the proposal for the book, and to Caroline Saslaw for her help in preparing the final manuscript. A very special thanks to Linda Serra for drawing the cartoons and for her love and encouragement.

Finally, I wish to thank the members of my family for their love and support, in this and many other endeavors, over the years.

Prelude

Music is the key!

Music has the power to evoke all kinds of images in our minds. I can recall the incredible excitement of purchasing my first classical recording – Tchaikovsky's *1812 Overture* – and picturing the ebb and flow of the battles as I listened to it. As a kid who grew up in the 1950's, I admit that Rossini's *William Tell Overture* still evokes memories of the Lone Ranger, and I can never forget poor Charlie, riding the subway day and night, in the Kingston Trio's *MTA Song*. But as an adult, another picture came increasingly to mind as I watched and listened to musical ensembles perform. The picture was that of functioning organizations – often incredibly well-functioning organizations such as symphony orchestras, jazz bands or chamber groups in professional or university level concerts, and sometimes struggling organizations as in the student bands and orchestras in which my children performed in elementary, junior high and high school.

A variety of obvious questions came to mind as I began to think of musical ensembles as organizations. How did they manage to keep all those players synchronized with one another? How did they manage to motivate organizational members to reach high levels of effort and achievement? Why did each ensemble select its particular repertoire and how did it achieve its own distinctive style? How did ensembles change their repertoire over time and by what processes did new kinds of music come into these repertoire? And when you put it all together, what distinguished the best ensembles from others?

As I thought about these questions, I realized two things. First, these were highly generic issues of interest to managers of organizations of all kinds, not just musical groups. Thus, if musical ensembles could be made to reveal their secrets, the lessons learned might benefit organizations in many other fields of endeavor. Managers should be interested, no matter what business they were in.

Second, I realized that the answers to these questions would not be the same for all musical groups, as they would not be for all kinds of organizations generally. Thus, there were probably no simple or uniform answers to the basic questions; different answers would apply to different organizations and circumstances. However, I was encouraged by another insight as well – that the immense variety of musical ensembles did a reasonably good job of mirroring the universe of organizations in general. After all, musical ensembles came in a wide range of sizes, they encompassed a full spectrum from amateur to professional workforces, they played music of many different styles and degrees of difficulty, they ranged in structural complexity from simple partnerships and small group structures, to hierarchies, to conglomerates combining orchestras and choruses, for example, and they played in all kinds of environments ranging from intimate rooms, to sedate concert halls, to boisterous outdoor settings – even the mobile settings of the high school marching bands in which all of my children performed. To a social scientist, variation is the sign of a fertile data field. So what better universe of organizations to contemplate than musical ensembles, especially as the members of this universe are all so visible to observe and (usually) pleasant to listen to!

The present text is not the result of a formal scientific study, but rather it is a systematic discussion of management principles based on direct observation of musical groups, discussions with colleagues, and readings of books and articles on music and reviews of music performances by professional reviewers. The chapters represent the ruminations of a researcher and teacher who is interested in the management of organizations and enjoys most kinds of music as an observer (and rank amateur banjo and harmonica player). As such, I hope I will be forgiven for any egregious misunderstandings of the musical realm or the leaps I have taken in applying the insights of this field to the general universe of organizational management.

This is an experiment that I hope will work, but it is not unlike other instances where insights from one field have been borrowed to provide new ways of thinking in another. In organization studies, for example, a variety of cross-over paradigms have provided useful insights – metaphors ranging from machines, to biological evolution, to garbage cans (see Morgan, 1997). Nor is this the first time that a writer or analyst interested in organizations has evoked music as a paradigm for understanding organizations. Indeed, a narrow but widening stream of organizational scholarship citing musical ensembles has at least 60 years of history, starting with Chester Barnard (1938) who characterized full orchestras and orchestra-chorus combinations as the largest examples of "single-celled" organizations which he saw as building blocks of all large formal organizations. This stream of scholarship has continued over the decades (see, for example, Kaplan (1955), Sayles (1964), Weick (1973), Faulkner (1973), Kanter (1989), Mintzberg (1998), and Albert and Bell (2002)) to name a few, and it has received boosts from a project at Harvard under Professor Richard Hackman to study symphony orchestras as organizations (Judy, 1996a) and the advent of *Harmony*, a professional journal devoted to the management of symphony orchestras.

As early as 1980, management guru Peter F. Drucker invoked music as a way of thinking about organizations:

> We have learned in the last twenty-five or thirty years that even the medium-sized business needs a top management team, and that the one single 'chief executive' is not adequate – the job requires too many different kinds of temperament, has too many dimensions, and embraces too much work to be done by a soloist. The proper analogy for the top management job is the small chamber ensemble, the string quartet, in which each player is an equal even though there is always a 'leader'. (Drucker, 1980, pp.230-231)

And one of the more whimsical applications of music to organizations was offered by Monson in his analysis of a university:

> ...if a university is a chamber orchestra where different instruments produce harmonious sounds, then the conductor must be the president waving his arms enthusiastically, the first-chairmen must be the deans keeping their charges in harmony, the audience must be the students applauding on cue, and the discordant rehearsal must be a general faculty meeting! (Monson, 1967, p. 23)

In the recent genre of management books, the jazz metaphor has gained great popularity. Max DuPree (1992) used it to draw out general lessons for organizational leadership, while John Kao (1996) did the same for creativity in business. Indeed a whole school of thought centering on the concept of organizational improvisation has been built largely around the application of practices from jazz (Bastien and Hostager, 1988; Lewin, 1998; Kamoche, Cunha and Cunha, 2002).

The music-related analysis in the organizational and management literatures ranges from use of music ensembles as metaphors for organizations in general, to analogies between organizational and musical decision making, to the particular study of musical ensembles as organizations. The present work tries to do a bit of each. Most of the analysis focuses on musical ensembles as objects of observation and for illustration and illumination of organizational and management principles and relationships. But the analysis is framed in terms of general problems and conditions of management that apply to all organizations. The idea here is to articulate insights from musical ensembles that may provide new ideas for managers of organizations in other fields.

There may be some places where the music metaphor stretches a little thin relative to the strategic and contextual variables and management strategies highlighted here. For example, on the issue of organizational size, musical ensembles never really grow to the dimensions of truly large organizations in the worlds of business or government.

Hence, there is a substantial risk associated with generalizing to organizations where, for example, some members of the organization never ever get to see the top executive. Still, lessons from musical ensembles probably have relevance, even in this case. Such large organizations are a bit like ensembles whose conductors are remote and personally inaccessible. Additionally, large organizations that recognize the problems associated with remote leadership may benefit by trying to simulate ensembles by breaking themselves down into smaller units in order to reconnect executives and staff.

Another area where the metaphor may be somewhat strained is the role of section leaders within large, formal musical ensembles. In the analysis below, we liken section leaders to department heads in other organizations. However, section leaders normally do not have formal supervisory authority over members of their sections, like division heads do in various other kinds of organizations. They tend more to be the top players in their instrument groups, selected primarily for their individual performance skills, reflecting the idea of the "natural task leader" as articulated by Young and Colman (1979). Here again, however, this situation is not unlike the selection of supervisors in many other organizations, particularly in professional service organizations such as universities, hospitals, arts and social service organizations. Moreover, no matter how they are selected and what formal authority they are given, section heads are looked to for leadership, and they serve as eyes and ears for the ensemble's top leader. These aspects of the section leaders' roles enhance the power of this metaphor to inform understanding of organizations in general.

A third example is the analogy made here between the musical score that an ensemble follows in playing a piece of music, and the formal plans and procedures most organizations use to support their work. Some would argue that the musical score is more than just a plan or procedures manual, and is in some sense the product of itself – *it is the music*, albeit in written form. The same cannot be said of a blue print to assemble a car or a protocol to carry out an emergency rescue. While this point is debatable, it again points out that no metaphor is perfect or complete. Metaphors, as Morgan (1997) indicates, highlight some aspects of the phenomenon we are trying to understand, while they neglect others. But they are useful so long as they help us derive new insights that would not have emerged otherwise.

In short, no transfer of knowledge from one field to another is ever perfect. But most fields of knowledge fail to expand very much without cross-fertilization of concepts from another. I ask only that readers keep an open mind on how well the ideas found here travel to their particular organizational circumstances or interests.

The general approach to analysis here is pretty straightforward. First, I identify four fundamental problems of management generic to any organization. These reflect my concert-hall ruminations previously noted:

1) How does an organization achieve the coordination of activities and resources required to produce its particular products or services?
2) How does an organization motivate the people that work for it?
3) How does an organization position itself in the marketplace, e.g., vis-a-vis

other similar organizations, in terms of style, product, customer base, or other "niche" parameters, in a way that allows it to survive and thrive?
4)   How does an organization manage innovation and change?

These four basic management challenges are addressed in sequence in each of the next four "movements." The structure of each of these movements is similar. After describing the particular management challenge and putting it within the context of ideas found in the literature on organizations, I identify a set of management tools and strategies that can be used to approach that challenge. Such strategies include formal plans and procedures, communications, incentives and rewards, education and training, the practice (rehearsal) of routines, and developing the capacities of leadership. The manner in which such strategies address each management challenge in the context of musical ensembles – for example, how coordination is achieved with written plans (musical scores) – is then discussed.

Next, I identify a series of contextual variables that affect the intensity of the management challenge at issue. For example, ensemble size commonly affects the difficulty of coordinating or motivating the players. Other contextual variables include the internal diversity of the organization (e.g., how many different types of instruments), the degree of professionalism of its players, and the difficulty of the music it must perform. Each contextual variable is analyzed for its implications in addressing the management challenge (e.g. how does size affect the difficulty of coordination?), and the efficacy of different management strategies and tools are considered as the context varies. For example, I ask – how do the requirements for utilizing written scores, internal communications, rehearsals, and formal leadership, change as an ensemble grows larger or becomes more internally diverse? In the first three movements, I also examine a few cross-cutting issues organizations face in formulating their management strategies. For example, to achieve coordination, in what circumstances is central leadership needed, and to what extent should reliance be placed on formal written procedures? These cross-cutting discussions allow us to gain a deeper appreciation both for the possibilities of substituting one management strategy for another, and for the ranges over which different management approaches may work best.

In the fifth movement, I recognize that the four management challenges are separate, but not separable, dimensions of overall organizational effectiveness. Thus, this final movement asks how the challenges of coordination, motivation, niche finding, and managing innovation and change, interact, and what trade-offs may sometimes be necessary in achieving one dimension of effectiveness versus another. The movement acknowledges that the four basic management challenges each reflect an aspect of organizational effectiveness, but none alone fully captures overall organizational performance. Thus, I ask how the four dimensions combine for organizational success, and what indeed distinguishes a truly excellent musical ensemble, and one which maintains its excellence over time, from one that is ordinary or whose greatness is fleeting. The emphasis here is primarily on the latter. In particular, this movement revolves around the theme of "evaluation and adjustment" through which excellence-seeking organizations monitor their performances and try to improve themselves over time.

In each of the five movements, connections are made between different types of musical ensembles and various other kinds of organizations in the public, nonprofit and business sectors. This is done in three ways. First, a matrix analysis is offered which is designed to show the correspondence between various stereotypical musical ensembles and organizations in other realms. This analysis also identifies alternative strategies for addressing the basic managerial challenges for each stereotype model. First, an initial matrix is offered which displays how different types of commonly encountered musical ensembles vary in terms of relevant contextual variables, such as size, heterogeneity, professionalism, and so on. This matrix also includes nonmusical examples corresponding to each musical ensemble stereotype. Then a second matrix is provided which prioritizes the managerial strategies appropriate to each musical stereotype, and by extension, to other organizations that can be analyzed by drawing parallels to those stereotypes.

Second, as a way of integrating the foregoing discussion, each movement offers one or two case studies of nonmusical organizations whose experiences are productively analyzed using musical ensemble analogs. These cases are short thumbnail sketches of organizations that range from large businesses, to government agencies, to large and small nonprofit organizations. Third, each movement provides a set of diagnostic questions that readers can ask themselves, in order to think through the managerial strategies appropriate to organizations of particular interest to them, using the conceptual framework offered here.

Not coincidentally, the structure of this monograph is designed something like a symphony (albeit an extended one with 5 rather than the more typical 4 movements). (I thank David Cerone of the Cleveland Institute of Music for offering this comparison.) In each "movement", I revisit many of the same themes – the various management tools and strategies, and the contextual variables that influence the different dimensions of management. Each movement offers different variations on these themes, some themes receiving more emphasis than others depending on how relevant they are to the management dimension under current scrutiny. For example, formal plans (scores) receive more attention in the first (coordination) movement, while incentives and rewards are more prominently discussed in the second (motivation) movement. Internal heterogeneity receives more attention in the third (niche-finding) movement while organization size receives more emphasis in the fourth (innovation and change) movement. Just as in a musical symphony, however, various themes appear and re-appear in various guises, and all are present in the final movement, hopefully helping to provide continuity and coherence to the piece as a whole.

Finally, a word here about audiences. The book was written with three groups in mind – scholars, students and practicing managers. For scholars and researchers, the book brings together a number of important concepts from the organizational and economics literatures and tries to extend our understanding of organizations by viewing them through a musical lens. It sketches a theory of management that the author/composer hopes will be orchestrated more fully, improvised upon, fine-tuned, and tested for its resonance in multiple organizational and research venues.

For students, this book can serve as a text on management and organization theory, especially if this subject matter is taught through the device of metaphors. I have used this material in my classes for several years, with substantial success, but it needs to be tested with other classroom conductors and ensembles of students. Finally, I would be more than thrilled if students of music can also benefit from this composition in their classes on managing and conducting ensembles.

As Ron Heifetz (1994) suggests in his book on leadership, there are "no easy answers" (or singular answers, for that matter). Still, the present book offers a way of understanding the management challenges faced by organizations in a wide variety of circumstances. So to begin, you the reader may wish to think of a favorite musical ensemble – symphony orchestra, jazz quartet, folk band or even rock group (my tastes don't go far beyond the Beatles but that is my own limitation) that might reflect the character of an organization with which you are engaged, then tune-up and play along.

First Movement: Coordination

When I said start your attack, I meant the music!

In his path-breaking essay "The Nature of the Firm" (1937), Nobel Prize winning economist R onald C oase a sked a v ery fundamental q uestion: I f o rdinary market exchange among individual buyers and sellers can in theory efficiently coordinate the allocation of economic resources through the price system, w hy do we n eed organizations (Coase, 1988)? Despite the pervasiveness of organizations in the "real world", economists had no solid answer to this question until Coase raised the issue. Coase's response, which led to the development of transactions cost theory, was to show that in some circumstances organizations are indeed more efficient in coordinating resources and human activities than are individuals interacting directly through markets.

This interchange among economists no doubt seems terribly esoteric to those of us who live and manage in the real world of organizations on a daily basis. We take organizations for granted, and although we often criticize their performance, we rarely question the need for them. Think of how much poorer the world would be if there were no symphony orchestras and a hundred professional musicians had to negotiate with one another and with audiences of music lovers every time there was a desire for a classical performance! In point of fact, of course, some musical performances do take place more or less spontaneously – without much formal organization or planning, for example in "jam sessions" of musicians who have not previously played together. And the manner in which such ensembles achieve sometimes extraordinary coordination is a matter of great interest (Eisenberg, 1990).

Nonetheless, Coase's question is just as important in the practical world of management as it is among academic economists, for two reasons. First, it bids us to ask – when do we really need to invest in the infrastructure and overhead of formal organizations and when might we be better off trying to coordinate activity without them? Second, it encourages us to inquire further by asking the obvious follow-up questions: *in what circumstances* do organizations do a better job of coordination than market transactions and exactly *how* do they achieve that coordination? Coase's answer to the former question was more profound than his answer to the latter one. By focusing on the "margins" of organizational activity, Coase anticipated the "shamrock organization" that Charles Handy (1990) has written about, in which organizations downsize to their essential core (what management analysts called the "core business") and contract out every function which costs more to carry out inside the organization than securing it on the outside. Coase, and later Oliver Williamson (1975), also identified the presence of uncertainty as a key factor underlying the circumstances where organizations are needed. If there is little clarity on what precisely has to be done or how performance is to be judged, then it is often best to employ people within an organization under general terms of service than to undertake complex market-based negotiations with them for various hard-to-specify inputs and outputs.

While economists have offered important insights on the questions of why we have organizations and when they are more efficient than markets, they have left the remaining question poorly explored: Exactly *how* do organizations achieve more efficient coordination than markets? What are the specific means at the disposal of organizations that managers can use to bring about high levels of coordination? Coase's answer to this question was fairly rudimentary:

> Within a firm these market transactions are eliminated, and in place of the complicated market structure with exchange transactions is substituted the entrepreneur-coordinator, who directs production. (Coase, 1988, p.35)

In other words, Coase saw the achievement of coordination in organizations as the result of top organizational leadership. In the metaphor of this monograph – the conductor does it!

We all know that coordination is more complicated than this, and it is the purpose of this movement to explore the multifaceted ways in which coordination is achieved in organizations. Coase was correct in observing that the essential purpose of organizations is to coordinate human activity in circumstances where markets cannot accomplish this as well. Furthermore, the metaphor of music makes it quite clear that "ensemble" is not only the essential purpose of organization but that it is one of the most important criteria for judging organizational performance. To approach perfection as an ensemble means working together so well that all members of the group meld into an inseparable whole. This is at least one of the things that distinguishes outstanding musical ensembles from lesser ones.   Thus, when *Plain Dealer* music critic Donald Rosenberg cited the resurgence of the Berlin Philharmonic as one of the world's great orchestras, he noted "...the Berlin Philharmonic's seamless glory..." and observed that "...The musicians work superbly as a unit..." (Rosenberg, 1996, p.9D).

The achievement of coordination in organizations is complex in at least two ways: First, it involves much more than the work of Coase's leader, but also a host of other organizational elements and strategies combined in just the right way – organizational plans and procedures; communications and working relationships among organizational participants; education and training of workers; rehearsal of tasks and activities; leadership at several levels; and indeed a clear vision of how things should work.   Second, there appears to be no simple formula for coordination. Different coordinating strategies apply to organizations of different sizes, workforces with different levels of professional competence, missions and tasks of varying complexity, and different kinds of operating environments.

The fact that musical ensembles vary in so many ways provides us with the opportunity to understand how coordination is achieved through alternative combinations of strategies and in various organizational circumstances. We have the luxury in music of observing large and small ensembles, ones with homogeneous as well as heterogeneous instrumentation, amateur as well as professional groups, and ones which play numerous types of music at varying levels of difficulty and in more or less accommodating surroundings.   While the strategies for coordination may vary substantially among such circumstances, there are also a number of common elements underlying the achievement of ensemble, no matter what the situation.

The Elements of Ensemble

Even if we accept Coase's idea of the entrepreneur-coordinator as a key to organizational coordination, it is clear that leader must take advantage of a broad spectrum of tools to achieve this objective. These "elements of ensemble" include a variety of familiar components including the use of written plans and procedures, assembling a mutually compatible organizational team, facilitating communications throughout the organization, ensuring that workers are appropriately trained or educated, practicing key tasks and routines, and providing leadership guidance at various levels within the organization.

Formal Plans and Procedures

Give a group of competent musicians who have never played together a modestly challenging musical score that they have never seen before and they will sit down and before long be able to play the piece together reasonably well. The better these individuals are at "sight reading" the better they will play together right off the bat. To those schooled in the rudiments of music, the score contains the basic instructions for different players to carry out their tasks (play their parts) in tandem with one another. The score specifies what notes each player is to play at a given time and how loudly or softly they are to be played, it specifies the pace at which the overall piece is to proceed, and it even offers guidance on the overall mood or feeling that players should try to create through their playing. Overall, scores can be seen as plans through which organizational action (music making) is supposed to unfold over time (Albert and Bell, 2002).

Substantial coordination is achieved by a clear instructional score whose parts are given to players sufficiently schooled to understand those instructions and interpret them competently. The quality of the score is thus an element in the achievement of coordinative precision. Indeed, it was the need for better synchronization that initially led to the development of written music in the first place, as European musical compositions became more complex. Around the year 1000, the stave system was developed for choirs to help choral members sing the proper notes in unison. As harmony and polyphony were developed, written music was used to specify rhythm so that different parts, with differing note values and combinations, could be synchronized in time. Eventually, systems were developed to distinguish the time value of individual musical notes and later, time signatures to specify overall tempo (Gammond, 1995). The history of development of Western musical scores illustrates both the possibility of coordination without such a tool (early on, for relatively simple music), and the increasing need for this tool to achieve coordination reasonably well when the circumstances (musical offerings) became more complex. The history also suggests that scores in musical ensembles, as for written procedures in any organization, are never completely comprehensive or determining. In various ways, ensembles learn to use the score as a foundation and to interpret and supplement it as needed to achieve a desired quality of performance.

Indeed, in improvisational jazz (and other musical venues) written scores are often eschewed. However, this does not mean that jazz ensembles operate without "plans". In the jazz context, the "song" and its concomitant set of chord sequences, along with the basic rules of jazz composition, define the boundaries within which the music is played (Barrett and Peplowski, 1998). Playing without written plans does have important implications for innovation and other aspects of performance, but it does not imply the absence of a common set of guidelines and procedures, though it does put additional pressure on other means of coordination.

Communication

A well specified score is of limited value in achieving coordination, even to well schooled musicians, if musicians cannot communicate with one another. Musicians must at least be able to hear one another in order to play together. This isn't quite as obvious as it seems, however. If a group of competent musicians with similar musical backgrounds sitting together with plugs in their ears and blinders to keep them from seeing each other all read a fairly straightforward score in the same way they might actually have a chance of playing reasonably well together for some period of time. However, they would certainly have trouble starting and finishing the piece, and beginning and ending phrases, together, unless they could signal to one another or were prompted by an outside agent (e.g., a conductor or a metronome or blinking light) on when to begin, and they would eventually lose synchronization with one another as slight differences in individual rhythms led to larger discrepancies over time. This became Beethoven's problem as his hearing worsened:

> His hearing was never very good, but as it worsened, musicians began to dread his conducting. They tried ignoring him and taking cues from the head violinist, but he managed to interfere and wreck the performances any way. One time, during a long soft passage, which he couldn't hear, he lost count; when he jumped high for a loud passage, nothing happened because he was much too early for the volume change. Finally, his hearing became so far gone that all delicacy was thrust aside in favor of the music. He was asked to please go home and not conduct ever again. Which is what he did. (Carlinsky and Goodgold, 1991, p.90)

Saxophonist Paul Winter's ensemble successfully mastered another dramatic situation where visual communications among musicians was difficult, in the sixth annual Summer Solstice Celebration in the Cathedral of St. John the Divine in New York City:

> The stage remained empty as the performers played from secluded corners of this magnificent edifice. Mr. Winter's keening horn melded with the pipe organ, played by Paul Halley; eventually the pan flutist Damian Draghici and the cellist Eugene Friesen joined in. Niamh Parsons stood in the nave and sang a plaintiff verse. The church's darkness precluded a visual experience. (Powers, 1999, p.B5)

Clearly Winter's talented musicians were able to compensate for the lack of visual contact by their mastery of the music itself and their ability to hear each others' musical cues, in order to synchronize in the darkness.

Ensembles achieve internal communication in several ways. First, musicians usually do need to be able to see as well as hear one another. They tend to deploy themselves in semi-circles or other spatial arrangements so that there are clear sight lines between members. In smaller ensembles, players will exchange glances and give each other signals on when to start a new section of the music or how to stay with one another through a difficult passage or a change in rhythm or mood. In larger ensembles, section leaders and the conductor will be watched for the signals they send to maintain the group's coherence throughout a piece.

It is interesting that passages in many pieces of music are often described as "conversations." In particular, improvisational jazz performances are sometimes characterized as dialogues among players of different instruments, employing a common language (Hatch, 1998). This metaphor at once describes the importance of communication among players in achieving precise coordination and also a particular strategy of serial coordination. The allocation of responsibility to one player and then another for sequential passages helps maintain the coherence of the music by specifying who is in charge at any particular point in time, and what the linkages are from one player's part to another.   In such a serial conversation, the players actually communicate with one another through the structure of the music itself.

But communication in ensembles is much more than signaling during a performance. Significant discussion of how to play a piece usually goes on among members of an ensemble during rehearsals and prior to performances and understandings reached during such preparations help individuals players maintain ensemble with their colleagues during performances. Moreover, the importance of communication highlights the significance of longer term relationships among ensemble players. Players, for example members of the Chieftains Irish band, who have worked together for long periods of time or who are personal friends of one another, can achieve higher levels of coordinative precision because they know each other's thinking and playing styles so well. This is why personnel changes can be so traumatic for long-standing ensembles, especially strong chamber groups. The Juilliard String Quartet appears to have surmounted such changes. This group has played exquisitely together for more than 50 years. In 1997, it faced one of its most serious challenges when the first violinist retired, the second violinist took over the first spot, and a new artist joined as second violinist (Rosenberg, 1998e).

The benefits of developing close working relationships among members of an ensemble point to the desirability of selecting compatible members at the outset. Hence, an important element in coordination is recruiting individuals who not only have the appropriate complementary musical skills but who have the personal rapport that enables them to communicate and play well together. In an interview, blue grass banjo player Pete Wernick observed of his fellow blue grass band leader David Grisman:

> ...he gets called back for encores after playing a long all-instrumental set. How does he do it?   I can see that he starts with really hot players....whatever he plays, the instruments are going to have a great tone and he is going to ... make it sound good. I think he picks players that feel and *hear* like he does... (McKay, 1996, pp.15-16)

Education and Training

It is obvious that the rudimentary elements of coordination – plans and procedures, effective communications and compatible players who know each other – presuppose a certain level of competence on the part of organizational members. Indeed, the degree to which organizational coordination is achieved depends substantially on the competence levels of individual participants in the ensemble. This is not just a matter of players' abilities to correctly understand written instructions or communicate in an informed way with one another.   The more members have their own capacities (instrumental skills and general musical knowledge) under control, the more attention they can pay to the needs of the group, the more easily they can adjust to the idiosyncrasies of other group members, and the more they can compensate for possible weaknesses in other parts of the ensemble. Moreover, the more highly skilled the players, the more easily they can adapt to the overall style of a particular ensemble. This is especially true at the professional level where ensembles such as a symphony orchestras differentiate themselves by how they interpret the tempo and phrasing of particular pieces of music.

For ensembles below the professional level, the continuing education and development of individual player skills also contributes significantly to the coordinative capacity of their ensembles. Some of this development is in the hands of ensemble leaders who can teach and coach as they lead.

We can already begin to see the "trade-offs" among different elements of coordinative strategy. Musicians with enough individual training can walk in off the street and play together in a "pick-up" situation even if they have not previously communicated with one another or studied the score. Their level of education or experience allows them to catch on quickly to the particular musical piece, to player preferences and to inter-player signaling, in order to achieve respectably coordinated ensemble playing. As noted by Eisenberg (1990), this is well illustrated by musicians with a common educational background in jazz. Cross-cultural music making provides a dramatic example:

> Last week at the Kitchen, several Japanese musicians who had been featured in a weeklong festival of new music from that country took part in unstructured improvisations with various American collaborators...Japanese and American musicians who were grounded in jazz were able to play together naturally, developing group improvisations that had both variety and direction. (Palmer, 1987, p.28)

Rehearsals

In an old joke, a tourist asks a New Yorker how to get to Carnegie Hall. The answer from the wizened native is "practice!" That stricture applies almost as much to group as individual playing. All other things equal, the most exquisitely coordinated ensembles are those that spend considerable time practicing and discussing their music together in rehearsals. Rehearsals are opportunities to facilitate communications among members of the ensemble and to achieve higher levels of mutual understanding on the character and details of the music. Thus, rehearsals allow musicians to move into performances with a common strategy and set of ideas in their minds (on mood, rhythm, dynamics and other aspects of the music), and an understanding of each others' moves so that they can react appropriately as they proceed through the performance. Rehearsals also provide opportunities to work out difficult passages, detect and correct mistakes, and interpret details in the score that may be unclear, so that errors and misunderstandings are minimized. In any case, rehearsals are all the more important in ensembles weak in other factors that affect coordination. An experience of the Ohio Chamber Orchestra some years ago provides testimony:

The Ohio Chamber Orchestra took a ragged ride through a lively stretch of American history Friday night... The music ranged from Scott Joplin's rollicking piano rags to Igor Stravinsky's sophisticated take on ragtime.. the performance as a whole lacked balance and cohesiveness...more rehearsal time was needed by the 25-member ensemble, which contained a mix of weak and strong players who do not perform together regularly. (Salisbury, 1998b, p.3-E)

Rehearsals may be adjusted to the level of difficulty or familiarity of the music. For larger ensembles, there is merit in rehearsing sections separately from the ensemble as a whole. Overall, as the experience of the Robert Shaw Chorale attests, rehearsals can make the critical difference in achieving coordination:

...The first rehearsals [of the *Messiah*] were spent with each part alone learning the correct pitches. Later, pairs of voice sections were rehearsed, each part having the opportunity to sing paired with every other part....Shaw's sectionals served a far greater purpose than learning difficult passages. They provided opportunities to work on rhythm, blend, balance, intonation, phrasing, musical direction and line, diction, and all the other ingredients of "polish" that resulted in the universally recognized brilliance of the Robert Shaw Chorale. (Mount, 1980, p.15)

Again, it is obvious that none of the coordinating elements can be viewed in isolation from one another. A highly educated group of players who have worked together for a long time may need less rehearsal time to achieve a high degree of coordination, and they may be able to use rehearsal time more efficiently and move more quickly into discussion of larger concepts of mood and gesture than another group that has to work out smaller technical problems.

Leadership

Certainly Coase's idea that the entrepreneur/leader has a central role in coordinating organizational activity is important. However, musical ensembles illustrate the subtleties involved in this notion. In one sense, the conductor of an orchestra appears to be all-powerful. One wave of a stick and dozens of musicians follow by playing in unison. In another sense, the conductor looks silly – waving a little wooden rod that makes no sound itself, while the members of the orchestra do the real work, sometimes seemingly oblivious to the conductor's antics (or possible incompetence or incapacity – as in Beethoven's case). Indeed, guest conductors have been known to follow their orchestras rather than lead them, and some orchestras have even played practical jokes on their conductors, performing music entirely different from what the conductor expected when he or she gave the downbeat to start playing! This may be a good way for an orchestra to wish its conductor a happy birthday, for example, but the situation can be more serious than that:

Sir Landon Ronald was ... done in by a memory lapse. He changed a symphony program, subbing Wagner's *Tannhauser* for Mendelssohn's *A Midsummer Night's*

Dream. When he reached the podium, he forgot about the switch. Sir Landon gave the downbeat for the Mendelssohn. The orchestra started the Wagner. Sir Landon fainted. (Carlinsky and Goodgold, 1991, pp.88-89)

Orchestras often rise above those notorious occasions when the privilege to conduct is given away as a prize, or to honor a benefactor, or for entertainment purposes – as in the case of the late comedian Danny Kaye, who despite his inability to read music humorously led the New York Philharmonic through the works of Beethoven, Ravel and other composers on several memorable occasions (Schonberg, 1981). Other distinguished orchestras have been guest-led by such characters as Big Bird and the San Diego chicken (Carlinsky and Goodgold, 1991). Clearly, musical ensembles, even large ones like symphony orchestras, can coordinate themselves with moderate success using various mechanisms discussed above, without benefit of (indeed sometimes overcoming) central direction. In the early days of orchestral performance, such ensembles were led from the key board and conducting was not considered so important as to require someone specializing in that function alone. Only after music became more complex, and orchestras became larger, did the conductor's role emerge and grow in importance:

In the seventeenth century, it was commonplace to accompany voices with instruments and the job of unifying the forces had become considerably more complex. The [church] cantor ...would now direct from the keyboard instrument and beat time...[Later] Responsibilities for controlling the orchestra were ... shared between the *Kapellmeister* on the keyboard...and the leader of the all-important violins...the *Konzertmeister* .... They would dictate the pace of the performance together, the *Konzertmeister* using his violin bow. It was not a wholly satisfactory arrangement and, as the keyboard contribution became redundant..., the single figure of the conductor emerged to take sole charge of controlling the orchestra.

It was a change that coincided with the time of Haydn, Mozart and Beethoven. Haydn...directed from the keyboard....Mozart also led from the keyboard, but Beethoven conducted from a podium in front of the orchestra, often visually conveying the emotions in his music as well as the musical essentials. (Gammond, 1995, p.22)

Even in modern times, the role of the conductor retains some ambivalence. Notably, the Orpheus Chamber Orchestra is famous for its operation without a conductor altogether:

Orpheus...not only plays without a conductor but rotates among its instrumentalists the traditional leader positions of concertmaster and "first seat" players. [Professor Richard] Hackman [of Harvard] thinks that Orpheus has achieved its greatness not despite the absence of fixed leadership but because of it: each member is compelled to take personal responsibility for the music. (Traub, 1996, p.101)

All this is not to say, however, that leadership has no essential role in organizational coordination. For smaller ensembles especially, leadership is often combined with instrumental playing. Someone in the group is usually looked to as the leader and consulted for prompts and signals on when to begin, how fast to go, how loud to play, when to stop, and other nuances. Or, leadership may be shared in some agreed upon fashion so that responsibility for maintaining ensemble always lies somewhere. Orpheus, for example, does not lack leadership, but leadership in that ensemble is a shared, collegial responsibility:

> ...Orpheus developed a system it calls "the core", in which the executive committee chooses a concertmaster, and each instrumental section a representative, for every piece... [W]hile Orpheus is a conductorless orchestra, it is not... "a leaderless orchestra." There is leadership, but it changes from piece to piece, and even *within* a piece. The trick that Orpheus has pulled off is to establish authority without establishing an authority figure. (Traub, 1996, pp.102, 104)

In the Orpheus system, the concertmaster is key:

> The person manages the rehearsal process for that piece – beginning each rehearsal, fielding suggestions from members about interpretive matters, deciding when spirited disagreements among members must be set aside to get on with the rehearsal, and taking the lead in figuring out how to handle transitions in the music that in a traditional orchestra would be signaled by a conductor's baton. (Hackman, 2002, p.194)

Even where there is a central leader or conductor, which is the normal situation for larger ensembles, leadership is also distributed throughout the organization. Instrumental sections – strings, horns, woodwinds, percussion – can each have their leaders. Indeed, the breaking down of the large ensemble into smaller, more homogenous units which can be more easily refined and coordinated internally and then connected with the playing of the whole group, is a key element in achieving a high level of organizational coordination. (That is one reason why Mount (1980) argued for sectional rehearsals.) Finally, individual virtuoso performers – a lead violin, clarinet, or trumpet or a singer or piano soloist – also take leadership in particular parts of musical compositions, where the soloist sets the pace and expects the ensemble (often even the conductor) to follow. Usually this works out well; sometimes it doesn't. In one concert in Ohio, the piano soloist was so fast, furious and unpredictable that the Cleveland Orchestra and its renowned conductor did all it could to stay with him much less polish the performance (Rosenberg, 1998c, p.4-E). By contrast, the careful attention which the accomplished piano soloist and the conductor of an orchestra in Michigan paid to each other led to a fine overall performance (Page, 1992, p.21).

What is it that leaders actually do in helping an ensemble achieve coordination? Faulkner (1973) cites the conductor's responsibility to set the tempo and maintain "proper ensemble and balances." (p.149) Gammond (1995) sums up the role of a conductor as providing four sets of instructions: tempo, dynamics (the volume of the sound), *rubata* or changes in tempo, and phrasing (indicating where to give emphasis so as to interpret the composer's intent). More dramatically, the *Oxford Companion to Music* (1970) asserts that "Conducting is generalship on the battlefield of music. Forces often large and very varied in their functions, have to be so controlled that they will combine together not only accurately but with unity of spirit" (p.240).

As the functions of *rubata* and phrasing suggest, while the score normally contains instructions about tempo and dynamics, this information may not be precise and may be subject to interpretation or adaptable to different tastes:

> The art of conducting, Mr. [Ilya] Musin said, lay in "making music visible with your hands". A conductor "must have expressiveness and exactness", he continued. "These are incompatible. The conductor's challenge, therefore, is to find a way of combining them." (New York Times Obituaries, 1999, p.A21)

Leaders help provide that interpretation and translate the general instructions about tempo into a specific pace at any given point in the performance. Obviously, there must be clarity about tempo in order to achieve a coherent, coordinated performance, although this clarity may be achieved either by conductor specification or by consensus among ensemble leaders and players. It serves no purpose to have different sections playing at different tempos unless this is a specific part of the plan! Interestingly, however, differential rhythms *are* sometimes part of the plan just as they are in nonmusical organizations. For example, the tempo in a large corporation of the basic research department, which must painstakingly advance the state of knowledge of a given technology, will differ substantially from that of the marketing or sales departments which must respond to current market conditions.

Multiple tempos obviously make the challenge of coordination all the more difficult. Here's how the Orpheus Chamber Orchestra grappled successfully with the challenge of a multi-tempo piece:

> ...Lee Hyla's "Trans" still had everyone in knots... "Trans" seemed to be testing the limits of the conductorless orchestra....[Hyla] had responded to the Orpheus commission by writing a piece that most conductors couldn't have handled properly, because of the difficulty of beating out two tempos at once. But he wasn't worried about the outcome. "They're such unbelievably professional musicians as well as good musicians", Hyla said. (Traub, 1996, p.105)

Interestingly, while leadership becomes increasingly important in such situations of great complexity, the Orpheus example also shows the advantages of distributed leadership to handle parallel challenges more easily by sharing responsibilities. In particular, in addition to relying on a concertmaster for any particular piece, Orpheus constitutes a "core group", consisting of principal players involved in the piece, whose function is to work out problems in advance and then to coach the rest of the ensemble on the nuances:

> The core meets prior to the first full-orchestra rehearsal to work out the basic frame for the piece being prepared. Then, when the rest of the orchestra joins in, these individuals have special responsibility for helping other members of their sections understand and implement the ideas the core has roughed out. (Hackman, 2002, p. 122)

Similar challenges are associated with leadership's role in controlling the dynamics of a performance. Dynamics not only involve modulating the sheer volume of sound over the course of a performance, but also coordinating the "balance" among relative contributions of the different sections and instruments at any given point in a musical piece. If the volume of the different instruments is not coordinated to ensure that they are heard in correct proportions, the piece as a whole will sound distorted. The melody in the string section may be drowned out by overplaying of the percussion instruments, or the delicate flute sounds may be overwhelmed by the horns. Leadership helps to specify and signal the relative contributions of different instruments at different times, and sectional leadership may be needed to maintain the proper levels within instrument groupings. Balance is also achieved by specifying the appropriate spatial layout of instrument sections, relative to one another. For example, low brass and percussion instruments are deployed towards the rear of a symphony orchestra so as not to drown out the more delicate sounds of strings and woodwinds.

Leadership helps to achieve coordination in other ways as well. As mentioned earlier, leaders give cues to instruct players on when to begin specific parts of the score so that all instruments start together. And leaders may detect and correct errant playing (hopefully at the rehearsal rather than performance stage!) In particular, leaders must ensure not only that correct notes are being played by all members but that everyone is interpreting the rhythmic instructions of the score in the same manner. Particularly at the amateur level, good leaders must be good teachers. Part of the work of both central and sectional leaders is to monitor the playing and to make corrections and adjustments as needed to ensure that all of the parts fit appropriately into the whole.

In all, there is no question that leaders make a difference in how well ensembles are coordinated, and indeed, in precisely how they utilize all of the mechanisms of coordination to achieve ensemble. Given the same score, for example, orchestras led by different leaders may produce very different results:

> The two Schubert performances could be described in terms of "more" and "less". Dohnanyi's account was more lithe and propulsive. Masur was less extreme in dynamics but more extreme in tempo and weight. The Cleveland performance was almost four minutes faster than the Philharmonic's, partly because Masur took a repeat in the Scherzo that Dohnanyi omitted. (Rosenberg, 1997a, p.5-B)

In summary, formal plans and procedures, communication, player compatibility, education and training, rehearsal and leadership are the key components, which in various combinations permit musical ensembles to coordinate their work efficiently. Moreover, these various elements complement one another over broad ranges of operation, so that a de-emphasis of one can often be suitably compensated by greater stress on another. The variety of circumstances in which organizations must achieve coordination, and the ways in which various means of coordination can be used in different combinations, are subjects to which we turn next.

The Circumstances of Coordination

Organizations differ substantially from one another in several ways that make coordination more or less difficult.   In this section, we examine five such dimensions – the size of an organization, its internal complexity or heterogeneity, the level of competence and professionalism of its workforce, the stability of its workforce, and the complexity or level of difficulty of the work the organization must perform.

Size

Larger organizations are generally more difficult to coordinate than smaller ones. Duets can coordinate themselves by simple communication between the two players. Chamber music ensembles, ranging in size from two to ten players, can work well without formal leadership; indeed chamber music is renowned for its democratic, nonhierarchical culture in which authority is distributed among players as needed.   In the 1980's, the Emerson Quartet was on the cutting edge in this respect:

> The members of the quartet have an innovative and, they believe, unprecedented approach toward internal hierarchy: Mr. Setzer and Mr. Drucker alternate in the first violin chair, changing during nearly every concert. Thus, the Emerson Quartet lacks a "second fiddle". However, certain strictures are observed. Each composition belongs exclusively to one musician – Mr. Setzer always plays first violin in Beethoven's Quartet in A minor (Op.132), for example, while Mr. Drucker plays first in the same composer's Quartet in E flat (Op.127). The six Bartok Quartets are equally divided. Mr. Drucker plays first violin in Debussy's Quartet, while the Ravel Quartet belongs to Mr. Setzer. (Page, 1984, p.H21)

Of course, one should not discount the possibility of breakdowns occurring in small, democratic ensembles. Young and Colman (1979) point out that "lasting deadlocks" can occur especially in even-numbered groups and that ensembles of four members are particularly vulnerable.   Such explicit conflict situations notwithstanding, larger ensembles require a fuller array of coordinative mechanisms and more intense application of those mechanisms, than smaller ensembles.   For example, symphony orchestras rarely if ever forgo having a conductor or allow players to perform without their parts of the musical score in front of them, although it is less rare for conductors to eschew using scores themselves.

Heterogeneity

More heterogeneous organizations are more difficult to coordinate than homogeneous ones. A men's chorus singing Gregorian chants has but one melody and one type of instrumentation to coordinate. Everyone has the same part and it takes just one set of instructions to keep them together. An orchestra of the same size is more complex; it has different types of instruments playing various parts that must dovetail with one another. A homogeneous chorus, even a sizeable one, may achieve coordination with a single choral leader and a simple score. A symphony orchestra requires a multi-part score, sectional as well as central leadership, and more practice, educational preparation and internal communication to make it work reasonably well. At the extreme, imagine the challenges of both size and heterogeneity that confronted the Cleveland Orchestra playing Mahler's Eighth Symphony:

> Gustav Mahler's Symphony No.8 stretches the resources of orchestras, choruses and vocal soloists like few pieces in the symphonic repertoire....[Robert] Shaw and the [Cleveland] orchestra transported the eighth to Carnegie Hall for the first of two performances that are sure to go into the Carnegie history books as colossal events. Where Severance [Hall in Cleveland] claimed close to 450 performers, Carnegie had nearly 700, including five choral ensembles... What a spectacle it was. The 562 choral voices belonged to the Atlanta Symphony Orchestra Chorus, Cleveland Orchestra Chorus, Cincinnati May Festival Chorus, Oberlin College Choir, and American Boychoir. Shaw, the choral magician, had taken only two days to transform these groups into a mighty aggregate of singers capable of roaring or scaling their voices to an almost imperceptible hush. (Rosenberg, 1995, p.12-E)

Shaw's leadership and his mastery of rehearsal strategies, as well as the competence of the various ensemble components, were obviously essential elements for successfully coordinating this very complex, heterogeneous mega-ensemble.

Professionalism

Organizations with more highly trained workforces are less difficult to coordinate than ones with more amateur, less schooled participants. Getting a grade school orchestra to play together is far more challenging than maintaining the ensemble of a professional orchestra. Ask any music teacher! Nor is this a matter of age or maturity alone, as the same can be said of coordinating an adult amateur group versus a professional one. Consider the experience of the Retired Men's Chorus in Yarmouthport, Massachusetts:

> The chorus has also had its share of concert mishaps. Sometimes, the group's director, Danny Rowntree, will signal the end of a song and a few men will keep singing. Once in the middle of [a] concert, "We were singing 'Let Me Call You Sweetheart' [and] we had to stop and start over," Mr. Schmitt [a member of the chorus] recalled. "But we had a lot of fun over it." (New York Times, 1987, p.51)

Professionals have their own sense of what is needed to make the whole operation work, they have internal standards developed through their individual educational and work experiences, and they have the technical preparation to understand and utilize the various elements of coordination (plans, communications, rehearsals, leadership signals, and so on) more effectively. Still, raw, motivated talent and nurturing leadership can often substantially overcome the skill limitations of amateur groups. The Cleveland Orchestra Youth Orchestra is one example of an ensemble with superb but unpolished young talent which has achieved great precision and performance quality, in challenging pieces such as Dvorak's Eight Symphony, under the guidance of a skilled conductor-teacher such as Steven Smith (Rosenberg, 1998d).

Instability

Coordination is less difficult to achieve in stable organizations where personnel turnover is low than in organizations where transience is high. This is a particularly sensitive area for musical ensembles, in several respects. First, it is the relatively rare ensemble that has sufficient financial support to be able to employ its members on a full time basis. Thus, there is always pressure for members to move in and out of different groups, following their individual artistic and economic interests. Second, in this dynamic environment, ensembles may make frequent use of "pickup" musicians who have particular instrumental talents but are not affiliated with any one particular organization. Third, for symphony orchestras at least, the "star system" that makes celebrities of famous conductors, leads to frequent changes of leadership. Many concerts are led by guest conductors, and some orchestras work with their own music directors relatively infrequently. These various manifestations of transience make the task of coordination more difficult because players do not get to know each other very well and may fail to develop close relationships with their leaders. As a result, communications are more difficult, signals and styles of operation must be relearned each time there is a change of personnel, and rehearsals must revisit the same ground more often. Ensembles that have enjoyed long term stability of personnel and have worked together intensely over a long a period of time have an advantage. The Guarneri String Quartet, for example, having played together for decades, achieved technical mastery over an impressive repertoire (Rosenberg, 1994c). Even a larger ensemble such as the Orpheus Chamber Orchestra benefits greatly from the fact that most of its players have worked together for years (Hackman, 2002).

Task Complexity

Organizations differ widely in the complexity of the work they must perform, and complexity is a major challenge to coordination. Certain kinds of organizations are, of course, better adapted to taking on highly complex assignments while others are better suited for simpler tasks. Professional symphony orchestras are more likely to be at home with the difficult compositions of Mahler, Shostakovich or Schoenberg, while amateur or high school groups are usually better advised to stick to a relatively more straightforward repertory. Fast and intricate music, with rapidly changing or unfamiliar tempos, rhythms, harmonies and keys will require not only ensembles with greater professional training, but more intensive use of other coordinative mechanisms as well – more intensive rehearsals, closer communication among members, more careful study of the score, and so on. Even with all this, however, the results may be imperfect if the challenge is strong enough. Even the Cleveland Orchestra continues to search for answers in pieces such as Charles Ives' "The Unanswered Question" even though they have played it many times (Rosenberg, 1998f).

Another aspect of task complexity is uncertainty. In certain musical situations, for example, the road map for performance is not well specified. Improvisational jazz ensembles, for example, may specify a particular song and even know generally how they intend to play it, but they determine on the spot exactly who will play what at any given time. Such ambiguity is an inherent part of the nature of certain kinds of work that cannot be completely preprogrammed for fear of losing some its special quality. Here, coordination is difficult because it must be achieved on a dynamic basis. In such circumstances, greater reliance on certain mechanisms such as communication and education may have to compensate for less dependence on formal plans, rehearsals or central leadership. Consider the difficulty Charles Ives's music has posed even for accomplished symphony orchestras:

> [Ives is] a composer apparently throwing craft to the wind, jumbling mismatched rhythms, keys and tunes against one another, exalting the fragmentary, and leaving all sorts of coordinations to work themselves out as best they may in performance. To invite the indiscipline, chaos and contradictions of experience into music – to give them so dramatic and visceral a presence – had to seem in some measure an affront. (Crutchfield, 1987b, pp.19,22)

In summary, coordination is more difficult in organizations that are larger in size, more heterogeneous in their internal composition, have lower levels of professional training in their workforce, have more transient work forces, and must perform work of greater complexity or ambiguity. The more intense these factors, the more heavily organizations must depend on each of the various mechanisms of coordination to achieve satisfactory ensemble. Moreover, the most effective combinations of the elements of coordination may vary with the situation. Indeed, some of the most interesting issues of coordination can be framed in terms of choosing the appropriate combinations of means of coordination under different circumstances.

Strategic Combinations for Achieving Ensemble

Suppose a maestro was commissioned by a "World Music Collegium" to advise all sorts of musical ensembles on how to coordinate themselves as well as possible. That maestro would have quite a problem. He would operate in a universe of ensembles that varies greatly along each of the five dimensions of coordinative challenge (size, heterogeneity, professionalism, instability, and task complexity).

Yet, the maestro would also have impressive tools at his disposal. He would carry in his portfolio infinite solution possibilities, consisting of adjustable quantities of each of the key elements of coordination (plans and procedures, communication, education, rehearsal, leadership) which can be used in varying combinations with one another. For each ensemble, the maestro would ask what particular combination of elements would come closest to achieving perfect ensemble. The answer in each case would obviously depend on the particular nature of the band or orchestra, its operating circumstances, and the music it is called upon to perform.

Like any other human being, the maestro would have great difficulty contemplating the infinity of combinations of organizational circumstances and coordinative solutions. But he would also discover that certain kinds of cross-cutting questions arise frequently, and that addressing these questions can provide guidance to broad clusters of his organizational clients. In particular, when is a central leader really necessary? And, when should an organization rely on a written plan versus other means of coordination?

When Is Formal Leadership Really Needed?

It is especially interesting to ask this question about musical ensembles of different sizes. In smaller ensembles, communications and practice can go a long way towards achieving a high degree of coordination without having to delegate one of the group members as the formal leader. Indeed, one of the attractions of small organizations (chamber groups) is the egalitarian environment that it can sustain without loss of coordinative benefits. In larger ensembles, some manner of formal leadership must emerge if only to ensure that signals on "what to do when" are not lost in a cacophony of competing voices. There is no clear watershed number of participating members above which formal leadership is absolutely necessary, but small chamber orchestras (10 to 20 members) usually have a conductor and even in smaller ensembles, one member often serves nominally as the leader.

As noted earlier, a now famous example of a fairly large ensemble (26 players) that performs exquisitely without a conductor is the Orpheus Chamber Orchestra. There is no doubt that Orpheus achieves a very high level of coordinative efficiency with excellent ensemble playing, but not without leadership. The leadership is collective and depends on several members of the group taking responsibility, working things out among themselves, and respecting each others' opinions. In all, the collective leadership in Orpheus requires greater dependence on the other dimensions of coordination than might be necessary if it had a designated conductor/leader. A very high level of individual competence and proficiency is required of the members, rehearsals are more prolonged than they would otherwise be, and internal communications among members is more intense and highly critical to the success of the group:

> Orpheus routinely spends thirty hours preparing for a two hour concert – three times as much as a typical orchestra. And yet it's precisely this painstaking process of arriving, almost unconsciously, at a shared vision that accounts for Orpheus's distinctive

sound.... I still don't quite understand how Orpheus works," the pianist Alfred Brendel...says. "I still can't understand how they play so unfailingly together. How do they divine what is going on?" The answer, he suggests, lies in the musicians' sense of trust, the intensity with which they listen to one another, and the responsibility each player takes for the entire score, and not just his own part. (Traub, 1996, p.104)

Orpheus does not operate without a conductor because it wishes to achieve better coordination than it might otherwise. It has other reasons for doing this, having to do with player satisfaction and overall musical quality. But Orpheus demonstrates that there is more than one way to achieve precision in organizations by utilizing different combinations of coordinative strategies.

Larger symphony orchestras invariably employ central leaders (conductors) and this size of ensemble also tends to have a differentiated leadership structure. Section leaders facilitate coordination at the level of different instrument groupings, helping to monitor individual players, so that conductors can concentrate on the larger issue of coordinating major orchestral parts.

Where, as in concertos, there are soloists who play major parts, often in front of the orchestra, or where the orchestra itself plays a supportive role in a larger context, as in an opera or concerto, the conductor may share leadership with others. A conductor and a concert soloist or opera singer must maintain coordination with one another, and the conductor must in turn keep the orchestra playing together and in tandem with the soloist. The operatic or the soloist situation is illustrative of organizational collaborations in which leaders bear responsibility not only for internal coordination but liaison with external autonomous partners as well. This can be problematic if the ensemble leader and the soloist differ in style or approach. In a recent performance of a Mozart violin concerto, for example, the soloist was forceful, precise and energetic, while the conductor had a more relaxed approach, requiring the soloist to adjust in various spots in order to maintain the continuity and momentum of the music (Rosenberg, 1998c).

The question of when formal leadership is desirable does not hinge only on the issue of coordination, and thus it will arise again as other dimensions of organizational management are considered in subsequent movements. However, coordination *is* a core management function and it is also the core of ensemble conducting. Indeed, the history of the emergence of conductors in musical ensembles indicates that it grew from this core function of coordination. Even as late as Mendelssohn in the 19th century there was a common notion that maintaining a minimum level of coordination was the main function of the conductor (Gammond, 1995).

Finally, it is interesting to briefly examine the downside of formal organizational leadership through the example of the orchestra conductor, especially in the contemporary era when conductors have become celebrities in their own right and are often away from their home organizations. It is not unusual now for star conductors to hold the principal conductor's post in several orchestras, splitting their residencies over the course of a year. This limits rehearsal times and can engender a degree of cynicism among players, arguably affecting the quality of performances (Faulkner, 1973; Gammond, 1995). This situation at once illustrates the essential role of top leadership in larger ensembles and the possibilities of compensating for this leadership when it becomes less available. For example, some orchestras rely more heavily on assistant conductors because their principal conductor is not always available. In essence, leadership lower in the organization emerges to compensate capacity limitation at the top. But there is another disturbing possibility as well: a reduction in one coordinative element may also cause reductions in another. Thus, a limitation in top leadership can lead to poorer plans, inattention to the education of members, breakdowns in internal communications, or shorter and less effective rehearsals. Although dependence on the direct contributions of top leadership to achieve coordination may be minimized through increased reliance on other coordinative elements, care must also be taken to ensure that a leadership framework is in place that will maintain the efficacy of all of the other coordinative mechanisms.

To What Degree Should We Play by the Book?

Organizations vary widely in terms of how much they rely on formal plans and procedures. Plans and procedures obviously contribute to coordination but they can also limit flexibility in dynamic situations. Again, size, heterogeneity, and task complexity influence where detailed plans and procedures are most helpful and where they can inhibit the achievement of coordination.

In very small organizations, one can envision achieving coordination without heavy reliance on formal plans and procedures. Once the music is known, small ensembles can operate well without scores, relying instead on memory, close communications and extensive practice to keep together. And operating without strict reference to the score allows a certain amount of flexibility and individual expression that smaller groups can accommodate without members' losing pace with one another. This is best exemplified by small jazz ensembles whose players rely heavily on their common understanding of the rules of jazz, as well as visual and aural communication to signal to one another where they are going with the music at any given juncture (Barrett, 1998).

It is rare, however, for larger ensembles to play without scores. There are several reasons for this. For one thing, not all musicians are able to completely memorize large, complex pieces without error, or to have mastery of skills required for improvisation. Thus, larger groups are less likely to be able to recruit entire ensembles of members who have such abilities. Moreover, smaller groups are more likely to attract players with soloist ambitions. Soloists must be able to play without the music in front of them, and they need the flexibility of forgoing strict reference to the score in order to indulge their own interpretive styles. But a large ensemble consisting of even virtuoso-level talent would probably need continual reference to written scores in order to play well together. Large ensembles simply cannot reconcile substantial numbers of idiosyncrasies in a short period of time without heavy reliance on a common reference plan.

One may well ask, however, what about the big bands and large jazz orchestras, especially those of the 1930s and '40s that were famous for their apparent spontaneity? Certainly these larger ensembles relied less on formal scores than classical ensembles of similar size. But they did use written musical scores, and they also played their music in a manner that relied less on ensemble playing and more on serial coordination of solo performances. The highlights of these ensembles were often the conversations of solo instruments as the musical spotlight was passed sequentially from trumpet to saxophone to clarinet to bass to drums, and so on. Here, reliance on scores gave way to improvisation, and ensemble playing became relatively less important. Emphasis on individual virtuoso players tended to distinguished one band from another. Speaking of Count Basie's band, successor Grover Mitchell observed:

> We've got Bill Hughes on bass drums, Kenny Hing on sax with us about 20 years; Melvin Wanzo on trombone since 1968, John Williams on baritone sax for 18 years and Charlton Johnson on guitar.... There are a lot of youngsters in this band [too] who will be future stars. (Scott, 1995, p.9-B)

For smaller ensembles, it is quite possible that above a certain level of coordinated playing, written scores become a hindrance to further coordinative refinement. When scores are completely memorized and digested, when players are of the highest individual quality and achievement, and when they have played together for a long time, perfection lies in fine-tuning and nuanced interpretation, even some implicit refinement of the written plan. That seems to be the case for small chamber groups that have achieved exquisite levels of ensemble playing. It is also the experience of some early music groups that value spontaneity and also emphasize some special coordinative advantages of playing from memory:

> When the music is internalized, you don't have this process of it going from the page to your brain and out to your muscles. You're free to play together better, to play more in tune. You can add more improvisationally to the music than you would otherwise. (Cohn, 1996, p.34 quoting David Douglass of the King's Noyse)

> After we started performing from memory...it gave us more musical freedom. We're more secure in the music. We listen harder, and we depend entirely on our ears, not on a sheet of music. (Cohn, 1996, p.35 quoting Mary Anne Ballard of the Baltimore Consort)

The experience of early music groups reemphasizes the point that trade-offs between formal plans and other means of coordination are possible and provide flexibility in achieving ensemble precision in different types of situations. Not only must players intensify their listening to one another, but rehearsals become all the more important:

> "Rehearsing over and over again is the best way to memorize," say Sequentia's Barbara Thornton, whose group has four medieval programs in its memory bank.... But group memory is a little more difficult to achieve [than individual memorization]. According

to [Mary Anne] Ballard, the first time the Consort performs a program, they always have sheet music in front of them. Then, little by little, it disappears. (Cohn, 1996, pp.35, 36)

Priorities and Trade-Offs

Our focus here on the issues of leadership and formal plans highlights our two central themes – that different organizational circumstances require different combinations of coordinating strategy, and that the elements of coordination work in tandem with one another, usually permitting helpful trade-offs where one element is lacking and another is more readily available. At one level, the relationships between circumstances and coordinating strategies can be summarized very simply from our discussion: As the organizational circumstances become more challenging, the more intensely must each of the coordinating strategies be employed. That is, the larger, more heterogeneous an organization, the less professional and more unstable (transient) its workforce, and the more complex its work, the more emphasis needs to be put on formal plans, internal communications, education and training, rehearsal, and formal leadership. That much is fairly obvious. The interesting question is how much relative emphasis to put on each of these coordinative strategies for different types of organizations. Answering this question requires that we characterize particular organizations in terms of their special circumstances and then assess how those circumstances influence the mix of strategic choices. For that purpose, the matrix in Table 1.1 considers several stereotypical musical ensembles and their circumstantial characteristics. Obviously the number of possible ensemble models that could be listed here is unlimited. A few are chosen to illustrate a wide variety of coordination challenges. In subsequent movements, this exercise is repeated for the other challenges of management.

Each of the listed ensemble stereotypes presents different coordination challenges. The professional symphony orchestra is typically large, has many different parts and undertakes complex musical tasks. But its work force is highly professional and relatively stable. Hospitals are similar in these respects. The challenge is to make the myriad, diverse complex parts to work smoothly together.

The amateur chorus consists by definition of participants who are not previously highly trained but who bring special enthusiasm to their work. The work itself is relatively straightforward consisting of music that the group enjoys singing. The membership of the chorus is relatively homogeneous and experiences moderate turnover. The analog suggested here, in terms of these variables, is that of a volunteer fire department, although the fire department would probably experience greater urgency in the act of performing its services. The essential challenge is to harness together the relatively raw energy of an enthusiastic, well meaning group and direct it to the accomplishment of a clear but still daunting task.

Table 1.1   Ensemble Attributes and Coordination

	size	heterogeneity	professional level	instability	task complexity	nonmusical analog
Professional symphony	high	high	high	low	high	hospital
Amateur chorus	moderate	low	low	moderate	low	volunteer fire department
Pickup jazz orchestra	moderate	high	moderate	high	moderate	consulting firm
High school marching band	moderate	moderate	low	high	high	restaurant
Professional string quartet	low	low	high	low	high	air force squadron

The pick up jazz orchestra is distinguished by its transience or instability, with players coming in and out as suits their availability. Musicians need to be fairly proficient to participate in such an ensemble and they represent a mix of skills on different instruments. A consulting firm that engages people of different talents on a project basis, depending on the particular contracts in hand, offers a nonmusical illustration of these characteristics. The challenge is to establish a framework in which skilled strangers with similar backgrounds can work well together in addressing a common task.

The high school marching band is distinguished by its amateur status and its transience, since students move in and out as they progress through their grades and then graduate, and by the difficulty of the task – producing coherent music while marching. A restaurant is similar in these respects. The work force is transient and mostly nonprofessional, and the meals, and the personnel who handle various aspects of them, are constantly in motion. The challenge is to overcome transience and movement, yet still get the job done in good order.

The professional string quartet is small and homogenous, and relatively stable in its membership. It is distinguished by the difficulty of the music it undertakes and the degree of professionalism of its membership. It resembles an air force squadron in these respects, flying in precise formation in order to accomplish its mission. The challenge is to get the members of the organization working so well together so that they can excel in a very complex task that requires great precision.

None of these musical stereotypes is completely characteristic of their counterparts in the real world, nor are the suggested nonmusical analogs exact. The stereotypes are nonetheless useful in thinking through the coordination strategies of different kinds of organizations. One way to analyze this issue is through the matrix in Table 1.2 which prioritizes the different coordination strategies for each ensemble type.

Table 1.2   **Coordination Strategies**

	written score	communication	education	rehearsal	formal leadership
Professional symphony	3	4	5	1	2
Amateur chorus	3	5	2	4	1
Pickup jazz orchestra	1	2	5	4	3
High school marching band	3	5	2	1	4
Professional string quartet	3	1	5	2	4

The matrix suggests that each of these widely varying ensembles should employ different strategy combinations to meet their coordination challenges. The numbers in the matrix represent a priority ordering of strategies, with "1" being the highest priority (or degree of emphasis) and "6" the lowest priority component of an overall coordinative strategy.

The professional symphony needs to rehearse and it must depend on direction by its conductor. The score is important but opportunities for internal communications are limited by size and spatial arrangements. Since players are professionally trained, limited improvement in coordination would be achieved by further education.

In contrast, the amateur chorus depends strongly on the choral director but also on training that can be provided to improve the individual proficiencies of the singers. The score is an important, common reference as well. Rehearsal is key and will improve play given that the forgoing elements are in place. Opportunities for internal communication are limited and have relatively less potential for improving coordination.

The pickup jazz orchestra offers minimal opportunity for rehearsals or for training of participating players. It presumes that participants have a basic proficiency and it uses the score (or songs) and basic rules of jazz as key coordinating mechanisms. Since much of jazz is based on improvised musical conversations, players will coordinate themselves during performances with a considerable level of internal communication. Formal leadership can be significant in helping to facilitate this communication and to reference key aspects of the score, by appropriate guidance and direction from the podium.

The high school marching band is highly dependent on rehearsals because it is limited in the extent that internal communications are possible or by the ability of the players to stay in touch with the conductor as the band moves about. The scores are helpful as well (although it is wise not to depend on them too much as they sometimes blow away in the wind!) Education is very important to these amateur players, and much of this can be provided by the conductor as teacher. In particular, the more proficient the players become with their own parts, the more easily they can pay attention to fitting their parts into the play of the whole ensemble.

Finally, the professional string quartet consists of highly proficient players who value an egalitarian environment. Hence, little gain in coordination is achieved by further training or by strong formal leadership. The written score provides a foundation on which to build coordination through rehearsal. Close communication among the players is critical, both in rehearsal and performance.

Case Studies

Herbert Kaufman's classic study of the U.S. Forest Service (1967) provides an excellent illustration of the array of mechanisms a complex organization can use to coordinate its operations. The Forest Service can be thought of as something like a military marching band. Its many different departments (instrument sections) are far-flung across the parade route, and cannot easily communicate with one another or be communicated with all at once; still, they all play together as they do their work in assorted local venues at any particular moment.

At that time of Kaufman's study, the Forest Service managed 181 million acres of national forest land, spread over 149 National Forests and 763 Ranger Districts throughout every region of the United States. Many of these districts are in remote locations, far from the eye of the central command in Washington, D.C. Yet, the Forest Service had a reputation as a smoothly functioning organization whose parts were well synchronized. Like the military band, the Forest Service exhibits a clear nominal hierarchy, with a central commander (conductor) and heads of each section. But, given the far-flung nature of this organization, direct central leadership control can be only one element in an overall coordination strategy. As Kaufman observed: "...so much of the work by which the objectives of the national forest administration are accomplished depends heavily on the Rangers" (p.47). In particular, great emphasis is placed on strategies that allow the Rangers to internalize what they need to know, so that they can operate in concert with one another without direct or immediate central supervision. These strategies include – in rough order of importance – education and training of the Rangers, emphasis on manuals of procedures (scores) for instructions on how to deal with particular tasks and situations, and practice drills (rehearsal) to ensure competency. Communications among Rangers and between Rangers and supervisors play a part too, but only to the degree permitted by the dispersed character of the organization. Similarly, central and distributed leadership play their parts as well within contextual constraints.

Like members of a marching band, Forest Rangers are subject to local events within their particular neighborhoods that may divert their attention and pull them out of alignment with the direction of the organization as a whole. Just as members of the brass section might develop their own internal comradery, or may be distracted by something unusual along the parade route that may lead them to miss a few beats on occasion, a Forest Ranger can be drawn into local issues or co-opted by local interests at odds with the policy of the U.S. Forest Service. One interesting device that the Forest Service uses to minimize this threat to well-coordinated performance is to rotate the Rangers into different locations and assignments over the course of their careers. It is as if members of the military band were to be given opportunities to learn multiple instruments and to do tours of duty in different sections of the band – woodwinds, brass, percussion and so on, so that they maintain an overall loyalty and perspective of the band as a whole. (Alternatively, one could conceive of the military marching band dividing itself into heterogeneous mini-ensembles for purposes of playing in different parts of a parade or in different venues simultaneously. In this case, players could be rotated among subunits without having to differentiate their instrument skills.)

The Forest Service manages to maintain a high level of ensemble in the face of serious contextual challenges, in large part because it employs mechanisms for maintaining an internal consensus and understanding about the work it is supposed to accomplish. From this basic premise, the organization is able to put in place managerial strategies, appropriate to its context, that keep its parts properly synchronized. By contrast, the more recent experience of AOL Time Warner illustrates what happens when an organization has insufficient consensus about what music it is supposed to be playing or how the parts of the organization are supposed to work together. AOL Time Warner was more like an orchestra-chorus combination, each division with its own membership, leadership, and style; each division with its own sense of what it wants to play; and neither division with a clear concept of how the two parts are supposed to fit together:

> ...bitter executives from the Time Warner side of the house say that some of the plans to synchronize their businesses with AOL's were flawed from the beginning. They say that so far many of the merger's promised synergies have cramped their businesses, including empty announcements about cooperation between Time Warner magazines and television networks; a proposal, still unfulfilled, to broadcast shows made by the Warner Brothers studio on Turner Broadcasting; and even a failed companywide push switch to AOL e-mail accounts. (Kirkpatrick and Rutenberg, 2002, p.19)

Without an accepted common set of concepts, none of the prospective managerial strategies of coordination could work: there was no clear score or song to work from; no music that could be practiced together; no common educational program from which choral and instrument (AOL and Time Warner) players could draw common understanding and inspiration; limited communication between the two divisions; and enormous challenges to top executives who might try to force coordination from the top. As noted by Rob Walker (2002): "There is....a gap between the theory of far-flung businesses working in seamless concert and the reality of protecting corporate turf. Reports have detailed the intense lack of interest among various divisional chiefs at AOL Time Warner in consolidating and ad-selling operations and cutting sweeping marketing deals across multiple units...."

Successful coordination of orchestra-chorus combinations, do often succeed – when the units understand each other, have common work to do in taking on Beethoven's 9th or some other clear challenge, have a sense of the intent and purpose of the whole organization, and work from the same play book. Without these elements, ensembles and their organizational counterparts can easily disintegrate.

Diagnosing An Organization

The experiences of musical ensembles contain many insights for managers of all kinds of organizations, but these insights must be adapted to specific contexts. One way of applying the musical metaphor to the coordination problems of a particular organization is to ask, what kind of musical ensemble does that organization most closely resemble? With respect to coordination challenges, is it like a large symphony orchestra, a jazz ensemble, a marching band, or an opera orchestra that supports the play on-stage? With a comfortable analog in mind, the two matrices discussed in the previous section may be constructed: first the circumstances under which the organization operates can be described (Table 1.1), and then the priorities for a combination of coordination strategies to address these circumstances can be considered (Table 1.2), as illustrated for the stereotype ensembles above. One may also find that different ensemble metaphors are needed to describe different parts of an organization. A university, for example, might view its academic departments as jazz ensembles and its student services division as a chamber orchestra. Large organizations are complex and multi-faceted and can benefit from this analysis at multiple levels. Once the particular components are analyzed separately, the operatic company can be put back together again for analysis of the whole production!

The forgoing matrix analysis provides a general sense of the nature of the coordination issues for a given organization and the priorities with which it can consider alternative coordination strategies. Whether the focus is on a particular part of the organization, or on the organization as a whole, it is also helpful to ask more detailed questions about the fundamental conditions that create coordinative challenges in the organization, and the combinations of coordination strategies that best apply in its particular circumstances. The questions below derive from the discussions in this movement. The experiences of musical ensembles suggest that these questions are appropriate for diagnosing and resolving coordination issues:

– Which are the largest sections or departments within the organization?
– Which sections are most diverse in terms of the types of work being done by their members?
– Which parts of the organization employ personnel with the least training and education relative to the work they must perform and the level of understanding they need of the organization's work overall?

- Which parts of the organization experience the most workforce and leadership turnover?
- Which areas of the organization have the most complex or least predictable work to perform?

The forgoing questions will help to locate the parts of an organization that may be weak links in the chain of overall coordination. In addition, one should ask about global aspects of the organization that affect coordination:

- Is the organization larger than it needs to be?
- Is the organization more complex than it should be, in terms of its specializations in capacities, skills, procedures and work tasks of different parts of the organization?
- Are all parts of the organization synchronized to the same overall rhythm or cycle of activity over time?
- Are some parts of the organization out of balance with other parts? Should emphasis be reallocated from some sections of the organization to others?
- Is the level of difficulty of the work of the organization incompatible with its capacity and level of expertise?

Affirmative answers to these questions suggest that the overall conditions under which the organization operates make the task of coordination difficult and may require modification.

Given a diagnosis, one may then consider the various coordinative solutions appropriate to the circumstances:

- How can formal plans and procedures be made more clear?
- How can interpersonal communications be improved within and among departments and key individuals, through changes in spatial arrangements, opportunities for conversation, opportunities to review and practice routines, and so on?
- Where does leadership need to be designated or cultivated to ensure that accountability for all tasks is made clear?
- How can practice sessions be designed to ensure that all workers know their parts and can work well with one another, within sections of the organization and in the organization as a whole?
- In what areas should workers be required to commit organizational plans and procedures to memory?
- How can policies be designed to increase workforce stability and reduce turnover?
- How can procedures be designed to select workers who are compatible and work well with one another?
- Where can education and training programs be best used to raise the technical and organizational skills and competencies of workers?
- Can the size and complexity of the organization as a whole be reduced?

Should the organization take on simpler work or reduce the number of its commitments?

- Can the organization, or large subsections of it, be broken up into smaller parts within which coordination can be refined? Would doing so yield benefits that outweigh the costs of coordinating additional parts with one another?
- How can the overall rhythm of the organization be made more clear to all parts of the organization?
- Should some parts of the organization be reduced and others increased to ensure greater balance?
- Is stronger central leadership needed or should leadership be shared more widely throughout the organization?
- If there are weaknesses in some coordinative mechanisms, such as communications or leadership, how can they be compensated by strengthening other mechanisms, such training or practices?

Bridge

It is clear that coordination is not the only issue that management must face in making choices of coordinative strategy. In particular, reliance on different combinations of plans, communications, education, rehearsal and leadership also has implications for the enthusiasm and motivation that organizational members may bring to their tasks, and to the flexibility that the organization can muster in adapting to new circumstances and developing innovations. In this larger picture, managers face even larger trade-offs than those involved in simply running a well coordinated organization. Without coordination, there may be no advantage to organization, but coordination alone is not in itself the final measure of organizational performance.

Second Movement: Motivation

Let me know when he looks this way!

When an individual is employed by an organization, he or she agrees to a bargain: A certain level of work is expected and a certain amount of individual autonomy is sacrificed in exchange for some package of compensation, benefits, opportunities and influence on organizational decisions. Although the nature of this package varies widely from case to case, such a bargain characterizes all employment relationships – whether the individual is a volunteer, a full time staffer, a part-timer, or a star professional and whether the organization is a small community group, a large corporation, or a government bureau. Moreover, although individuals may be highly self-motivated, the nature of the bargain and how it is implemented and managed, will influence the individual's morale, conscientiousness, inclination to excel, and desire to contribute to the organization's mission. In sum, a fundamental challenge for an organization's management is the motivation of its work force.

A critical element in this challenge is the fact that when individuals become part of an organization, they are asked to make personal contributions in a situation where the rewards of performance are usually attributed to the organization as a whole. The credit for an exquisite performance of Beethoven's *Eroica Symphony* goes to the Cleveland Orchestra as a whole, and perhaps individually to its conductor, and to solo performers, but separate credit is not easily parceled out to each of the ensemble players. In this sense, individual members of an organization can be seen as contributors to what economists call a "collective good".

A characteristic of collective goods is that one can enjoy their benefits without paying for them or otherwise contributing sufficiently to their support. If a talented young music student decides to play her flute in a public park, passers-by can listen whether or not they decide to put a coin or two in her open music case. Or, if a group of alumni decide to form a chorus to sing at the annual reunion, those attending can enjoy the show whether or not they volunteer to join in. The implication of this attribute of collective goods is that people are likely to "free-ride" on the efforts of others, and, consequently, collective goods (music in the park or at the reunion) will be under-supplied.

Thus, if members of an organization are not rewarded in a manner commensurate with the value of their efforts, then the contributions they ultimately make to the provision of those goods may fall short, emerging as deficits in the level and quality of their work. In his classic analysis of collective goods, Mancur Olson (1965) concluded that there are basically three ways to overcome this "free rider" problem – "social pressure", "coercion" or "selective incentives." Social pressure, which Olson asserted works best in relatively small groups where people know each other well, can be effective as a motivational element even in larger professional ensembles. No one wants to stand out like a clanking, ill-fitting bolt in a well-oiled machine. However, even in this context, under-performers may succeed in hiding behind the work of others rather than playing in an obviously incorrect way.

Use of coercion assumes that the organization has enough control to force the individual to contribute a certain level or quality of effort. For example, governments use the police power of the state to require people to pay taxes or go to jail, in order to support government-provided public services. In organizations where staff have little choice of comparable alternative employment, management may have considerable coercive power. Alternatively, in (hopefully most) organizations where coercive options are limited, the focus is largely on the second alternative – selective incentives. The use of selective incentives involves rewarding individuals in a manner that is correlated with their individual efforts so that they will contribute as much and as well as they can to the organization.

It is easiest to think about selective incentives in terms of material rewards. For example, a contributor to a public radio station can be given a gift tote bag emblazoned with the station's logo as a token of thanks for support. Or, for employees, compensation can be structured so that there is a direct relationship between individual performance and level of pay. However, the notion of selective incentives can be broadly interpreted to include not only material compensation, but various other means of recognition, acknowledgment and encouragement that highlight an individual's contributions and help align his or her interests with those of the organization.

The question of aligning individual and organizational interests is the subject of a field of study among economists and organizational scholars known as "principal and agent theory". In this framework, we can characterize the workers in an organization as the agents with which the principals – management – contract to carry out the work of the organization. Since workers' and managers' interests may not be precisely the same, the challenge to management is to structure the conditions of work so that employees behave in a manner consistent with organizational interests and put forward their best efforts. To do this, managers must obtain the information they need to monitor workers' performance, and they must, as Olson suggests, structure appropriate rewards and penalties to influence workers' behavior.

Various conditions may influence how effectively principals can control agents and what particular strategies are most effective in different situations. These conditions include how easily principals can identify and measure the contributions of agents, how closely agents' and principals' interests coincide with one another in the first place, whether the principal-agent relationship is a permanent or transient one, and whether agents are worried about their reputations outside the immediate organizational setting (Pratt and Zechhauser, 1991).

Musical ensembles nicely illustrate the issues surrounding worker motivation, and the ideas suggested by collective goods and principal-agent theories. While musicians are commonly highly self-motivated because they intrinsically enjoy their art, they play in ensemble combinations that vary widely in how well their individual contributions are recognized and how well they can be held accountable for their individual efforts. There is no hiding or slacking in a vocal duet where an error or an omission can stand out like a tuba among flutes; however, singers in a chorus of 100 voices all singing the same tune face an entirely different situation. Between these extremes is a myriad of ensemble combinations, each with its own challenges to maintaining high player motivation and effort.

Certain characteristics of musical ensembles highlight the challenges of motivation. Here, paralleling the previous movement, we discuss five of these dimensions: the size of the ensemble, its internal heterogeneity of instrumentation and musical parts, the level of professionalism of its participants, the degree of stability in its work force, and the character and complexity of particular jobs within the organization. Given the nature of collective goods, we can expect that the larger an ensemble, and the more homogeneous and transient its workforce, the more difficult it will be to maintain high levels of individual contribution to the organization's performance. And, we may expect that the more professional the workforce (and the more competitive the market for professional positions), the more self-motivation and concern over reputation is likely to compensate for inadequate organizational incentives. The nature of particular jobs within the organization may also reflect some of these considerations. If players are part of instrument sections that are large or which play only supporting roles, the motivational challenges may be more severe. Or, if the work itself is too difficult or too easy, or if it is highly formal and allows little room for individual discretion, initiative, or creativity, motivational challenges may be greater because intrinsic satisfaction is lower.

Musical ensembles are rich in the variety of their approaches to the challenges of workforce motivation. They utilize a host of strategies for selecting who becomes and remains a member of the organization; for matching work assignments (parts) to players' skills and preferences; for differentiating the status, working conditions and responsibilities of individual players; for distributing leadership responsibility among players; for monitoring, recognizing and rewarding the contributions of individual players both in practice and in performance; and for inspiring players through example, peer support and challenging assignments.

Ensembles pursue a variety of different approaches to motivation partly because of the range of circumstances in which these organizations find themselves, and because various components of motivational strategy can be substituted for one another within broad areas of discretion. Differences in management philosophy among ensembles also contribute to this variation. This will become clear when we consider two cross-cutting questions that emerge from this discussion: To what degree does reliance on central leadership and hierarchical arrangements hinder or help solve the motivational problems of ensembles? And, in what circumstances is a system of sharing authority, status and glory among players in an ensemble preferable, in motivational terms, to one in which status and authority are the rewards of competition?

The Circumstances for Motivation

It is the unusual worker who can do his or her best under all circumstances. The task of management is to adapt motivational strategies to organizational conditions so that free rider problems and other disincentives to performing well are overcome.

Organization Size

The larger the organization, the potentially more severe is the problem of free-riding characterized by individuals who coast, hold back their best efforts, or are otherwise less than fully dedicated to their work. Members of large groups realize that their individual efforts constitute only small parts of the group's effort and may go unnoticed or unrewarded. In this circumstance, ensemble members can count on others to pick up the slack while avoiding accountability for their own performance. Moreover, the larger group may afford greater anonymity to individual members, hence avoiding the social pressure of colleagues or neighbors that would push them to shape up. In a large chorus, for example, singers with uncertain mastery of the tune or with little enthusiasm for the piece may decide to sing in hushed tones or simply mouth the words, without being detected. (Indeed, choral conductors of amateur or grade school choruses have sometimes encouraged poor singers to fake it!) Similar behavior could not be indulged in a trio or a quartet where each individual's contribution is easily noticed, even if all singers have the same parts. The free-rider problem is less severe in small groups where shirking is less difficult to detect and peer pressure from other members of the group is more likely to keep each individual player sharp (or flat, as the case may be!)

Heterogeneity

The more homogeneous an organization is internally, the greater will be the free rider problem. It is easier for a tuba player to shirk in an ensemble of 100 tubas than in an orchestra of a hundred musicians playing a variety of instruments of which only a few are low brass. (The potential for such behavior would seem substantial for example in the various tubafests that take place in cities such as Akron and Cincinnati, Ohio and San Jose, California during the Christmas season. However, in this case, erratic playing is not considered a terribly serious vice, and all manner of tuba players participate simply for the fun of it.) Though it is most significant for large ensembles, this homogeneity effect holds for groups of all sizes. Even a trio can experience less motivational difficulty if the three parts are differentiated by instrumentation or musical parts. For large homogeneous ensembles such as a chorus of male tenor voices, the motivational challenge is eased if the ensemble is divided into different sections, each with a different part to play, although the challenge will remain substantial if the sections are themselves large. For example, string orchestras commonly have fairly large, homogenous, first and second violin or viola sections in which individual contributions are hard to isolate.

Professionalism

If members of an ensemble each "march to their own drummers" the motivational challenges associated with free-riding may not be as serious as they otherwise might be. Individuals who pursue music as a career, for example, are most often substantially self-motivated by the love of the art, by desires for self-improvement, and by aspirations to secure the most desirable appointments. These motives help to align individual interests with that of the ensemble whose presumed purpose is to produce the best possible music. As Pratt and Zeckhauser (1991) put it: "If we can get work that we like, we needn't worry about our boss's standing over us" (p.14). However, even among professional musicians in major symphony orchestras, motivational problems remain. For example, the New York Philharmonic experienced such problems in the 1980s (Henahan, 1983).

If individuals aspire to solo careers or to positions of leadership within the ensemble world, especially if plum positions are scarce, they will be more likely to try to stand out among their peers rather than to hide or shirk responsibility. Indeed, they will seek out opportunities to shine. Similarly, such individuals will be less likely to risk their reputations by putting forth less than their best efforts. Thus, we may expect the motivational challenges to be less severe in professional ensembles or ensembles composed of aspiring artists than in ensembles where individuals do not aspire to professional recognition or have given up on advancement. Even so, the potential for shirking impacts even at the highest levels of professional achievement. As reviewer Peter Goodman puts it: "It sometimes happens that performers slack off when they are not playing in one of the major locations, idling a little while preparing for a big effort somewhere else" (Goodman, 1987, p.II-8).

To the contrary, one may surmise that ensembles composed of highly accomplished or ambitious individuals might lead to problems of internal competition rather than slack. In some circumstances, efforts may be required to keep competitive urges under control in order to foster cooperation and internal composure. This effect seems less likely in smaller groups where individuals can more easily share attention and receive individual credit than in larger ones where they must subsume their interests and identity to that of the group. In this connection, there may even be a difference between trios and quartets. Goodman continues: "There's a tradition that chamber trios are assembled from prominent soloists who enjoy playing together and therefore choose occasionally to tour or record, as opposed to string quartets, whose delicate balance demands four musicians who work constantly as a unit to maintain the required blend" (Goodman, 1987, p.II-8).

The situation of amateur and volunteer members of ensembles is more ambiguous. On the one hand, amateurs join ensembles for the love of music and for the social rewards of participation. Thus, their interests may be intrinsically aligned with that of the group and they are unlikely to be as sensitive to the issue of individual recognition as professionals. For these reasons they are less likely to slacken their efforts in situations where such rewards are lacking. On the other hand, amateurs and volunteers may be less driven towards overall ensemble achievement and may feel less compelled to participate if the costs become too high:

> The [University Circle Chamber Choir] volunteer group is made up of 44 singers selected from the University Circle Chorale. Some are students at the Cleveland Institute of Music and Case Western Reserve University. Others are older adults from Greater Cleveland.

> Susan Davenny Wyner....the ensemble's musical director and conductor, has not attempted to forge the enthusiastic group into a choral instrument of smooth blend and pure intonation. Standing in a scattered arrangement rather than unified sections, the singers hold their pitch well enough to perform *a cappella*. But individual voices frequently pop out of the texture, and different vibratos are sometimes at war.

> The program consisted of 18 selections from seven centuries of music...Had a professional choir attempted such a wide range of repertoire, it would have been expected to make some distinction among historic and national styles. But Wyner was content to let her singers sail from the Renaissance to the present without delving beneath the surface of the music or exploring the essential differences between pieces...The idea, apparently, was to enjoy reading through the rich variety of chorale literature. Singers and conductor communicated pleasure in performing together. (Salisbury, 1994, p.8-F)

Some amateurs, however, may be driven by their own internal quest for excellence and achievement and may indeed be subject to the same motivational tendencies and inducements as professionals:

> "It's helpful for the youngsters to have the chance to play in a band with professionals and semi-professionals", [Rufus Kern, founder of the Huntington Community Band] said. "...Of the 75 to 85 musicians who regularly perform in the six summer concerts, one-third are students, one-third community members who just like to play music, and one-third professional musicians, who make $30 a concert... [It gives me}...the chance to play challenging music that I wouldn't normally get to play in school concerts", added Diahann Kline, a high school clarinetist... "If it weren't for the band, I'd never get to play this kind of music at all", says Ken Sottys...a trumpet player who teaches in a private school...and performs with jazz and pops combos. (Delatiner, 1985, p.LI 11)

Instability

Transience in an organization has much the same effect as size or homogeneity. If players have no permanent association with the organization it becomes easier to shirk, escape detection or accountability, and avoid peer pressure. The itinerant musician may be the opposite of the one time shopper who can be easily exploited by the unscrupulous merchant (Pratt and Zeckhauser, 1991). Since that musician has no long term obligation, he or she may not be conscientious in performance. On the other hand, if the itinerant is a long-term job seeker and professional, the incentive to perform well may be quite strong. For example, the Orpheus Chamber Orchestra uses free lance players for pieces requiring larger ensembles, or as substitutes when regular players are unavailable. Many of these free lancers have developed close relationships with the orchestra and are prime candidates when openings for regular positions occur (Hackman, 2002). Labor market competition also plays a role in motivating freelance players:

> Mr. Wilson, who is 35 and lives in Washington Heights in Manhattan, can change musical styles in the space of a subway ride, traveling from one job to the next. He has to. He has some 2,000 competitors in the New York area alone, according to the American Federation of Musicians. "Most musicians freelance in a number of bands because you don't have that many steady working bands...", Mr. Wilson says. "I try to bring an openness to every situation." (Orgill, 1996, p.24)

Finally, in ensembles with stable memberships, players will know each others' styles, habits and capacities well, and will be more attuned to deviations from best performances than they would be if they were among strangers. Thus, the monitoring aspect of maintaining motivation is more manageable in less transient situations. Still, the impact of transience on motivation is not necessarily an excuse for mediocrity. Witness conductor Marin Alsop's experience with the Long Island Philharmonic:

> "When I finally went to hear the Philharmonic after I was appointed music director, I

found the playing really uninspired....It wasn't really anyone's fault, I guess. Just real dull playing, something very sleepy about it all. I wanted to get up and shake everybody, even the audience. You can't just play notes! You have to play the *music*. And that's much more difficult."

"I want to turn the Long Island Philharmonic into the best orchestra it can possibly be," she continued. "Now, I know it's made up of freelance musicians but, believe me, I've been a freelance musician myself, and it *is* possible to inspire them. If a conductor comes onstage 200 percent prepared and completely committed, somehow that's contagious and the players give their all." (Page, 1992, p.6)

Task Complexity

As we have recognized, some ensembles are more heterogeneous than others, in terms of their instrumentation and the diversity of musical parts played by their members. As a result, some players occupy positions that are more vulnerable to motivational lapses than others. Some players, for example, such as first violins, clarinets, flutes or trumpets, are more likely to carry the melody line and may even have solo parts from time to time. Others, such as second violins, violas, cellos and basses, and low brass, are more likely to provide background harmonies and perhaps counter-melodies. Percussion instruments may be prominent in driving the rhythm of a performance, but some may have long periods during a performance in which they have nothing to do but follow along until the next clang of the cymbal or bang of the drum. Instrument players in the more supportive and less intense roles will generally be more motivationally-challenged because their contributions are less prominent and they are less likely to be singled out for compliments or criticism. (Unless, of course, the clang of the cymbal comes in at the wrong time!)

The cymbal player and the first violin in the same orchestra may be subject to different extremes of motivational difficulty. In a difficult piece, the violin player might be challenged by immense complexity, leading to frustration and loss of confidence or morale, while the cymbal player might be frustrated and bored with not enough to do. These considerations carry over to work of the orchestra as a whole. A piece of music that is too complex or difficult for the ensemble to master may be disheartening for all its members, leading to loss of motivation and slackening of effort. A piece of music that is too elementary or uninteresting, or played too often, may not be taken seriously, also leading to malaise. Thus, a matching of the ensemble's capability to the level of difficulty of the music it attempts to perform, is an important and delicate management responsibility. The ensemble must be challenged without being frustrated and capable of mastery without being bored.

Experiences of classical ensembles at various points in music history when composers introduced radically new forms, illustrate the issue. The orchestras in Italy provide illustration perhaps in the extreme:

The rough-and-ready state of orchestras in the country that gave birth to the symphony and the concerto may better be explained by Italians' individualistic not to say anarchic spirit. This trait, healthy and productive in countless ways, can be fatal to group effort. Italian orchestra musicians frequently interrupt rehearsals to fight with each other or to talk back to conductors. "Dmitri Mitropoulos dropped dead on the podium while trying to get us to play Mahler, back in 1960," says one veteran member of La Scala orchestra – the sadness in his voice tinged with unmistakable pride. (Sachs, 1987, p.21)

Gianni Baratta of the Emilia-Romagna orchestra in Italy faces the same frustration:

> One of my hopes is that the orchestra will gradually become less recalcitrant than most 'traditional' ensembles with regard to contemporary music. (Sachs, 1987, p.26)

Another aspect of the work that can affect motivation is its degree of formality. If a piece is fully specified with no room for individual interpretation or experimentation it may be less interesting to accomplished players than one that allows more artistic freedom. A jazz ensemble, for example, may follow the basic plan of a classic piece by Duke Ellington but will have room for improvisation and individualized interpretations. A symphonic rendering of Mozart's Jupiter Symphony leaves less freedom for individual maneuvering or ensemble interpretation. The degree of formality of a piece may cut both ways, however. A piece that is under-specified or which contains unresolved ambiguities may lead to frustration and exasperation, and even unwillingness to perform it:

> Ultimate unplayability is offered by Schumann, who writes on one page "as fast as possible" and on the next "faster". Don't ask me. (Holland, 1999a, p.B3)

Refrain

A variety of factors may intensify the challenge of motivating workers in an organization. The world of musical ensembles illustrates that large size, internal homogeneity, lower levels of professional competence, transience, less intense or prominent job assignments, and organizational tasks that are too difficult or too easy, can exacerbate problems of motivation. Interestingly, however, some of these challenges contain the kernels of their own solution. Thus, ensembles can devise strategies for engaging their workers that simulate smaller scale, greater diversity, greater stability, more sensitivity to skill level, and greater attention and recognition of individual effort.

The Elements of Motivational Strategy

Managerial approaches to motivation may be thought of in four overlapping stages: recruiting motivated players; matching those players to appropriate work assignments; assigning status and responsibility to players and their leaders; and monitoring individual performance so that rewards and recognition may be appropriately distributed.

Recruitment

Selecting players who are self-motivated, believe in the purpose of the organization, set high standards for themselves, show enthusiasm for their work and are personally compatible with one another goes a long way towards achieving an ensemble whose membership can remain highly motivated and productive. As Pratt and Zeckhauser (1991, p.15) put it: "Those who share one's objectives tend to carry them out." However, ensembles recruit their members and weed them out in a variety of ways, not all of which are fully conducive to maintaining high morale and motivation.

Smaller groups often come together of their own volition when a few musicians with common interests, tastes or ideas, decide that they have something special to offer and would like to work together. This process of formation is likely to lead to highly motivated groups. And when members of such self-selected groups no longer feel excited about playing with one another, the ensembles are likely to dissolve of their own accord. Rock groups are particularly well known for coming together and coming apart this way:

> Rock never stops, and neither does the parade of reunited and resuscitated rock bands. The four-act "Rock Never Stops" tour, which hits the Nautica stage tomorrow night, is proof of that...

> "It's nostalgic rock, but it's good nostalgic rock," Night Ranger guitarist Jeff Watson said cheerfully. His band known for mighty anthems and lavish power ballads, had a solid chart run in the mid-'80s....before calling it a day in 1989. There was no animosity when guitarist Watson and Brad Gillis, bassist/vocalist Jack Blades and drummer Kelly Keagy went their separate ways.... "When we got bumped out in the early '90s by the grunge stuff, interest was already waning... Fitz [keyboardist Alan Fitzgerald] had left the band and our numbers were down and it just wasn't feeling fresh or good and we needed a break. And it was a good break. Coming back together was a blast." (Pantsios, 1999, p.17)

Larger and more formal ensembles are likely to have more systematic ways to engage new members. In some cases, the process may be gradual. Some players may initially be engaged as pick-up musicians on a part-time basis to satisfy the requirements of particular performances. Eventually some of these musicians may be employed on an ongoing basis as the permanent members of the ensemble become familiar and comfortable with their playing, or when an opening occurs and/or the ensemble becomes able to afford them on a permanent basis. The Long Island Philharmonic in the 1980s illustrated this process:

> In music circles, (violin soloist) Mr. Tarack said, the caliber of the [Philharmonic's] work is a given. He has no trouble, he said, recruiting from "New York City's tremendous pool," although 80 percent of the musicians who were there at the beginning remain on the orchestra's roster, and at least 50 percent of the entire orchestra is from Long Island... Although the Philharmonic is still considered a "freelance orchestra", since its season is too limited for full-time status, this consistency has produced the kind

of sound that only comes with musicians playing together regularly under one conductor. (Delatiner, 1986, p.LI 21)

In other instances, such as the better established symphony orchestras, players will be engaged through a highly formalized audition process (Lehman, 1995). The tradition of blind auditions, in which potential recruits are heard anonymously from behind a screen, offers both motivational advantages and disadvantages for ensemble players. On the one hand, this system strengthens the legitimacy that each player brings to the organization. Because their positions are achieved by merit of individual performance, without favoritism or prejudice as possible influences, chosen members gain respect for their skills. All ensemble members may be inspired to maintain their own skills as a consequence, and internal morale will not be undermined by suspicions of unfairness or disappointment in the capacities of one's colleagues. Moreover, selection in this manner helps ensure that members' skills are matched to the difficulty of the music that the ensemble intends to perform.

On the other hand, the blind audition system selects players in an artificial setting devoid of important aspects of the organizational environment. It does not test for skill in ensemble playing nor does it screen for personal rapport with other players, dedication to the ensemble's particular goals, or understanding and appreciation of the style and tradition of the ensemble as a whole. Put into the real organizational environment, the skilled individual player who passes the blind audition with flying colors may not get along well with fellow players, may underachieve in a group setting, may undermine a sense of unity or purpose, or may demoralize or undermine his colleagues in other ways. This is perhaps one of the reasons that certain distinguished orchestras such as the Vienna Philharmonic choose their players from the "family" of students of current players. Such a system has other obvious problems, such as establishing barriers to outside candidates who may be truly outstanding. Overall, the selection process can be difficult no matter what system is used:

The first session of auditions for the Symphony – judged by Tilson Thomas and a committee of players – produced no hirings. "I like the 'big' musicians with expansive personalities, who I can then tone down when necessary," Tilson Thomas says. "They [the orchestra] were used to choosing 'team players' who blend in more easily. We were not yet at the same place, so we made no choice." (Schiff, 1995, p.31)

Work Assignments

Players usually come to musical ensembles with established competencies on particular instruments. Thus, it is rare, though not unknown, for members to be assigned to different instruments than they had initially in mind. I can still recall the experience of my oldest son Seth when he first joined his elementary school band. He wanted to play saxophone but all the sax positions were taken so his teachers convinced him to try the baritone horn (which at the time was bigger than he was!) As a good sport, Seth took on the horn quite well and eventually moved onto the trombone, but his initial enthusiasm was dampened a bit by not having the instrument he originally preferred. Seth's experience was not unique. Consider that of Grover Mitchell of the Count Basie Orchestra:

> I really wanted a trumpet, but they assigned you ones they needed in their bands. They tried to stick me with a tuba. Finally, they gave me a trombone, because they said my arms were so long. I was 6 foot 3. I didn't get into playing the trombone, though, until I heard Tommy Dorsey play it on the radio. (Scott, 1995, p.9-B)

Even within instrument sections, however, the differentiation of musical parts and status levels can affect, and be used by management to strengthen, motivation. Specifically, given the motivational (free rider) problems that stem from large, homogeneous groupings, ensembles can stimulate their players towards greater individual effort by differentiating their parts. Thus, a large violin section can be broken down into two or three subsections, each playing complementary but different musical lines. Since each of the subgroups is smaller, members' contributions are easier to monitor, each player has greater individual impact, and free rider incentives are less severe. Naturally, this approach requires selection or adjustments to musical scores to permit such differentiation. Nonetheless, it is a strategy that can be used to maintain morale and effort within large instrument sections.

A related problem within larger musical ensembles is that some instrument sections play more prominent parts than others. Notably, lower register instruments such as basses or tubas, or percussion instruments, normally play supportive roles. As a result, they may receive less attention and become lax. But this problem may be ameliorated by appropriate differentiation of musical parts. Thus, musical pieces can be chosen, at least on occasion, to reverse the normal order and put supportive instruments in the spotlight. This is what the All-Star Excursion Band did in a concert at the Cleveland Museum of Art where the percussionists took the lead in singing the tune (Wolff, 1999).

An extension of this differentiation strategy is to ensure that opportunities for singular parts or solos are distributed throughout the ensemble so that players not normally in the spotlight have a chance to shine. This can be more of a problem for players of certain instruments than others:

> ...orchestral repertories of the late eighteenth and nineteenth centuries involve markedly larger cohorts of string players than they do of wind and brass players...While an oboist or trombonist aspires to be an orchestral musician, a large cohort of their string colleagues aspire to be the successors of Itzhak Perlman and the Guarneri Quartet...

> ...[But] while the wind, brass, and percussion players get to hear themselves in the orchestra as the performers of individual lines in a musical texture, the string players spend their lives submerged in choirs of sometimes dubious intonation. (Freeman, 1996b, p.13)

The irony here is that players of instruments normally in support roles may have a better chance to shine than players of lead instruments, simply because of the numbers involved in each instrument section.

Again, the strategy of distributing the glory depends on piece selection, but it is not uncommon for performances to highlight lower register and percussion instruments that normally play supportive roles. The model, for ensembles of modest size at least, is the small chamber group. In a 1987 performance, the Kronos Quartet appears to have achieved a standard wherein all players received individual attention in some manner:

> Each player stood out as an individual Friday; along with the shared energy of commitment, one remembers especially the unusual intensity in tremolo of David Harrington (first violin), the emotional frankness of John Sherba (second violin) in his sudden solo in the Berg [Suite], the haunting moans and wails of the viola (Hank Dutt) in the Alfred Schnittke's String Quartet No.1 and its evocatively handled "whistling" solo in the Sallinen, along with the unusually thoughtful and varied treatment of several contrasting pizzicato passages by Joan Jeanrenaud (cello). (Crutchfield, 1987a, p.49)

In ensembles that play popular music, there is much more flexibility in adjusting musical arrangements to share performance attention among different instruments. In jazz ensembles, of course, the practice of individual solos is well-developed and players of all instruments get their turn, including bass fiddles and drums.

In summary, the differentiation of ensembles into subgroups with specialized parts and periodic highlighting of the performance of subgroups or individual members who are normally not in the spotlight, may serve to significantly ameliorate the motivational problems associated with large, homogeneous, and supporting sections of the organization. The assignment of particular work tasks in an ensemble affects motivation in several other ways as well. It determines how well each player is matched to the work (instrument) that he or she enjoys. It also determines how well each player's skills are matched to the level of difficulty of the task. While players normally want to be challenged and to play at the limits of their skills, assigning someone to first violin who is not yet capable of playing the more difficult parts for this position can lead to frustration and disillusionment.

Status and Responsibility

Introducing sub-groupings within homogeneous instrument sections creates new opportunities for differentiating individual status, responsibility and rewards within an ensemble. For example, to be a first violin rather than a second violin, or to be first or second chair in one's section rather than a ninth or tenth chair, is a recognition of accomplishment, and the chair and subsection system serves as an incentive structure to motivate individual players towards higher levels of performance. But this system also has its limits and drawbacks:

> A violinist or violist...may spend two hours every day practicing scales and orchestral passages, but as soon as he or she sits within the orchestra, other colleagues' lack of

interest in careful preparation makes it difficult to determine if the practicing has accomplished anything. So long as a string player can aspire to a position on a higher stand, with the anticipation of a possibly higher salary, he or she may well practice diligently. But once a musician decides that he or she will never be promoted beyond the inside of the fourth stand and that it is unlikely that the conductor will ever hear poor playing, dull routine sets in, leading to less than satisfactory performance and to the visual appearance of men and women who no longer care about what they are doing. (Freeman, 1996b, p.13)

As with the system of blind auditions, the chair system can work both ways, depending on how it is managed and who belongs to the ensemble. For one thing, as Freeman observed, the system can be de-motivating if players give up on it. For another, the system can be used inappropriately in a punitive way by an autocratic music director.   Nonetheless, if lower-chaired musicians are permitted to challenge occupants of higher chairs, and chairs are periodically reassigned through objective reevaluations, the inducement for the challenger to move up and the threat to the incumbent of demotion, may serve to spur each of these participants to maintain and improve their skills. However, without such periodic reevaluation, improved occupants of lower-ranked chairs or subsections may become frustrated and discouraged, while incumbents of higher chairs or subsections may become lax and complacent. There is also danger that too harsh a competitive system may injure the self-esteem and confidence of distinguished veterans. The challenge system seems to work well in ensembles of young players who revel in the competitive challenge and whose egos are resilient. It was a matter of great fun and excitement each time one of my children came home from school and announced a successful challenge for a higher chair; and it was fully expected that the honor might not survive the next round of competition.

But such a system is more problematic in a professional venue where careers hinge on status, recognition and respect, and where co-workers value a collegial relationship with one another. While the threat of reputation loss serves as a powerful incentive for longstanding veterans to maintain their high positions, actual experience of such losses can also have demoralizing consequences both for the veterans themselves and other ensemble members who fear being in that position in the future. This consideration argues for a system wherein incumbents maintain an edge in the competition but cannot be guaranteed their positions if performance differentials between incumbents and aspirants become too large. In any case, managerial judgment must determine the balance of status competition and respect for veterans that should prevail in such situations:

Like other American orchestras, now that mandatory retirement ages have been declared illegal, the Chicago Symphony has an abundance of superannuated musicians, an audible problem in the upper strings. Mr. Barenboim's contract forbade him to fire anyone in his first two years as music director; now he is able, but disinclined to do so.

"I hope that a musician who has served an orchestra of this level for a long time has enough musical consciousness himself or herself to know that the time has come for them to go," he said. "You cannot really expect me or anybody else in my position to go to somebody who has been playing in this orchestra for 40 years, giving the best of themselves – their whole soul and body – and say, 'Now you have to go because you are not good enough anymore'. It should never arrive at that." (Miller, 1994, p.27)

There is some evidence, of course, that excessive emphasis on status and competition within ensembles of high professional achievement can be counterproductive. As noted earlier, smaller chamber groups value their egalitarian culture. And even in larger groups such as the Orpheus Chamber Orchestra, the notions of hierarchy and status are dispiriting to these highly accomplished, self-motivated players:

> One of the great crises in the group's history occurred in the early eighties, when one violinist began to act like a virtual dictator every time she became concertmaster, brushing aside all differences of opinion with maestro-like brusqueness. This was a violation of the Orphean categorical imperative, and it led to an atmosphere of rancor and tension. (Traub, 1996, p.104)

Intrinsic to the allocation of status and responsibility within an organization is the distribution of authority and leadership. As with the differentiation of work tasks and sharing of recognition, leadership can also be shared and distributed within an organization. Sharing of top leadership responsibility is more common in smaller groups where individuals can take charge of particular performance pieces and the job of leader can rotate according to what piece is being played. The Orpheus Chamber Orchestra has extended this idea to larger groups, appointing a different concertmaster and different instrument section leaders for each piece that it plays (Hackman, 2002). Indeed, there is no reason why, except for the administrative complexity, entirely different assignments of chairs throughout the ensemble cannot be made for different pieces or categories of music; this would recognize, for example, that some players have more expertise in Beethoven, while others are more masterful at Stravinsky. Such a system might have important motivational benefits, endowing a substantial fraction of an organization's members with responsibility and recognition and helping to overcome potential free-rider effects. However, such an approach can also be tricky (e.g., by what process are assignments made?) as well as discouraging when particular individuals are not capable of the responsibilities asked of them. Again, the Orpheus experience speaks to this:

> About fifteen years ago, two violinists were removed from the concertmaster rotation. It was, Nardo Poy, a violist, recalls, "a very painful issue," especially since the excluded violinists had been with Orpheus from the outset. "We had to decide: Do we accommodate people's feelings, or do we accommodate the group's wishes to have the best leadership possible at all times?" On that occasion, the musical imperative won out over the etiquette of group interaction. (Traub, 1996, p.104)

The alternative of centralized leadership under a strong musical director is associated with ambiguous motivational consequences as well. Strong leaders of prestigious ensembles, because these ensembles represent unique employment opportunities for accomplished players, often have coercive power in their sticks. George Szell of the Cleveland Orchestra had a reputation as an autocrat who could browbeat his players into achieving magnificent results. But other leaders do manage to inspire their troops in less oppressive ways:

> [Esa-Pekka Salonen]...leads with an assurance, dynamism and interpretive clarity that the musicians [of the Los Angeles Philharmonic] seem to find inspiring. And in virtually everything they played – particularly the Bartok Concerto for Orchestra and the Lutoslawski Symphony No.4 – they responded with a level of energy and excitement that one hears too rarely at orchestral performances. (Kozinn, 1994, p.B1)

Thus, inspirational central leadership cannot be dismissed as an important element of motivation. If conductors can articulate the ensemble's vision and goals, and embody its spirit, they can often inspire their players to make their best contributions to the group. In orchestras, this extends beyond the conductor to the second in command, the concertmaster, as well. For example, Daniel Majeske, long time concertmaster of the Cleveland Orchestra was credited with maintaining the traditions of George Szell, long after that maestro's tenure (Rosenberg, 2000).

Monitoring Performance

We have already touched on many of the ways in which performance is rewarded within ensembles and how these ways affect the proclivity of players to put forward their best efforts. The emphasis in this discussion has been on how ensembles can overcome the anonymity of large undifferentiated groups so that individuals can be induced, through rewards, recognition, or indeed by subtle or overt intimidation, into contributing their utmost to the collective product of the organization. The ways ensembles can do this are manifold. They can select self-motivated and talented players to begin with; they can assign the work in a manner that ensures that individuals are challenged and not frustrated, and hence derive intrinsic satisfaction from its performance; they can allocate status in a way that exploits players' competitive spirits and drives for excellence; they can divide up responsibilities for tasks and leadership so that individuals and small groups receive appropriate attention and recognition of their individual efforts; and they can empower leadership with the opportunity to inspire excellence and discourage substandard performance.

One reason that these various approaches work is that they offer players individualized rewards for contributing to the collective good of the organization. Thus, solo opportunities and status positions are examples of the "selective incentives" that Olson (1965) recommended to overcome the free-rider problem. But an equally important reason, also emphasized in principal-agent theory, is that they improve the ability of organizational leadership to monitor individual performance more closely so that individual contributions to the collective good can be isolated and identified. This is an obvious prerequisite to implementing individualized, selective rewards or penalties. Thus, individuals, not groups, compete for entry into the organization or for advancement to higher status positions; and auditions and chair-competitions provide leaders with the chance to evaluate players one at a time. Differentiating musical assignments and assigning solo parts also puts the spotlight on individuals, so that leaders can more easily determine, in practice or in concert, who is contributing what to overall performance. And decentralizing leadership, through section chairs, or sharing leadership through rotating positions, brings the monitor into closer range with individual members who are being observed as they perform their parts.

Strategic Balances in Achieving Motivation

Musical ensembles illustrate many ways for organizations to structure their practices and incentives so that individual interests become better aligned with overall organizational needs and players are motivated to put forward their best efforts. Nonetheless, ensembles also reveal some interesting tensions that arise in finding the appropriate combinations of motivational strategies. One of these tensions is the degree to which ensembles rely on centralized leadership and hierarchical structure versus more collegial arrangements. Another is the degree to which they rely on competition as a motivational strategy compared to cooperation and sharing.

Hierarchy and Central Leadership

As noted in the previous movement, hierarchical arrangements and central leadership arise as efficient means of coordinating the work of members of larger ensembles. Without designated leadership and division of authority, larger groups can become chaotic and difficult to keep on track. The motivational consequences of this management approach are more ambiguous, however. Formal, authoritative leaders can be inspirational and supportive, fair in their dealings and constructive in their guidance, lifting the spirits of group members and urging them on to make their best efforts. Moreover, a formal leadership structure – with subgroup and section leaders, a concertmaster and a conductor – can serve as ladder of opportunity containing incentives for members of the ensemble to excel so that they may be considered for future advancement. These motivational benefits of leadership and hierarchy are obviously more relevant to larger groups in which extended hierarchies are possible and where formal leadership is needed to address coordination problems. In some cases, such advancement is successful and in other cases it is not. Eugene Ormandy and Leonard Bernstein are well known for launching their conducting careers by successfully exploiting opportunities to fill in for ill conductors at short notice (Goodman, 1985b). Other, such as Maurizio Pollini, the Italian pianist, have had less successful experiences trying to make the leap to the rostrum (Holland, 1985).

To a certain degree, coercive or overbearing authoritarian leadership may succeed in eliciting greater effort from group members. George Szell was ruthless in his demands on Cleveland Orchestra players and in making personnel changes until he got what he wanted. But he was an inspired genius who had a clear vision for achieving excellence, and those who signed on and remained loyal to him gave their best and shared, at least vicariously, in his glory (Rosenberg, 2000). Still, formal leadership and hierarchy can also be demotivating if it is sufficiently oppressive and if it displaces individuals' sense of responsibility for the organization as a whole. If members of the Cleveland Orchestra lived in fear of George Szell and if they knew they had few alternatives for employment in such a prestigious organization, they had no choice but to respond to his scowls and do their best to satisfy his demands. However, many would argue that there is a limit to which such an approach can motivate and inspire better playing. The source of this limit is the fact that a top-down, command and control, hierarchy may not be able to take advantage of the inner resources of talented organization members. This appears to be a particular problem in symphony orchestras:

> This arrangement makes matters awkward for the orchestral musician who desires to improve the quality of the orchestral product. The musician must not challenge the conductor's tempi or interpretation; he or she cannot even suggest that there might be a pitch or ensemble problem, much less how the conductor might fix it. (Levine, 1996, p.18)

If, as Michael Haber of the Orpheus Chamber Orchestra describes it, a symphony orchestra operates like "one brain and two hundred hands", then the enthusiasm players bring to their performances will be limited to that of automata – responding to the stimulus of the brain (conductor) but bringing to bear none of their own inspiration or enthusiasm (Rosenberg, 1996). Worse than that, lack of control by musicians in an orchestra can lead to player stress:

> During rehearsals or concerts, musicians experience a total lack of control over their environment. They do not control when the music starts, when the music ends, or how the music goes. They don't even have the authority to leave the stage to attend to personal needs. They are, in essence, rats in a maze, at the whim of the god with the baton....Extensive research has demonstrated that lack of control is a major cause of stress. (Levine, 1996. p.20)

Individual enthusiasm can be more effectively engaged if ensemble members have some control and assume responsibility for themselves. As Alfred Brendel observed, one of the elements of success of the Orpheus ensemble is "...the responsibility that each player takes for the entire score, and not just his own part" (Traub, 1996, p.104). That general sense of responsibility for the organization's overall performance is jeopardized when leadership is given over completely to dominant individuals with formal leadership authority, and players are absolved of it.

The question then becomes – under what circumstances will de-emphasis of formal leadership and hierarchical arrangements bring motivational benefits? The answer appears to hinge on two key variables – size and level of professionalism. Size obviously affects the feasibility of running an organization informally and democratically. As the Orpheus ensemble has found, ways can be devised to decentralize and share leadership responsibilities in a fairly large group, certainly one on the order of two dozen individuals. Larger groups require greater formalization, but leadership styles and strategies can also be shaped so that members' alienation is minimized. Indeed, even in a formally organized hierarchy the organization chart can be turned upside down so that the conductor becomes a servant of the players rather than the other way around, i.e., a reversal of who is principal and who is agent. This reflects the experience of the Colorado Symphony which was recently reorganized as a musician-controlled organization in which the music director became, in effect, an employee of the players. The Vienna Philharmonic and the London Symphony Orchestra are also self-governing in this way. They operate without a music director and engage their own visiting conductors. In such arrangements, the many players do delegate their authority to the (current contracted) leader for operational purposes, but they maintain a sense of ultimate control and individual welfare.

It remains a question, however, as to what kinds of organizations can best derive motivational benefits from nonhierarchical arrangements. This hinges on the issue of responsibility as well as maturity. Musicians of the Orpheus Chamber Orchestra or the Colorado Symphony are highly skilled professionals who can inspire each other and are capable of making or evaluating the technical and creative decisions required of their ensembles. The same would not necessarily be true of an amateur group or a student ensemble. In these cases, an effective leader serves the important functions of teaching, inspiring, coaching, encouraging and indeed disciplining members towards their best efforts. This carries over even into the professional realm:

> ...if instrumentalists make mistakes it is not because they want to but because they don't understand or have difficulties; so you must help them to overcome them...when you are conducting an orchestra you have to match your approach to the temperament of the players... (Judy, 1996b, p.35 quoting Pierre Boulez)

The propensity and talent of the leader to teach thus has much to do with whether the hierarchy has discouraging or inspirational consequences.

In summary, the questions of hierarchy and formal leadership hinge on comparing the benefits of potentially inspirational, encouraging and supportive central leadership that may emerge under a formalized approach, with the motivational energy that can be released when ensemble members assume responsibility for themselves. The latter appears more likely to dominate in smaller organizations and ones in which members have achieved high levels of competence and professional achievement.

Competition and Collaboration

Musical ensembles also have mixed experiences with competitive and collaborative approaches to managing their personnel. Clearly, ensembles depend critically on close cooperation among their members, and members must encourage and inspire each other if the best group performance is to be achieved. Yet, ensembles also utilize competitive strategies to spur their personnel – competitive auditions, competition for seats in a section, competition for solo parts, and competition for leadership of sections. Clearly both competition and cooperation can have positive and negative motivational effects. Reliance on cooperation always runs the risk that individuals will slacken their efforts and not carry their fair shares of the load. But cooperation and collaboration can inspire and provide the mutual supports that individuals may need to put forward their best efforts. Alternatively, reliance on competition runs the risk of building resentment or frustration among losers, and undermining cooperation between colleagues where that cooperation is critically needed. Yet, competition appeals directly to individuals' self-interests and can potentially draw out individuals' best efforts.

Again, the most effective balance of cooperative and competitive strategy appears to depend on circumstances. In smaller ensembles, competition may be unnecessary and destructive. In a quintet or an octet, everyone knows and can hear each other, and social pressure will operate to spur each individual towards his or her best effort and towards working well together. Creating permanent rankings or statuses in such small groups may stir resentments that can easily flare into conflicts and confrontations when individuals work in close quarters with one another. Even where skill levels are differentiated and the score requires allocation of musical parts of differing prominence among the players, the practices of rotating leadership from piece to piece and sharing the solo opportunities recommend themselves.

Small ensembles can make good use of competitive strategy at the audition stage, however. A small ensemble is a select group by its very nature, and when it comes time to recruit new members, existing members can be jointly involved in overseeing a rigorous competition for entry into the group. Once selected, the new member can feel that he or she has earned the respect of existing members and can be accepted into the collaborative milieu thereafter.

Within larger ensembles, competitive strategies become more attractive. Opportunities for advancement come more frequently in larger groups so that losers in one round of competition can look forward to bettering themselves at a later stage. Moreover, competitive approaches have the advantage in large groups of introducing an important element of objectivity into decisions about individual reward and recognition. While competition for chairs and solo parts must be judged by someone, they may be less subject to perceptions of favoritism if formalized into competitive procedures with established rules and criteria.

As noted earlier, competitive procedures may also work better in situations where egos are less easily bruised or where downside risks can be minimized. For example, in ensembles consisting of members with distinguished reputations, holders of high status positions must be displaced with dignity and rewarded in alternate ways for their good service. This is necessary not only to maintain the morale of the displaced individuals, but for the entire membership of the ensemble as well. Individuals want to feel that they work for a compassionate and sensitive organization, and that they too will be treated with appropriate fairness and respect in such circumstances.

Priorities and Tradeoffs

As for coordination, it is clear that an organization can employ various combinations of strategies to motivate its participants. In this movement, we have identified a variety of motivational strategies: recruiting self-motivated players; designing work assignments that provide opportunities for players to shine; providing incentives to achieve higher status; sharing leadership responsibilities; monitoring and rewarding performance; and emphasizing pride in collective achievement of the ensemble as a whole. In general, all organizations can benefit from these strategies. Motivation will improve as more highly motivated participants are selected; as work assignments provide more opportunities for individual recognition; as greater opportunities exist for individual advancement and status; as leadership is shared more widely; as individual performance is monitored and connected with individual rewards; and as collective achievement inspires all participants. Again, however, ensembles facing different circumstances are able to exploit these strategies to varying degrees. Hence, the emphasis they put on each of them will necessarily differ from one type of ensemble to another.

Following the themes of the previous movement, we have considered a variety of organizational circumstances affecting motivation in this movement: size, heterogeneity, professionalism, instability and task complexity. The matrix in Table 2.1 is a variant of the one presented in Table 1.1 in the last movement, for a variety of ensemble stereotypes that face different motivational challenges. The stereotypical big band jazz orchestra, typical of those in the 1930s and '40s, was moderate in size – fairly large, but smaller than a full sized classical orchestra. It contained a variety of instruments, including woodwinds, brass, and percussion. Typically, it employed professional musicians, some of whom would be regulars and others who would also have other jobs and might come and go. The task at hand was a complex one, involving fairly intricate parts for each instrument section, including improvised passages, as well as weaving together of the contributions of different instrument sections. The suggested analog is a university which consists of diverse disciplinary departments staffed by professional faculty and some part-time adjunct faculty. The teaching of each discipline is a complex task, and integration of multiple, disciplinary curricula into the overall educational plans of students with different majors and minors, is also complex. The motivational challenge is largely to engage participants in a menu of work that is challenging and interconnected, but in a manner that maintains flexibility and room for individual achievement, and causes a minimum of frustration.

The tubafest is a periodic (usually annual) event consisting of many (sometimes hundreds) of mostly amateur participants all playing variants of the tuba, including sousaphones, tubas, and baritone horns. Although there are many regulars in these events, many others participate from time to time. The music played in tubafests is usually simple, to accommodate the variety of skill levels, and to celebrate certain community themes such as the winter holiday period. The suggested analog is a student protest movement which also can be large, amateur, communal, involve diverse participants, and must focus on basic tasks like holding a rally or a march. The essential motivational challenge is to keep participants enthusiastic and contributing, given the large diverse group, the collective nature of the output, and the limits to providing individual rewards.

Table 2.1   Ensemble Attributes and Motivation

	size	heterogeneity	professional level	instability	task complexity	nonmusical analog
Big band jazz orchestra	moderate	high	high	moderate	high	university
Tubafest	high	low	low	high	low	student protest movement
College wind ensemble	moderate	high	moderate	high	moderate	department store
Men's church choir	high	low	low	moderate	low	government license bureau
Barbershop quartet	low	moderate	low	low	low	small, neighborhood law firm

The college wind ensemble is something like the professional jazz orchestra in its size and heterogeneity. However, its participants are more transient, have lower levels of training and face a more structured set of tasks, since the music is generally more formal and calls less frequently for improvisation. Players in the wind ensemble are students who generally are volunteers although some may be required to play in the ensemble as part of the curriculum for their music majors. Over time, student turnover reflects a relatively unstable work force. The suggested analog is a retail department store which has various departments with sales people who are trained in the individual requirements of their particular product inventories as well as in store-wide procedures. Here, vagaries of the labor market and the limits of long term career opportunities cause the workforce to be relatively transient. Tasks are relatively straightforward and specified by written procedures. The essential motivational challenge for this type of organization is to maintain the interest and dedication of participants in light of the high turnover and the structured nature of the tasks at hand.

The men's church choir is relatively large, homogeneous, and transient, though perhaps less extreme in these dimensions than the tubafest. It also consists of mainly amateur players singing relatively simple music. The suggested analog is a government license bureau where officials at every station are responsible for doing the same tasks of issuing certain kinds of licenses according to pre-specified requirements. All of the license bureau employees share in the overall reputation of the bureau, just as members of the choir derive satisfaction from the collective output of their singing. The essential motivational challenge here is to motivate individuals within a milieu that makes it difficult to recognize individual effort and achievement.

The barbershop quartet is a very small organization, with a relatively homogeneous internal composition – although there is clear differentiation of roles within the context of male voice ranges. Typically, participants are dedicated amateurs singing relatively simple and straightforward music. Moreover, the group tends to be stable with little turnover among participants. The suggested analog is a small neighborhood law firm whose partners work together on cases. Each partner has expertise on particular aspects of the law and cases are relatively common and straightforward. The essential challenge is to motivate individuals while maintaining the egalitarian milieu which all participants value.

As in the previous movement, none of these stereotypes is completely characteristic of their musical counterparts in the real world, nor are the suggested nonmusical analogs exact. Again, however, they are useful for prioritizing motivational strategies best suited to organizations that resemble each stereotype. Table 2.2 suggests priorities among alternative motivational strategies for each ensemble stereotype. The matrix suggests that different types of ensembles will tend to rely on substantially different combinations of motivational strategies. The big band jazz orchestra is large and diverse enough to substantially motivate players by the promise of more prominent work assignments, e.g. solos and more prominent parts within instrument sections. It can also easily monitor and reward players for their performance. Changes in status can accompany changes in work assignments. Over the long term, recruitment can play a role as an important strategy for achieving and maintaining a motivated workforce. Recruitment can become even more effective if the ensemble as a whole has acquired a good reputation for its overall performance, hence attracting players seeking a prestigious and challenging place to work. However, the relatively large and diverse, transient, individualistic character of the ensemble makes it more difficult to rely on pride of collective achievement or sharing of leadership responsibilities as primary motivational devices.

The tubafest is substantially different. It is so large, homogeneous and lacking in professional characteristics that few of the conventional motivational strategies can be effective. Opportunities for monitoring and rewarding individual performance, sharing leadership or offering status incentives are few. To a certain extent work assignments can be crafted to help motivate individuals to contribute and improve themselves – for example, by breaking down the group into sections with parts of differing prominence. Even greater reliance can be put on recruitment of motivated players. Tubafests tend to be open enrollment affairs with little control over who participates, but those who do participate tend to do so out of self-motivation. In this context, management can be pro-active in identifying and recruiting potential players who might not be aware of the opportunity and who might bring both enthusiasm and skill to the ensemble. Finally, it is the irony of an ensemble like a tubafest, that despite its large size, and hence the inability of its individual players to claim much of the credit for the ensemble's overall performance, that the ensemble may have to rely primarily on pride of collective performance as the key to motivation. Individuals participate voluntarily because they want to be part of the larger whole, and they get their kicks from the festive environment and from hearing what 500 tubas trying to play together actually sound like. Management that can focus the attention of the group on this collective milieu and achievement may have the most success in motivating individual players.

Table 2.2   Motivation Strategies

	recruitment	work assignments	status incentives	sharing leadership	monitoring and rewarding performance	pride in collective achievement
Big band jazz orchestra	4	1	3	6	2	5
Tubafest	2	3	4	5	6	1
College wind ensemble	1	2	4	6	3	5
Men's church choir	2	4	6	3	5	1
Barber-shop quartet	5	1	6	2	4	3

As a transient and selective group, with participants coming in and leaving every year, the college wind ensemble can put substantial emphasis on recruiting motivated players. Moreover, as a fairly large and formal ensemble with substantially differentiated parts, it can also utilize work assignments (i.e., more or less prominent parts), monitoring and rewarding of individual performance, and allocation of status (first and second chairs, etc.) as effective devices to manage motivation. Although school spirit may be invoked, motivating through pride of collective achievement is more difficult because the group keeps changing composition and because participation is only one of many activities and responsibilities undertaken by individual students. Finally, motivation through shared leadership is difficult because the ensemble is basically part of an instructional regime in which the faculty leader must maintain essential authority and cannot easily delegate that authority.

The men's church choir is a communal organization in which participants are motivated less by private than collective factors. Thus, pride in a job well done is the immediate key to maintaining motivation while recruiting individuals with a communal spirit is the primary avenue for ensuring motivation over time. By sharing leadership responsibilities in the ensemble, credit for performance can be spread around, reinforcing the group spirit. Given the communal character and the size and homogeneity of the group, allocating work assignments, monitoring and rewarding performance, and offering status incentives, are less effective motivational strategies for this type of ensemble.

Finally, the barbershop quartet is obviously a very small and also egalitarian ensemble in which there are few opportunities to motivate through status incentives or the formal monitoring and rewarding of performance. (Performance monitoring happens more or less automatically through the close interaction and inevitable mutual feedback among the players.) In addition, since turnover is likely to be very low, and disruptive when it occurs, recruitment is not a strategy that can be extensively utilized either. Promoting pride in collective achievement of the group is effective since each participant can claim a substantial fraction of the credit. Moreover, sharing of leadership responsibilities can enhance this mutual claim of credit for performance. Finally, it is interesting that even in an ensemble this small, differentiation of skills (voice registers) and parts allows for effective use of work assignments as a motivational strategy. Overall repertoire can be shaped, and individual performance pieces chosen, to favor those who are contributing most.

Case Studies

Melville House, a small, institutional program for troubled teenage boys, opened on Long Island in 1972 (Young, 1985). It was staffed and managed by a small group of five close colleagues with complementary mental health, social work and business skills, all of whom believed that better and more innovative programming was needed to help teenage boys with severe behavioral problems. Three of the five members of the group had been professional staff members in a local state mental hospital, where they developed their concepts and understanding of the problems facing troubled boys.

Motivation was an extremely important dimension of Melville's survival and early success. The members of the group had decided that the array of services heretofore provided by the state were inadequate and they were determined to challenge those services with something new. Yet, they required public funding to make a go of it. Not surprisingly, many bureaucratic barriers were thrown in their path, including difficulties in finding appropriate housing property in a local community that would tolerate their program and clientele; obtaining approval from governmental regulatory bodies for bringing their group home up to code; securing necessary licenses; and remaining financially solvent during periods of delay between state reimbursements; and so on. Most of the team members had easier, more secure and more financially rewarding jobs before undertaking Melville House. They needed to make up in internal motivation what was lacking in external encouragement.

As an organization, Melville resembled a small chamber group with differentiated instrumentation, such as a string quintet. The different skills of its staff complemented one another, they enjoyed working together, they believed in the same organizational mission, and they relished the mutual challenge of undertaking a new and difficult repertoire. While there was some sense of seniority and deference within the ensemble as a result of different levels of experience, education and age, the group functioned as a team, held together by mutual respect and genuine affection, rather than a formal authority structure.

The members of the Melville team could be described as highly motivated, and that motivation was maintained by the sharing, collaborative milieu that they had established, rather than formal structural mechanisms. Perhaps of greatest importance, all members of the team shared a collective pride of achievement. What Melville House accomplished in helping troubled boys was indivisible, with substantial credit and pride accruing to all of the ensemble members. Also of great importance was the fact that each member of this ensemble had a rewarding work assignment, i.e., a prominent part to play reflecting his or her particular skills. Moreover, the members of the ensemble shared leadership – depending on the task at hand, one or the other team member could take the lead and had the opportunity to excel and receive recognition. By contrast, more formal organizational mechanisms played a much smaller motivational role: there was little formal monitoring and documentation of each others' performance; there was no explicit recruitment program to attract new team members or discharge ones that did not perform, and there were no formal promotional or incentive programs through which members of the team could achieve greater status. In keeping with its likeness to a small chamber group, Melville House's success in motivating its players relied on egalitarian measures that promoted mutual respect and recognition, and pride of collective accomplishment. As evidence of its success in exploiting these motivational strategies especially appropriate to small chamber groups, Melville faced a dilemma after six years of operation in connection with whether the organization should expand its services and pursue a growth strategy. The members of the ensemble knew that becoming an orchestra rather than a chamber group would substantially change the character of the organization and require a new regime to maintain its high level of mutual dedication and enthusiasm.

The Salvation Army is also an organization that could be described as embodying high motivational levels of its members (Watson and Brown, 2001). But the Salvation Army is a large organization, more like a full symphony orchestra than a chamber group. It encompasses large numbers of paid employees and volunteers. As such it relies more on formal organizational mechanisms for motivation, especially: systematic recruitment of like-minded individuals who derive meaning and satisfaction in the religious beliefs and the self-sacrificing values of Salvation Army members; reinforcement of those religious and organizational values through educational programming; formal systems of goal setting and evaluation to assess performance and to promote individuals to positions of greater responsibility and status; and certainly strong central authority – based on a long tradition of charismatic and visionary leadership dating back to the 19th century.

While the latter may be the primary motivating mechanisms, the Salvation Army also engages some of the strategies of a chamber group – especially building collective pride in the achievements of the organization as a whole, and (recently) undertaking decentralization so as to create local work situations that allow for individual creativity and risk taking, and sharing of overall organizational leadership responsibility.

Perhaps the best analog for the Salvation Army, in terms of motivational issues, would be a community-based symphony orchestra. Much of its workforce is (initially at least) amateur, indeed volunteer, and even the professional core staff have been attracted to the organization because of their beliefs and love of the concept rather than any established record of virtuosity or sophistication in their working skills. Thus, the Salvation Army is able to motivate by attending primarily to their members' emotional satisfaction while providing modestly for their basic material needs and financial security. Still, the size and complexity of this organization requires that motivational systems be put in place that play to the particular values and rewards of its constituents. It is an army with a heart, but it is still an army which depends on informed central leadership to implement appropriate, formal motivational strategies.

Diagnosing An Organization

As in the last movement, it is useful to ask: what kind of musical ensemble does my organization of interest most closely resemble? In connection with motivational issues, is it like a jazz orchestra, a tubafest, a college wind ensemble, a men's church choir, a barbershop quarter or some other type of ensemble? With a comfortable metaphor in mind, one can proceed to construct an appropriate row in each of the two matrices of Tables 2.1 and 2.2, by first describing the circumstances under which the organization operates (Table 2.1), and then considering the priorities these circumstances require for employing a particular combination of coordination strategies (Table 2.2), just as we have done for the stereotype ensembles above. Again, different ensemble metaphors may be needed to describe different parts of the organization. The repair shop in an automobile dealership may be more like a jazz orchestra while the sales department may more closely resemble a men's church choir. Indeed, large organizations are often complex and multi-faceted and may benefit from this kind of analysis at multiple levels.

The matrix analysis should yield a general sense of the nature of the organization's motivational issues and the appropriate emphases to be put on alternative motivation strategies. Whether the focus is on a particular part of the organization, or on the organization as a whole, it will also be helpful to ask more detailed questions about the fundamental conditions that create motivational challenges in the organization, and the combinations of motivation strategies that best apply to its particular circumstances. The experiences of musical ensembles suggest that the following questions are appropriate for diagnosing and resolving motivational issues, bearing in mind that each organization is different and solutions will vary accordingly.

First, certain areas of an organization will be more vulnerable to motivational problems then others. In order to focus on these areas, managers can ask themselves the following questions:

- Which parts of the organization feature relatively large numbers of workers doing similar kinds of work?
- Which parts of the organization have high turnover or depend on part-timers, consultants or other auxiliary workers?
- Which parts of the organization are dependent on workers who are not tied into professional career tracks?
- Which parts of the organization are responsible for supportive work where slippage is less noticeable?
- In which parts of the organization are worker skill levels mismatched with the difficulty of the work?
- In which parts of the organization is the work highly programmed and limited in the degree to which workers have discretion or can use their own creativity?

Parts of the organization that meet one or more of these criteria are likely to be the ones most vulnerable to motivational problems and which merit managerial scrutiny. With the potential targets identified, management can then ask itself about the applicability of a variety of strategies and solutions that ensembles employ:

- Can departments or sections be broken down into smaller groups, and can work within sections be further differentiated and individualized?
- Are there ways to allow more individuals to stand out through "solo" opportunities or leadership on particular projects or functions?
- Can the skills and preferences of workers be more precisely matched to their work assignments?
- Can additional ways be found to recognize and reward the contributions of individual workers?
- Are there ways to make the work more interesting or to give workers more discretion in shaping it?
- Can more robust advancement ladders be developed within large departments?
- Are there ways to highlight the work of supporting departments or to develop

projects where members of supporting departments have more prominent roles?

– Can the organization as a whole reshape its agenda so that work becomes more interesting and challenging or less frustrating?
– Can worker recruitment processes be improved to attract individuals better matched to the work at hand, more self-motivated, more attuned to the mission of the organization, and more comfortable working in teams?
– Can leaders be selected who can inspire by example and will not discourage or cause resentment among workers through autocratic behavior?
– Can leaders do a better job of articulating the vision and goals of the ensemble in a manner that inspires its players to contribute to its collective achievement?

Third Movement: Finding and Maintaining a Niche

Maybe the audience is better on the next block!

Achieving coordination and motivating the workforce are bedrock tasks of management. Yet superb ensemble and high motivation do not ensure organizational success. Even more basic is the requirement that the organization be doing something that people are willing to support. Without resources there will be no organization to coordinate and no workforce to motivate.

This is not to say that all organizations must produce something that is marketable in the conventional sense. Organizations support themselves in a variety of ways. A few are lucky enough to have internal resources provided to them by some act of past generosity or from surpluses accumulated over time, e.g., endowments created by year to year savings or donated by philanthropists or charitable organizations that wish to have a particular activity or program carried out in perpetuity. Some musical ensembles, such as the Cleveland Orchestra, are well endowed. In the short run, this can insulate against the need to prove one's self constantly in the eyes of financial benefactors or customers, but it also provides flexibility to experiment and take risks.   Other ensembles are supported directly by those who do the organization's work, i.e., volunteers who carry out most of the organization's activity and who, in return, reap personal benefits or satisfaction from the contributions of their labor.   Many musical groups operate in this mode: Amateur ensembles often play solely for their own satisfaction, and even professional ensembles involve a substantial element of playing at modest wages (discounted from what its players might earn elsewhere),   for the love of it. However, most organizations depend primarily on financial resources derived from their external environments – either through sales of services or goods in the marketplace, maintaining a systematic flow of voluntary contributions, or through government support derived from taxation and ultimately mandated by voter-approved public policies.

Whatever their circumstances or chosen strategies, all organizations must find "niches" that can command the internal or external resources to sustain them.   The closest exception is the endowed organization that may choose to live off past generosity or accumulated wealth.   But even here, it is the rare endowed organization that finds it wise to stand still.   Most endowed organizations tend to use their financial corpus as a base on which to build, and building requires appealing to those who can supply new resources.   The alternative can be problematic: well endowed organizations can become insulated, grow flaccid and unresponsive to changes in their environments, and ultimately become targets for criticism, reform, restructuring or dissolution (e.g., see Hirschman, 1970 and Guthrie, 1996).

Achieving a viable niche is a much more serendipitous challenge than the core tasks of coordination and motivation.   While coordination and motivation are essentially inward-looking management challenges subject to substantial management control, niche-finding requires looking outward into an uncertain, often changing environment.   Still, there are important connections between the internal character and operations of an organization and how it finds its place in the world at large.   Organizations, even fledgling groups, are not completely free to select any niche that appears, on the surface, to be attractive or remunerative.   To the contrary, organizations must build on their internal strengths and capacities if they are to exploit external opportunities and be successful.   It is the nexus between internal strengths and external opportunities that best defines successful niche-finding.

"Niche" is essentially an ecological concept derived from the study of natural, biological systems: organisms find their places in nature as predators and sources of nourishment in the food chain, and as competitors for limited natural resources to sustain themselves.   The application of this metaphor to the social world is imperfect (Gould, 1996) and requires modification (Hannan and Freeman, 1989). In nature, biological niches are filled out through random mutations and subject to the harsh standards of Darwinian survival, while in the social world there can be more conscious planning and control, less dependence on random occurrences, and even the sustenance of inefficient forms over long periods of time by tenacious or obstinate supporters or through the protection of legal or social constraints that immobilize resources and inhibit their transfer to more productive uses.

Still, the ecology metaphor provides important insights for organizations. A well coordinated and highly motivated organization that simply duplicates the programs of another, even if it is efficient and energetic, is liable to fail if the resource environment cannot support both, while a less polished organization that produces something unique may have greater success. For example, the Retired Men's Chorus in Dennis, Massachusetts is far from a flawlessly performing ensemble but it has prospered for twenty years on the basis of its large repertoire of songs and its popularity among senior citizens (New York Times, 1987).

On the other hand, some have blamed the contemporary struggles of American symphony orchestras on too much duplication and narrowing of the repertoire:

> We in the world of symphony orchestras are the custodians of staggering wealth; nearly 300 years' worth of incredibly diverse music. We are not, however, doing a very good job with our stewardship. It is more than half century since Virgil Thompson noted that the active orchestral repertory was overwhelmingly dominated by "the 50 pieces." It may be that "the 50" are really 77 or 113, but what Thompson deplored has not changed much. We lavish amazing expenditures of money, skill and spirit on nursing just a tiny part of the available repertory. (Steinberg, 1999, p.1)

Nonetheless, the specialized niche of classic works, both originals and imitations of those works, undergirds an important segment of the organizational ecology of musical ensembles. Composer Steve Reich laments:

> ... if I had a dime for every trace of *The Rite of Spring* I've heard in movie soundtracks, I'd be rich...I don't think imitations will sap the power of the originals. If anything, because of familiarity with the sound, the original will come through more clearly...Ezra Pound once said that a classic is something that remains new and the best work is capable of re-creating the context of its times. (Page, 1992, p.120-121)

The choice of repertoire, and ultimately niche, reflects an ensemble's particular resource base and market position. A well-endowed ensemble, or one which is the beneficiary of substantial, unrestricted voluntary support, has more flexibility to experiment with new works or musical genres than an ensemble that relies more heavily on box office revenues, and it must closely align itself with (or somehow shape) popular tastes. As economist Burton Weisbrod (personal communication) puts it, the latter is likely to play Tchaikovsky's *1812 Overture* more often (and presumably John Cage's *Concert for Piano and Orchestra* less often) than the former.

The essential idea that the ecology metaphor contributes is that organizations must find their places within their environmental contexts. This may involve defining a new niche that no other organization has previously occupied. It may involve finding vacancies in the present landscape of known possibilities or competing for occupied places with other organizations by offering the same products or services in a better way. The borderline between the process of creating a new niche and searching for a viable, existing niche is very fuzzy.

Producing a known product more cheaply or at higher quality may involve a change in the production process or a new variation in the product itself. For example, the contemporary movement to play baroque or classical music on original instruments created a new niche despite the fact that the compositions being played were the same pieces by Mozart, Bach and Vivaldi. It remains to be seen whether this niche competes with or is complementary to playing early music on modern instruments (Rosenberg, 1998h).

The Elements of Niche-Finding

While some of the conventional elements of management may play a lesser and indirect role in the task of niche-finding than in the tasks of coordination and motivation, most are still important. Plans, communications, incentives and rewards, education and practicing (rehearsals) do contribute to effective niche-finding. Leadership is even more important.

Formal Plans and Procedures

As we have seen, musical scores, and songs and standard rules in jazz, while playing critical roles in the coordination of ensembles, serve only as a foundation to the final product of musical performance. Scores, for example, must not only be implemented to achieve the physical output of (hopefully well-coordinated) sound, they must be *interpreted* to give the music a particular flavor. Composers do much to guide ensembles with their scores, so that certain moods, rhythms, and melodic effects are achieved. But written scores go just so far in providing instructions for playing, and indeed instructions on scores can even be overruled or modified by ensembles that choose to do things differently. It is this room for *interpretation* of the score, or of the composer's intent, that may allow an ensemble to achieve a special niche in the world of musical performance. Thus, two ensembles that play the same music may play it differently in ways that elicit support from alternative constituencies with different tastes. In classical music, for example, it is common to refer to the "Philadelphia sound" or the "Chicago sound" in differentiating the symphony orchestras in those cities. An ensemble's lack of such identification may even be a signal that a problem exists, and that the ensemble has not achieved any special distinction. Indeed, some bemoan contemporary homogenization of orchestras across the board:

> Thirty years ago, Russian, French and Czech orchestras still had quite special sounds, and there was a radical difference between, say, the Cleveland Orchestra and the Philadelphia, or the Concertgebouw Orchestra and the Vienna Philharmonic. Gradually, the characteristics are being ironed out. (Griffiths, 1999, p.32)

The process of interpretation falls largely to the leadership of musical ensembles, especially of large ensembles, or is developed through internal discussion in smaller, more collaborative ensembles. Another strategy of niche-finding is to search for fresh scores themselves, i.e., to find essentially different projects or plans that the organization can undertake. For ensembles, this includes the uncovering of lesser known or forgotten works by recognized composers, or exploration of the works of unfamiliar composers. Some ensembles achieve unique and sustainable niches by emphasizing differing repertoire or combinations of programming than those offered by other organizations. The search for different repertoire may also fall to ensemble leadership or emanate from a deliberative process within collaborative organizations:

> "I'm going to seize on the orchestra's limitations and celebrate them", [Hugh Wolff, music director of the St. Paul Chamber Orchestra] said. "It's a 34-player orchestra, and we're not going to play Brahms symphonies. Given that, it's incumbent upon me to search the widest possible spectrum for suitable repertory. One of my pet peeves is that the big orchestras have really narrowed their repertory. They've eliminated Bach and Handel partly out of fear of being stylistically embarrassed. But I feel at St. Paul we must go all the way back to 1600, the start of orchestral music. Sure, we have modern instruments, but it can be done in an informed way." (Schwarz, 1991, p.25)

In jazz, of course, the song and the rules of improvisation are the linchpins of performances, but not necessarily the sources that differentiate one ensemble from another. Certainly, the Duke Ellington bands were unique in part because they specialized in the leader's compositions (his songs), played the way he wanted them to be played. However, for many if not most jazz ensembles, the real distinctions derive from their liberal interpretations of (various) songs, and the creative ways in which those improvisations reflect spontaneity and new sounds and ideas that evolve from their performances over time.

Communication

Especially in smaller organizations, a sustainable niche may be found through a process of internal dialogue among key players and leaders. Organizational participants may have different ideas about what the organization can do best and what might be appealing to organizational supporters. Moreover, communication enables ensemble members both to try different interpretations in the current repertoire and to experiment with new pieces – two ways in which ensembles may grope towards finding a unique place for themselves.

Through communication, ensemble players may discuss what is meant by particular instructions in the score and how these instructions are best carried out. Or they may argue over whether they agree with the composer's instructions or have a better idea of what to do. They may also identify gaps in the score – necessary information that has been left out and needs to be filled in by the players in the process of implementing the score. The manner in which the gaps are filled or the instructions interpreted will have the effect of differentiating one ensemble's playing from another's. And those interpretations that appeal to potential organizational supporters may constitute viable niches that the organization can exploit for continued sustenance and development. The players in the Orpheus Chamber Orchestra spend countless hours deliberating over how to play a particular piece, often to unique effect. Members of improvisational jazz ensembles "speak" to each other in real time, as the performance proceeds, sometimes leading each other into new musical territory that they can ultimately claim for their own (Weick, 1998). On the lighter side, the players of the Johann Strauss orchestra have great fun conspiring with one another on how to play Straus's music as outrageously humorously as possible, carving out their special niche in the musical world in the process (Rosenberg, 1998f).

Education

We have seen that for purposes of coordination, the more technically proficient an ensemble's players, the more easily they are able to synchronize with one another. Thus, management is well-advised not only to recruit highly trained players but also to encourage their continued development. A similar observation can be made with respect to niche finding. For this purpose, however, the *breadth* of education rather than its *depth* or emphasis on technical proficiency is of equal or perhaps greater interest. Education that exposes players to different types and styles of music will widen their awareness to a fuller set of possibilities for their own playing. Especially in areas like popular, jazz and folk music, players tend to listen to their contemporaries and often borrow ideas, techniques and even particular pieces from one another. Peter Paul and Mary borrowed songs introduced by Bob Dylan, the Kingston Trio and the Weavers, for instance. Formal education can contribute on a wider scale by exposing players to significantly different types of music, e.g. instructing classical players on how to listen to jazz or vice versa, or by presenting broad historical perspectives that allow players to put their own music into context and expand their understanding of its possible variants. The bands formed by composer Toshiko Akiyoshi are beneficiaries of such a broad perspective, combining big band bebop with elements of Japanese traditional music to produce a unique sound (Owen, 1995).

As a strategy, education will contribute to niche finding only if players are viewed as collaborators in determining the direction of the organization. If the ensemble is run by an authoritarian conductor, the players' ideas will hardly matter. But collaborative ensembles such as the Orpheus Chamber Orchestra depend heavily on their players to explore possibilities and shape the ensemble's particular style and repertoire. In this context, broad player education can contribute to a more robust niche-finding process.

In jazz, education enters the picture in another way. Players intensively and broadly schooled in the state of the art are better positioned to go beyond that to establish new musical niches for themselves. One must know the rules, conventions, and theory of today's music in order to recognize the limits of, and experiment outside, the conventional boundaries. In management professor Bill Pasmore's words:

...if a musician only knows one song, one beat, or one style, he or she can't be part of the emergent synergy that is jazz (Pasmore, 1998, p.563)

Rehearsals

As we have seen, practice sessions serve a variety of purposes. They enable the working out of coordination problems, and they can assist with motivation by allowing closer attention to particular players and subgroups. Rehearsals can also contribute to niche-finding because practice sessions represent opportunities for experimentation and change. In rehearsals, organizational members and leaders can say, "let's try it like this and see how it sounds." Major variations in style or repertoire are not likely to arise from rehearsal sessions, but small but important changes in tone, rhythm, volume, balance among instruments, and other nuances, can result which cumulatively help define an ensemble's special sound. This can be a serendipitous process, especially in a collaborative organization where leadership is facilitative rather than directive and participants are open-minded about the outcome rather than driven by preconceived ideas. But it is the serendipity itself that may be most important to ultimate success in finding a unique niche. "Management by groping along," a phrase introduced by political scientist Sarah Liebschutz (1992) , utilizing mechanisms such as collegial rehearsal sessions, is sometimes the best way to find creative solutions to the niche problem. For more risk-taking groups, some of this experimentation may even take place in live performance. The Grateful Dead, for example were known for doing this (Pareles, 1987b). Indeed, in jazz this is as much the norm as the exception. Even in these contexts, however, rehearsals can serve the purpose of working out some ideas in advance, ultimately moving a group towards some distinctive possibilities for themselves.

Incentives and Rewards

We have seen how reward and incentive systems help management motivate an organization's workforce. The challenge of niche-finding is not so obviously addressed by incentive structures. It is possible to provide specific rewards for individuals to come up with new ideas that may prove to be viable, but such an approach is tenuous at best. Successful niche-finding not only requires creativity; it also requires consensus and cooperation and a sense of the organization's place in the world. If the organization's members cannot buy into a suggested new direction, and if top management is not involved and supportive, it is unlikely that players' suggestions will lead to defining and pursuing a successful new niche. Incentive schemes that put players into competition with one another for rewards may even undermine the possibilities for coalescing around a common approach.

Incentives and rewards do have their place in niche-finding, however. Ensembles that depend on the creativity of their members to find a successful repertoire or style must create an atmosphere in which risk-taking is encouraged and individuals are not penalized or embarrassed for suggesting ideas that may ultimately be found unworkable or unattractive. An authoritarian environment in which a strong leader intimidates players is not one in which creative ideas for variations in repertoire or style are likely to emerge. Even an egalitarian environment in which some players are nonetheless permitted to dominate conversation or undermine others' efforts may be unsupportive of successful niche-finding. Rather, the organizational environment must be one of mutual respect, openness and tolerance if players are expected to be comfortable contributing their best ideas and receptive to the proposals of others. The London Symphony Orchestra suggests a possible model:

> In many ways, the LSO operated like a large family: members had generally congenial relationships, they care about one another personally as well as professionally, and they freely exchanged information and opinions...Consistent with the spirit of self-governance, members looked out not only for their individual interests, but also for the well-being of the orchestra as a whole... (Lehman and Galinksy, 1994, p.8)

Leadership

The LSO is also an ensemble in which leadership is crucial to the niche-finding process. The orchestra's artistic and marketing plan is the responsibility of the managing director, though accountability is to the players:

> ...As players became increasingly confident of [managing director] Gillinson's judgment, they granted him greater autonomy to act on their behalf pursuing the orchestra's artistic, organizational and financial goals. Most players felt that the hallmark of Gillinson's administration was his ability to "persuade without bulldozing," to foster agreement about objectives, and to exercise creativity in overcoming challenging financial problems. (Lehman and Galinsky, 1994, p.10)

Leaders can suggest and interpret plans, facilitate dialogue among players, provide or recommend educational experiences, administer productive rehearsal sessions, and create an atmosphere in which risk-taking is encouraged, all in the interests of supporting ways to identify, explore, experiment with, and confirm viable alternative programming. In some ways, leaders can inhibit successful niche-finding by interfering with open processes of communication and collaboration among ensemble members. In other ways, however, leadership is essential to the niche finding process. Niche-finding requires understanding of the organizational environment, historical trends, and technical possibilities. Leaders of organizations are often expected to have command of these subjects and are looked to for ideas grounded in long experience, deep comprehension, and technical mastery. Jeannette Sorrell's leadership of the early music group Apollo's Fire is a good example. This group has secured a special place in the landscape of musical fare in the Northeast Ohio region and in the field of early music. Apollo's success is due in no small part to Ms. Sorrell's extraordinary historical and technical knowledge of early music repertory and instrumentation which guides how the group's programs are adapted to available performance venues ranging from churches, to converted barns, to the splendor of Severance Hall (Salisbury, 1998c).

Certainly music directors of most symphony and chamber orchestras, and even leaders of smaller and more popular groups are expected to provide such expertise. The issue here is not only knowledge and perspective or even creativity per se. It is also what is commonly called "vision" – a mental picture of what makes the organization special, what characteristics make its style and repertoire unique, and where it fits into its overall field of activity. Sometimes, vision is inextricably linked to the style or genius of a particular (charismatic) leader. The Supremes could not survive without Diana Ross nor could the Grateful Dead without Jerry Garcia. But in many other instances, especially with larger organizations, visionary leaders do succeed not only in leaving their special imprints on the organization, but in creating viable niches that outlive their own tenures. While the styles of the Cleveland and the Philadelphia orchestras have changed under successive administrations, and while there may be a contemporary trend towards homogeneity among major symphony orchestras, there is still something defining about the Philadelphia and Cleveland "sounds" developed under the leaderships of Eugene Ormandy and George Szell, respectively, that continues to support viable places for these organizations in the ecology of great orchestras. To the contrary, other orchestras that have not succeeded in developing or retaining a distinctive sound are likely to suffer most in today's commodified world of omnipresent technology and global competition.

The Circumstances of Niche-Finding

Organizations of varying characteristics and operating in different environmental circumstances are likely to require alternative niche-finding strategies. Moreover, the possibilities for finding a successful niche are richer in some fields of activity and in some historical periods than in others. Organizational size, internal diversity, level of professionalism, the complexity of work in the field in which the organization participates, and the stability of the organizational environment, all affect the viability and direction of niche-finding and the kinds of approaches that are likely to be succeed. Dynamic environments are more likely to feature unfilled niches that represent new opportunities for alert organizations. But they also create uncertainties for organizations wishing to hold onto their existing niches. The advent of Rock and Roll in the 1950s opened up a whole new space for popular ensembles (starting with Bill Halley and the Comets and continuing on through the Beatles and beyond) while it constricted the space available for traditional popular music groups (eventually causing the popular Hit Parade television show to go off the air, Snooky Lanson, Dorothy Collins and Giselle MacKenzie notwithstanding!)

Organization Size

The collaborative processes of niche-finding, involving effective internal communications, collaboration and experimentation in practice sessions, are more likely to be viable for smaller organizations. Larger organizations require more formal processes and more directive leadership in order to keep them focused and productively engaged in exploration of alternative styles and repertoires, and maintenance of a distinctive character. It is possible to simulate the benefits of smaller size by breaking down larger organizations into smaller working groups and bringing the results of small group processes together systematically into an overall consultative decision-making process. That is, leaders in large organizations can create structures and processes to enable small group deliberation, and they can be systematically supportive in their management approaches. But this still requires strong leadership to design and manage a facilitative, collaborative and consensual regime overall. Moreover, even in a facilitative environment, top leaders will still be valued for the ideas, information, guidance and vision they can offer. Overall, therefore, larger organizations will put greater reliance on leadership to successfully identify, articulate, implement and maintain their niches. Indeed, recruitment of leaders will often center on the question of what vision they will bring to the organization in order to secure its future:

> The band in the late 1950s and early 1960s had a unique sound, one of the classic musical styles of the twentieth century. [Count] Basie maintained the integrity of this hybrid style until just weeks before his death. Since then Thad Jones, followed by Frank Foster, alumni of the 1950s band, have maintained the Basie institution with dedication. (Owens, 1995, p.231)

In a real sense, Jones and Foster had to understand and appropriate Basie's vision in order to maintain the niche of his ensemble.

Internal Diversity

Organizations composed of widely diverse members and sections, are likely to have a more difficult time defining their niche, for two reasons: The possibilities for such organizations are likely to be more numerous, and the orientations and preferences of their members are likely to be more divergent. A homogeneous ensemble such as a chorus or a brass band is necessarily more specialized in terms of repertoire and stylistic possibilities. Such groups are largely confined to the literatures and traditions associated with their particular instrumentations. Moreover, the members of such ensembles are likely to have similar musical backgrounds, interests, tastes and preferences. The search for a viable niche will thus be relatively simple if also more restricted. Such groups sometimes attempt to stretch their possibility sets by adapting other literatures to their own instrumentations. Thus, banjos and harmonicas can play classical music and symphony orchestras can play the Beatles. Successful thrusts of this kind are relatively rare, however, since they are often distinguished only by their novelty, or they run into technical difficulties:

> The Powell Quartet at Weill Recital Hall Saturday afternoon made the sound of four flutes in concert more attractive than the prospect of it. Perhaps the least comfortable moments of this program were in a transcription of the Overture to "A Midsummer Night's Dream" – in which the prominent part Mendelssohn assigns to flutes is bloated to almost unbearable shrillness without support from below. (Holland, 1988)

Heterogeneous organizations have the advantage of being able to try many different combinations of style, emphasis and repertoire associated with their varied internal makeup. A full symphony orchestra can range in its emphasis from works that rely mainly on strings to those in which percussion or brass are the dominant features. The universe of possibilities is very wide, although literature that addresses many of the theoretical combinations may not be robust.

The wider range of niche possibilities is modulated by the greater tensions that are likely to exist in heterogeneous organizations. The parochial interests of different parts of the organization may surface when alternative possibilities, providing for more or less prominent roles for different subgroups, are proposed. Woodwind players will be unhappy with repertoires dominated by string pieces, and string players may blanch at repertoires favoring brass. Compromises may be required to balance the interests of the different sections, if agreement and commitment to a common understanding of the organization's best niche is to be achieved. As a result, the leadership factor again looms large in heterogeneous organizations. Here, there is little substitute for leadership vision, for knowledge and understanding of the many possibilities, for guidance and facilitation of the processes for achieving a common understanding among members, and for making choices that can balance internal interests without compromising the niche that is sought for the ensemble as a whole. Indeed, for heterogeneous organizations to take advantage of the wider set of possibilities available to them, they require effective leadership that can help make the difficult choices that sometimes favor one group over another. The alternative is to rely so heavily on compromise and consensus that the benefits of wider choice are lost.

Another way in which internal diversity can be brought to bear on niche-finding is by bringing a combination of different styles of music into one ensemble. In such cases, internal diversity is created by design rather than being something that must be managed or kept under control. So-called "fusion" groups illustrate how new niches can be created by combining the elements of different kinds of ensembles in order to play music derived from a mix of different genres. An example is the Romulo Larrea Tango Ensemble which integrates tango with classical techniques and jazz by combining a classical string quartet and a traditional tango trio (Salisbury, 1999).

Professionalism

The level of competence and training of organizational members will also affect the niche-finding process, but in ways that are not entirely transparent. Professional ensembles with highly trained players are likely to have wider knowledge and greater skills to explore different styles and repertoires. At the same time, the members of such ensembles are likely to be more specialized, favoring compositions of particular composers or periods of music, and of course, particular instruments. The flexibility of highly professional ensembles can thus be limited by the attitude and orientations of their members and the large investments these individuals have made in attaining high competence in narrow areas, thus limiting the range of niches they are willing to explore. Organizations with less highly trained workforces may be more limited in terms of talent, breadth of knowledge, and basic competencies, but they can be more flexible and wide-ranging in their willingness to explore within their ranges of capability.

The paradox here is that ensembles with more highly trained members, because of their deeper and usually wider knowledge, often have greater capacity to experiment outside their traditional areas of operation. Thus, the potential for successfully achieving new and unusual niches is greater for these groups if they dare to venture, perhaps with the prodding of inspired leadership, outside their domains of comfort. Marin Alsop appeared to achieve this with her Concordia Chamber Symphony which combines classical and jazz music and found a solid core of support among audiences and financial contributors in New York City (Page, 1992).

Task Complexity

Organizations operating in fields where the work is highly complex may be more limited in exploring alternative niches than those where work is simpler. The reason for this is that changing niche in a field of complex work may requires changing whole interrelated systems of working parts, moving from one set of protocols and plans to another. Any such shift is likely to require major efforts and investments. Thus, a symphony orchestra accustomed to specializing in music of the Romantic period may have a difficult time decreasing its substantial investment in this area and adapting to a repertoire dominated by twentieth century music where tonality and rhythmic synchronization yield to unpredictable, but no less intricate, juxtapositions and sequences of familiar and unfamiliar sounds. Members of such an orchestra would have not only to learn new individual tasks and skills but also new ways of relating to one another to achieve a successful overall performance:

> I once heard one of the world's best orchestras, though not one accustomed to playing much new music, with a distinguished conductor, take on a program that included an extraordinarily difficult piece by Milton Babbit, the Webern Symphony and three other tough 20th-century pieces, all being played by that orchestra for the first time. It was

infuriating, a waste of the talents of everyone on stage, because not one of all those interesting and worthwhile pieces was justly treated. (Steinberg, 1999, p.34)

Simpler fields of endeavor may support greater adaptability. Folk singing groups can range widely in their explorations of blue grass, traditional, country and ethnic music, because all of these paradigms are relatively straightforward in themselves, and talented musicians, grounded in the basics of melody, harmony and rhythm, can, with serious effort, mix and adapt from one to another, individually and in groups. Bela Fleck & the Flecktones is a leading example, combining pop, jazz, bluegrass, country, classical and other modes of music in their various genre-blending performances. While few ensembles may achieve the range or virtuosity of Bela Fleck's group, the numerous potential combinations of the musical genres in which they dabble offer potentially viable niches for many other ensembles as well.

All this is not to underestimate the advantage of highly polished ensembles that have established themselves in a narrower, possibly complex, musical genre such as classical chamber music. Such ensembles may hang on tenaciously to their established niches and fight off new competitors. But they can take those niches for granted only to the extent that the complexity of the task is sufficiently intimidating to newcomers, the environment continues to support the genre, and they remain superior performers. Groups like the Guarneri Quartet have held their niches for long periods of time by force of these factors.

Instability

Organizational and environmental stability generally make a manager's life easier. Stability allows managers to fine-tune operations, policies and relationships knowing that the organization as a whole is reasonably well-adapted to its extant conditions and that radical shifts may not be necessary. Thus, in ensembles, players can learn to work more closely together where turnover is low and they have time to learn the nuances of each others' ways. And players can be motivated by long term reward and advancement systems where they have some reasonable expectation of staying with the organization over a long period of time and that the organization itself will not radically alter its reward system over that time.

Niche-finding is one area, however, where instability can help the astute manager because environmental instability and dynamism create new opportunities. As Hannan and Freeman (1989) observe: "Stable and certain environments almost surely generate low levels of diversity" (p.9). That is, environmental stability allows the winnowing down of organizational possibilities to a few types that are best suited to the particular stable conditions, while dynamism and uncertainty encourage experimentation with new forms and tolerance in the short-run of forms that may not survive the competition once conditions settle down.

This situation has different implications for different types of organizations. For well-established organizations, environmental instability can be threatening because conditions under which the organization flourished may give way to new conditions for which it may be poorly suited. The history of symphony orchestras seems to reflect this experience. These ensembles developed during a period of high popularity and low cost for live symphonic music (DiMaggio, 1986), but they now exist in a period of limited demand and escalating costs (Baumol and Bowen, 1966). Indeed, modern symphony orchestras have been called "museums" of past artistic achievement, unresponsive to contemporary musical tastes or innovations. This situation has undoubtedly contributed to the serious financial jeopardy in which many symphony orchestras find themselves. Some have suggested that the contemporary crisis of symphony orchestras must be solved by revisiting their programmatic niches, finding performance offerings more responsive to contemporary tastes and interests (Wolfe, 1992).

Despite the threat that instability poses for established organizations, such organizations still have some advantages over smaller, less-well established ones. Established organizations normally have higher levels of organizational "slack" or reserves which they can call upon in periods of crisis and change (Cyert and March, 1972). An established organization that is alert enough to trends and uncertainties in its environment can use its organizational slack as a cushion for implementing change in a more controlled, deliberate, planned fashion (Hirschman, 1970). For example, the Boston Symphony is one of many established orchestras that have differentiated their programs to expand their popular appeal, through outdoor concerts and auxiliary "pops" programming. Overall, however, symphony orchestras have also tended to narrow their programming in response to competition from smaller, specialized ensembles which have usurped portions of their formerly broader repertoire:

> Having largely given up years ago on regular and frequent performances of contemporary music, the Philharmonic and other orchestras are busily abandoning early music, too...This gradual breakup of the orchestral repertory among various performing groups has shifted the balance of power: If, not long ago, a handful of great symphony orchestras – Berlin, Vienna, Chicago, Philadelphia and so on – were recognized as undisputed champions of large-scale instrumental playing, attention has now spread to a wide range of orchestras of various sizes...that are competing for, and attracting, public attention and record-buying dollars...

> ...symphony orchestras are now caught in a bind: If they try to maintain a broad repertory, then they willingly go head to head with the specialists; but if, as appears to be happening, they narrow their purview, there is the risk of losing listeners...Perhaps the symphony orchestra will have to be...reconfigured so that it becomes several groups at once, each presenting a different part of the repertory.

> In the meantime, the large orchestras are in a state of flux. The growth of the specialty ensembles and the accessibility of all kinds of music on recordings have changed the function of the symphony orchestra. While it may remain the most technically accomplished and the wealthiest musical organization in a given city...it no longer must serve up a broad repertory to sate the musical appetite of its audience...

...If the product of a narrow repertory is a more thoroughly realized and convincing performance at the concert hall, it will be only for the good. Toward that end, symphony orchestras just may have a chance to regain some of the luster they had years ago, when these giants stood as unrivaled exponents of the entire repertory. (Kimmelman, 1987, p. 24)

Smaller, newer organizations are also threatened by environmental change, and less well insured against uncertainty than their more established counterparts. However, fledgling organizations are likely to be less set in their ways, more nimble and flexible, and hence faster to catch onto and adapt to environmental shifts. Moreover, such organizations have more to gain from environmental uncertainty than larger ones because a dynamic environment may create new opportunities that will allow them ultimately to grow into major institutions with significant resources:

When Chuck Berry appeared at the Newport Jazz Festival in 1958, breaking the jazz world's unofficial taboo against rock-and-roll, many critics accused the festival of dumbing down in an attempt to draw bigger and younger audiences. Forty years later, an appearance by Sonic Youth at what is nominally a jazz festival hardly raises an eyebrow, because audiences for fringe rock and out jazz are increasingly the same. There is a type of rock fan who wouldn't dream of going to hear latter-day be-bop at the Village Vanguard or Lincoln Center but who regularly shows up at alternative venues for performances by neo-screamers like David S. Ware and Sabir Mateen. More than anything, these listeners value all-out sonic assault, and they don't care if it comes from tenor saxophones or guitars. (Davis, 1999, p.31)

The risk of environmental instability to both established and fledgling organizations, and the degree to which each is able to take advantage of uncertainty, depends on the relative strength of two competing processes under which potential niches in the organizational ecology become filled: *adaptation* versus *selection* (see Hannan and Freeman, 1989). Under adaptation, existing organizations adjust to environmental uncertainty and fill out the new niches that become available as a result of environmental change. Under selection, existing (established and fledgling) organizations which are ill-suited to new conditions change too slowly to survive and new niches are filled out by emergent organizations that come into being specifically to fill vacancies in the shifting ecology.

In biology, with the possible exception of humankind, the Darwinian selection process dominates. In the social sphere, it is a matter of controversy and empirical study as to whether adaptation or selection is the more important process (Hannan and Freeman, 1989). For social entrepreneurs promoting new ventures, the selection process may be of primary interest – how to find and exploit new niche opportunities in the face of environmental change (Young, 1983). For managers of existing organizations, however, adaptation is of primary interest – how to maintain an existing niche or find a new one quickly in order to foster organizational prosperity or avoid disaster.

The case of the Colorado Symphony Orchestra offers an illustration of both the managerial and entrepreneurial perspectives (Freeman, 1996a). Environmental pressures and internal rigidities that prevented adaptation to deteriorating economic conditions caused the demise of the Denver Symphony Orchestra. The players in this orchestra later formed a new ensemble called the Colorado Symphony Orchestra (CSO), built on the ashes of the old one, but newly adapted to extant conditions that permitted a wider variety of programming and lower costs through shared governance and financial risk-taking between community board members and the players themselves. The CSO case illustrates that the selection process is powerful in eliminating organizations that occupy niches no longer well-supported by their environments. However, the CSO case also shows that managerial strategy that is sufficiently sensitive to extant conditions can forestall and even exploit changes in that same economic and social environment.

Strategic Issues in Niche-Finding

The literature on strategic planning makes clear that organizational leaders and managers are expected to monitor their environments and to periodically assess how well their organizations are adapted to those environments (e.g., see Bryson, 1988). When internal strengths and weaknesses are poorly aligned with external threats and opportunities, the organization is expected to make changes, either directly in its niche (its products, services or mission) or in its internal capacities to support the activity required by its current niche. Skeptics have questioned the utility of formalized strategic planning, especially in a rapidly changing environment, but "strategic thinking" which conceptualizes the relationship of the organization to its environment is clearly an ongoing management imperative for all organizations (Mintzberg, 1994).

The experience of musical ensembles reveals that there is no single, obvious way in which these organizations successfully adapt to their environments and find their particular places in the sun. A unifying theme, however, appears to be the search for distinction or uniqueness. Economists call this "product differentiation" – finding ways to make your organization's product or service different from those of all other organizations, so that you have a degree of market power and no other organization's offering can be considered a perfect substitute. Marketers who promote "branding" have the same idea (Kotler, 1997).

Achieving Distinction

Distinction may be achieved in a variety of ways. Musical ensembles may specialize in the particular quality of their sounds (e.g., the Philadelphia sound or the Chicago sound), the repertoire which they select (e.g., early baroque music), the kind of technology they use (e.g., playing early music on original instruments), or indeed the particular community they serve (e.g., the Suburban Symphony in Cleveland). In each case, the selected niche builds on internal strengths and preferences (e.g., the special inspiration of a charismatic conductor, the expertise in early music, or the interests of volunteer musicians in a particular community).

Copy-cat behavior is also well known in the musical world. When niche leaders define something new and highly popular, others may follow to exploit any excess demand that the original group generates or even surpass the innovators. For example, groups like the Kingston Trio and Peter, Paul and Mary followed on the heels of the Weavers who had established a new popular niche for folk music in the 1950s. While the Weavers had "first mover advantage", as economists would say, the newcomers could build on what the Weavers had established, to offer sounds that many considered even more exciting.

More straightforward "imitations" may also succeed in establishing themselves. Thus, Beatles imitations and Elvis rock bands persist, especially after the originals are no longer around to perform. But even in these cases, there is usually some distinctiveness to the ensembles that allow them to sustain a particular niche (if only to claim they are the best at imitation!) In music, and in most other fields, most organizations seek to avoid having their services become "commodities" in the sense that they cannot be distinguished in some substantial way from their competitors. Even bands that play for weddings and bar mitzvahs try to set themselves apart from the competition, although these may come the closest to being commodities in the musical performance arena. As in other fields, establishing a "brand name" for one's product is a key to ensemble success:

> In today's world, a brand for an orchestra is just as important as for any other good...Such orchestras as the Vienna Philharmonic or the Berlin Philharmonic are associated with world-class quality and other attributes. The names of these orchestras have developed into brand names, even if those orchestras do not actively promote their brands...

> With its surprise encores and the friendliness it exhibits towards its audiences, the Detroit Symphony is creating a certain favorable image in the mind of its audiences. It is building a brand with this image to differentiate itself from other orchestras, and from other performing arts groups in Detroit...orchestral institutions in any city have to think hard about the qualities and values they want people to think of when they hear or see the orchestra. (Kerres, 1999, p.51)

While one might argue that the Detroit Symphony has a local monopoly, clearly it competes in a much broader market – with other local arts and entertainment options, and through technology and travel with orchestras in other parts of the country and the world. Even within Detroit, therefore, the distinctiveness of the orchestra is important.

Priorities and Trade-Offs

Following the logic of previous movements, we have considered a variety of organizational circumstances affecting niche-finding: organizational size, heterogeneity, professionalism, instability and task complexity. The matrix in Table 3.1 signals the variety of niche-finding challenges faced by a number of interesting alternative ensemble stereotypes.

Table 3.1   Ensemble Attributes and Niche-finding

	size	heterogeneity	professional level	instability	task complexity	nonmusical analog
Pops orchestra	high	high	high	high	moderate	local accounting firm
Amateur rock band	low	moderate	low	moderate	moderate	small software company
Community chamber orchestra	moderate	high	moderate	low	high	YMCA, JCC
Fire department band	low	moderate	low	low	low	Habitat for Humanity
Children's choir	high	low	low	moderate	low	advocacy association

The pops orchestra is similar in structure to a classical symphony but has chosen to specialize in playing a different genre of music geared more to general public tastes and audiences. In some sense, therefore, the pops orchestra is defined by the niche it has selected. Yet within this genre, particular pop orchestras will need to differentiate themselves in this already specialized market, in order to compete for audience attention. Certain pops orchestras such as the Boston Pops are known for their excellence and for a certain personality developed under charismatic leaders such as Arthur Fiedler. Other such ensembles may need to take different routes to success. As relatively large, internally diverse organizations, and ones which exhibit substantial turnover among its members, pops orchestras are unlikely to find their special niche through internal deliberations except perhaps within the top leadership of the organization. Visionary leadership, trial and error, and some risk taking are likely to be necessary in finding a special place for such an ensemble. The possibilities include developing a certain overall style, emphasizing a certain sub category of popular music, or perhaps becoming associated with a particular community that can take special pride in its accomplishments. The Cleveland Pops Orchestra, for example, is overshadowed by the reputation of its classical counterpart, and by better know pops orchestras at the national level, but it enjoys a strong following in the Cleveland community itself. A nonmusical analog to the pops orchestra is a local accounting firm that may do very good work, which may have national aspirations, but whose clientele are basically local businesses and families.

The amateur rock band has a very different problem finding its niche. This ensemble is small, encompasses only moderate internal diversity – limited to a few different types of players (perhaps just strings and percussion), may be fairly stable over a reasonable period of time, and need not be involved with music that is highly intricate. Its problem is to find a really different sound, style or repertoire that will distinguish it from the myriad of other such aspiring groups, and endear it to some proportion of the (young) audience of rock music listeners. While its players are not necessarily highly sophisticated technically, this ensemble has the luxury of undertaking extensive experimentation and internal dialogue, drawing on the ideas of all of its members. Nonmusical analogs might be a small software firm, or a boutique consulting group, where the principals need to provide a product or service that is unusual in some way that inspires a loyal following that can grow over time.

A community chamber orchestra can be fairly large, perhaps two dozen members, and is diverse in its instrumentation. It is likely to consist of players with a mix of skill levels, some professionals and some motivated and fairly accomplished amateurs. Such an orchestra will try to play fairly challenging classical music and has the advantage of some stability, given its community base and orientation. Like the pops orchestra, the niche of the community chamber orchestra is already pre-defined to a substantial degree. Its base in the community implies that it serves as a vehicle in which local musicians can participate and from which local residents can derive listening pleasure. However, such definition does not guarantee success since both local players and local music lovers have other options. The orchestra still needs to be special in some other way. Given its relatively large size, internal diversity and mix of skill levels, this ensemble is likely to depend on visionary leadership and internal dialogue among a core group of the more skilled and highly educated players, in order to find its special niche. While its repertoire is likely to be constrained by the skill mix and the tastes and expectations of the local community, it has room to explore different areas of both classical and popular repertoire and also different characteristics of performance that might distinguish it – perhaps unusual instrument combinations, or emphasis on the works of certain popular but less frequently played composers such as George and Ira Gershwin, Richard Rogers or Scott Joplin. Nonmusical analogs include YMCAs and Jewish Community Centers which are also rooted in their communities, employ diverse skills in order to provide a variety of recreational, fitness and social activities for their members, engage both professional and volunteer workers, and face the complex tasks of mobilizing and scheduling a wide variety of complex tasks and events within their facilities. Like their musical counterparts, these organizations too need to distinguish themselves within their community settings in order to assure their continued support, given the alternatives available to their members.

A fire department band serves a number of different purposes. It helps the fire department project a friendly image to the community and it boosts the morale of its own members. It is intended to offer entertainment for the community, especially at public events such a parades or on summer evenings. And it serves as a recreational vehicle for its member players. Such bands are generally fairly small, they embrace a modest variety of different instruments generally within the brass and percussion families, and they consist of players either from the department or the local community who are amateur musicians. These bands play relatively simple music and they are fairly stable in membership, given the sources from which they draw. Since each community has just one fire department, and hence probably just one fire department band, and since there are general expectations that this ensemble will play popular pieces for brass instruments, such as marches and polkas, the niches of these ensembles are also somewhat pre-defined and to some extent, assured of support. Again, however, some distinctiveness and distinction is necessary if support of the department is to be maintained, and if members are to be willing to continue to participate. Such bands may compare themselves to counterpart ensembles in order to help define their places in the musical landscapes of their communities. They should offer something different from high school marching bands and something that adds to the quality of community events. They can aspire to a higher level of achievement as well, seeking to compete for distinction among fire department bands in the state or region, in order to bring local pride to the community. To do that, the fire department band needs to find a repertoire or quality of play that makes it better in some ways than other fire department bands.

As participants in small, relatively homogeneous and relatively stable ensembles, members of fire department bands can deliberate productively among themselves, and experiment to find and improve their particular styles and repertoires. The more accomplished musicians among them may be able to provide some vision or inspired leadership, though none are likely to be professional musicians. If a professional leader can be engaged, he or she is likely to carry an inordinate proportion of the responsibility for finding the appropriate niche. Habit for Humanity is a nonmusical analog. Volunteer workers come to this organization to build (relatively simple, straightforward) housing for the poor. Workers have some construction skills but few are professionals. The organization employs professional supervisors to design, oversee and inspire the work. Interestingly, the mode of work itself helps define Habit for Humanity's niche – the very fact that it produces housing using volunteer amateurs. In the same way, the fire department band also achieves a certain uniqueness by virtue of the fact that many of its players are firefighters.

A children's choir is likely to be a large group – children of all members of a church or all children within a certain grade level of a public school. While varying in talent and socio-economic background, its members are relatively homogenous in terms of organizational parameters – they are all kids using their voices, and they obviously have not yet achieved high levels of professional skill. And to accommodate their large size the ensemble is unlikely to undertake highly complex music. In this context, niche finding is likely to depend strongly on visionary leadership of the choral director or music teacher.

As with other examples, the niche of the children's chorus is largely predefined but still needs to be secured, justified and possibly further differentiated. Schools or churches may not tolerate children's choruses that do not achieve some minimum level of performance and do not engage the attention of their listeners. Again, the niche may be quite solidly established by the character of the participants – a chorus may be one of the few available venues in which parents can hear their children perform in a public context. But as with fire department bands, children's choruses can aspire to more – competing against those of other schools and churches to achieve a degree of recognition that reflects well on their home institutions.

Nonmusical analogs to the children's chorus include advocacy associations which promote the interests of their members. These may be labor unions, public interest groups, professional or trade associations, and so on. Such organizations are relatively large and stable, consisting of members with similar interests and needs, amateur in the sense that members are not specially skilled in articulating their interests in the public arena, despite the fact that their task (message) is relatively simple. Defining their niche, so that they can stand out and be taken seriously, depends strongly on visionary leadership that can frame the message and mobilize the membership so that it speaks with one strong voice.

Again, none of these stereotypes is completely characteristic of their counterparts in the real world of music, nor are the suggested nonmusical analogs exact. Still, they are useful for prioritizing niche-finding strategies best suited to organizations that resemble each stereotype. The matrix in Table 3.2 describes the relative emphases for alternative niche-finding strategies of each ensemble stereotype.

Table 3.2   Niche-finding Strategies

	internal dialogue	trial and error	diverse, educated players	visionary leadership	encouraging risk-taking	interpretation and selection of scores
Pops orchestra	5	6	3	2	4	1
Amateur rock band	2	1	5	4	3	6
Community chamber orchestra	3	5	4	1	6	2
Fire department band	1	2	6	5	3	4
Children's choir	4	3	6	1	5	2

The matrix suggests that different types of ensembles will tend to rely on substantially different combinations of niche-finding strategies. The larger ensembles such as the community chamber orchestra, the children's chorus and the pops orchestra will tend to lean more heavily on the vision of their leader (music director) to bring a distinctive style or character to the ensemble, e.g., by molding the ensemble's repertoire in a particular way, or by offering especially compelling interpretations within that repertoire. Visionary leadership can also serve a teaching function in these groups, coaching players to shape the sounds of the ensemble in some distinctive manner.

In the case of the (professional) pops orchestra, bringing in accomplished players of diverse musical backgrounds can also contribute to niche-finding, as such players may suggest interesting new combinations of instrumentation, rhythm and other musical parameters. An atmosphere that allows risk taking would facilitate this kind of experimentation. However, since the pops orchestra is fairly large and engages busy professional players who have little spare time, it is unlikely that sustained trial and error or internal dialogue in rehearsals would be primary tactics for developing a niche strategy.

The community chamber orchestra is not as large as the pops orchestra and perhaps not as pressed for rehearsal time. Hence, internal dialogue can play a larger part in shaping niche strategy, incorporating community members' own ideas about what they want to play or how they can otherwise distinguish themselves. Since many members are likely to be amateur players without high mastery of their instruments, risk taking and trial and error with different musical techniques and styles is unlikely to be very productive. However, listening to the ideas of some of the more accomplished players who may come from diverse musical backgrounds could lead to interesting results. If classical, jazz and popular musical backgrounds are all represented, the orchestra might develop a reputation for an eclectic repertoire or one in which techniques from one genre are incorporated into another. Beatles music for full orchestra or jazzed up Bach, for example, are not unrealistic, and even potentially popular.

The children's choir offers fewer possibilities for cultivating the ideas of members with diverse musical backgrounds, or encouraging them to take risks. Children are naturally experimental and unregimented, but the challenge with a children's chorus is largely to achieve discipline and coherence, not encourage diverse behaviors. Members of such choruses, depending somewhat on the particular age group, are unlikely to have already had sufficient training and education to contribute productively to shaping the character, style or repertoire of the ensemble. However, trial and error can play a part in niche-finding in this case, if the leader/music director is willing to experiment with a variety of different musical styles and repertoires to determine what combinations excite, inspire and hence might ultimately distinguish the ensemble. Children, for example, might be excited by a repertoire that features the latest theme music from popular movies or television shows.

The amateur rock band and the fire department band are more likely to favor internal dialogue, trial and error in rehearsal, and risk-taking in their niche exploration, given the smaller size of these ensembles and their probable lack of professional leadership. And given the amateur nature of these groups, they are unlikely to benefit from the contributions of members with diverse musical backgrounds or be in a position to put their particular imprimaturs on standard repertoire. Exceptions occur, of course. Rock bands are often formed by individuals with great, if often raw, musical talent and charisma as well. Fire department bands are sometimes fortunate to engage talented players from the community and accomplished volunteers willing to provide them with musical leadership. In such cases, more emphasis can be put on visionary leadership and musical interpretation as strategies for niche-finding.   Those possibilities notwithstanding, the strength of the rock band will be in its boundless energy and time to experiment, for its players to communicate intensively with one another as they play with different possibilities, listen to others' music together, and to allow each member to express ideas without fear of being ridiculed. Similarly, the strength of the fire department band will be a relaxed atmosphere in which players can talk to one another, find the repertoires that they enjoy playing together, and put forward suggestions for new pieces. Since it is more likely to play standard pieces than the rock band, the fire department band will emphasize selection and interpretation of repertoire more than the rock band is likely to do.

The point of this discussion is not to claim in any hard sense that the forgoing combinations of strategies are necessarily the right ones for any particular rock band, community chamber orchestra, and so on, or their analogous nonmusical organizations, but rather to illustrate the fact that appropriate niche-finding strategies will vary from organization to organization. Comparing an organization to a certain kind of musical ensemble (stereotype) can help in the formulation of a niche by reasoning through the priorities of niche-finding strategy components and combinations appropriate for that ensemble.   Although there is likely to be more variation between categories of organization (i.e., between ensemble stereotypes), appropriate niche-finding strategies are also likely to vary within categories, depending on the particular combinations of size, heterogeneity, professionalism, stability and task complexity manifested in a particular organization.

A Case Study

Girls Incorporated is a charitable organization that provides recreational, educational and developmental services for girls (Young, 2001). It consists of a national headquarters organization and more than 80 affiliated locally incorporated affiliates nationwide. It is an organization with a long history, originally called Girls Clubs of America, established in 1945 by nineteen local charter member girls clubs. One can think of Girls Incorporated as a large, professional chorus with each of its members (affiliates) singing the same tune and contributing in the aggregate to the volume and quality of performance at the national level.

Before 1980, Girls Clubs of America (GCA) had a clearly defined niche. It ran girls clubs, which were local facilities where girls could come to enjoy themselves, engage in a variety of recreational and social activities, and learn how to be good citizens and homemakers. The turbulent social environment of the 1960s and '70s challenged the relevance of these traditional services.   At the same time, larger organizations such as the Girl Scouts, increasingly competed with GCA for members.   In the 1980s, GCA was faced with a severe crisis that required it to immediately reexamine its place in the world. The much larger Boys Clubs of America became co-ed and changed its name to Boys and Girls Clubs of America. While Girls Club of America sued for name infringement and won a modest cash settlement, it ultimately decided to change its name and try to redefine a niche for itself that would not be overwhelmed by the competition.

Given the large, decentralized character of the organization, and the relatively homogeneous nature of its affiliates, Girls Incorporated could not depend entirely on internal dialogue, or modest tinkering with current programs to get the job done. It needed bold new ideas that depended more on visionary leadership, risk taking and the bringing to bear of new concepts from diverse sources. That leadership came from a strong national executive director and key members of the national board of directors. One of the initiatives taken was to establish a National Resource Center that would do research on issues facing girls in contemporary society and devise new and innovative programming approaches. The programs generated by the Resource Center were field tested in affiliate organizations, and new kinds of affiliates and partnership organizations were also engaged to implement and develop the new initiatives. The new programs addressed such issues as drug abuse, career choices for women, pregnancy prevention and educational opportunities. Through a process of visionary leadership, participation of new players from diverse educational backgrounds, and a new atmosphere that encouraged significant risk taking by affiliates, Girls Incorporated devised a unique and special repertoire grounded in innovative programming addressed to the needs of underprivileged girls. In the process, it has had to give up some of its old music, despite some loyal followers who continued to value it. It has managed to survive and prosper with a new audience of stakeholders and participants, finding a place for itself outside the performance space of its larger and more conventional competitors.

Diagnosing An Organization

The niche-finding experiences of musical ensembles suggest a number of areas where managers can begin their searches for distinct, sustainable places in their own environments. The following diagnostic questions should be helpful:

- What are the various interpretations that can be given to the organization's products and the manner in which it does business? Which alternative interpretations might add a new attractiveness and uniqueness to the organization's repertoire?
- What kind of "brand name" can the organization devise for itself that would capture the special character of its repertoire or the particular way it carries out its business?

Successful niche-finding will require engaging the organization's people in the search process. In this connection, managers can ask:

- How can the organization's workers be brought more fully into the process of interpreting how the organization's mission, procedures and product repertoires are best described and promoted?

- How can organizational participants be more broadly educated about the field in which the organization works, and in related fields, so that they have a wider view of the possibilities for the organization's repertoire?
- How can the diverse perspectives of the organization's various participants be brought into collaborative interaction with the organization's leadership so as to consider the widest possible array of options?
- How can the organization encourage risk-taking so that its workers will not be reluctant to share new ideas, even if they radically depart from current ways of doing things? How can an egalitarian setting be devised so that differences in status will not suppress open interchange?
- How can organizational leaders be encouraged to articulate a distinct "vision" for their organization which combines a full appreciation of internal talents and strengths, a deep understanding of the environment in which the organization must sustain itself, and some special measure of creative genius?
- How can professional staff be encouraged to push the boundaries of their specializations and to interact constructively with individuals from other specializations, and disciplines, and with talented amateurs?
- In a rapidly changing organizational environment, how can organizational leadership and staff be encouraged to give up old, comfortable niches and define and compete for new ones?

The manner in which the organization is structured will also affect the success of the niche-finding process. Hence managers should ask:

- In a large organization, how can divisions and working groups be utilized to capture the creative advantages of smallness?
- In a large organization, how can leadership bring the energies of diverse small groups together into a process of consultative, consensual decision making that is guided by the larger interests of the organization as a whole?
- In a diverse organization, with many specialized groups, what are the different ways in which the talents and expertise of these groups can be combined to give the organization as a whole a greater distinctiveness?

Fourth Movement:
Innovation and Change

In a gaff that probably caused him grief when he got home, former President Richard Nixon once said in a nationally broadcast speech: "This country can't stand pat!" (Pat was the name of the first lady.) Nixon was referring, of course, to the fact that nations resist change only at their peril. The same applies to organizations. Change occurs whether the stewards of organizations are prepared for it or not. The economy changes, the technology of doing business changes, the tastes and preferences of suppliers and customers change, and so on. And change often takes place in ways that are mostly out of the control of an organization, or even a whole nation. Nonetheless, the stewards of an organization must be prepared to address change, lest they be taken by surprise and overwhelmed by it. To remain fixed in a changing world, even if at some point in time one is among the best, usually means flirting with long term irrelevance and demise. While abandoning tradition or historical values can also be a serious mistake, even successful tradition-bound organizations must adapt over time (Salipante and Golden-Biddle, 1995)

Managing change is a multifaceted endeavor, consisting of at least two parts. First, the notion of change means identifying new ways of doing things. An organization cannot cope with external changes unless it has alternatives to the status quo that it can potentially pursue. The identification and implementation of new ways of doing things is called *innovation* – the theme of the present movement. The second part of change management is the process of *evaluation and adjustment* (Nelson and Winter, 1982) or what organizational scholars have called *organizational learning* (Senge, 1990). Learning involves taking stock of where you are relative to where you want to be, and then making adjustments to come closer to your goals. Learning is related to change because when environmental circumstances change, the organization must be able to measure how much it is being left behind (or how much its lead over other organizations is diminishing), and hence what corrective actions it must take. Learning is also related to innovation because often an organization learns that it cannot catch up or dash ahead by doing things in its usual way – it must innovate or change its traditional methods. This is what organizational scholars call "double loop" learning (Senge, 1990).

Discussion of *evaluation and adjustment* is reserved for the next and final movement of this presentation because it encompasses not only the challenge of coping with change, but also the general issue of achieving organizational excellence in all dimensions of management. The present movement focuses specifically on *innovation*.

Innovation

To innovate is to do things *differently*, hopefully better, than they have been done before. For management, this can be problematic. Good organizations commonly seek to improve what they are doing. But this often means doing the same things over and over until they get it right; in this process, innovation can even be seen as a diversion which can throw the quest for fine-tuning into discord.

Nor is innovation necessarily prompted by a desire to improve. Innovation comes about in a variety of ways and may serve various purposes or no purpose at all. To paraphrase a contemporary scatological bumper sticker, "innovation happens!" It may be the result of unpredictable, serendipitous circumstances and unforeseen events, or simply human desires to be creative, playful and inventive. The best that managers may be able to do, if they consciously seek innovation, is to establish conditions under which such creativity is encouraged and where people are receptive to change and new ideas. Such was the case for the bebop quintet led by Max Roach and Clifford Brown in the 1950's:

> After [drummer] Roach ends his solo there follows the most extraordinary portion of this excellent performance [of *Blues Walk*]. For the next five choruses Brown and [tenor saxophonist] Land engage in a musical dialogue that has never been surpassed on record ....The smoothness with which this musical dialogue proceeds suggests that they preplanned it all, but they did not... the conversation... begins well, but sputters along during the last three choruses. Uncertainty reigns supreme as the players struggle with shorter and shorter phrases, almost all of it different from that used in the final version. (Owens, 1995, pp.217-218)

Innovation is a cross-cutting phenomenon that interfaces in a variety of ways with other dimensions of management responsibility.   Consider coordination. Some of the strategies that we have considered for coordination – such as the use of standard plans and procedures, extensive rehearsals and central direction – may suppress innovation by minimizing individual variation and experimentation. To the contrary, however, innovation can sometimes be achieved because ensemble is so perfect that organizational members are locked into each others' behaviors and can follow each other flawlessly into uncharted territory.   For example, in an interesting study of a jazz quartet, Bastien and Hostager (2002) showed how the expansion of shared knowledge through a consensus on rules, procedures and practice, allowed the ensemble to explore uncharted musical territory – invent a new song – while maintaining its coordination.

Motivation and innovation are also linked in this way.   Novelty and freshness that stem from innovative activity can be an important motivator for participants in an organization.   To work in an exciting organization can be more stimulating and energizing than working in a smoothly running organization where one may be treated well and rewarded appropriately but where the work is routine and bounded.   Yet innovation can also be chaotic, destabilizing and disruptive, and discouraging to those caught in its whirlwind.   Often, a balance is needed to provide basic stability without oppressive routine.

Niche-finding is perhaps most closely related to innovation.   Organizations can excel in standard market niches with classical styles and repertoires that break no new ground.   So innovation is not essential to finding or maintaining a viable niche, at least not for the short term.   But organizations often do create new niches for themselves *by* innovating.   For example, through incremental innovations they may "differentiate their products" as economists would say, so that their repertoires are slightly different from those of their competitors and they enjoy a modest gain in market power as a result.   Few music groups succeed without first finding their own unique styles.   Product differentiation is an incremental process, but small changes accumulate.   Over time, evolutionary changes that come about through differentiation and incremental adaptation to new conditions can lead to major shifts, even if managers are not looking explicitly to innovate:

> "We've been in the recording studio for over 25 years", says [bassist Teddy] Gentry. "You just find your sound and then redefine what you do best each time you go into the studio. I've never looked at Alabama as traditional country, but we are country boys, and when we sing, it sounds like country no matter what kind of a beat we've got to it. So, we never quit looking for a new way to express our sound." (Capozzoli, 1999, p. 1-E)

Innovation can also destroy niches. When Rock and Roll's popularity overran conventional "Hit Parade" music in the 1950's, demand for the latter shrank considerably. But there was little that managers of conventional music groups could do about it. Few of them had the capacity to transform themselves into rock groups. They could only continue to compete for the reduced ecological space remaining for their style of music. Innovation was not a panacea. In music as in other fields, innovation can be a force of creative destruction (Schumpeter, 1934) in which the old is destroyed and new forms are created. This is generally a healthy process for fields as a whole, but it can spell disaster for individual organizations, even if they are well run.

Finally, innovation itself can be a niche. Some organizations are pace-setters and, by design or reputation, succeed by drawing support from those who equate value with progress and state of the art methods and products. Maintaining that special position requires an organization to constantly innovate or risk losing its distinctiveness:

> In their work together with the New York Art Quartet, Mr. Tchicai and Mr. Rudd brought uncommon elements to free jazz, as if holding to its original promise of liberation from predictable routines. Collective improvisation was a cherished ideal in early free jazz, but aside from greater parity between horn soloists and their rhythm sections, this was often just talk. For the New York Art Quartet, collective improvisation was a raison d'etre, the band's musical starting point. (Davis, 1999, p.31)

Overall, innovation is potentially important for managers in a number of ways. If the environment is changing rapidly then innovation is a route to maintaining a viable niche. If a comfortable niche is achieved by establishing the organization as a pace-setter then continual innovation is required to retain that position. Innovation can also contribute to maintaining motivation through the rewards of novelty, freshness and the excitement of pioneering. But motivation and coordination problems can also arise where innovation becomes too prominent a part of the organizational regime. Finally, innovation is an inexorable imperative that eventually affects all organizations. Sectors or industries in which innovation does not occur eventually decline or are overtaken by other sectors that do innovate. In this sense, innovation can be seen as a collective responsibility of leadership in all organizations that share a common focus. In short, organizations must attempt to manage innovation or risk being managed by it.

Innovation comes about through a number of related organizational processes. The economist Joseph Schumpeter (1934), in his study of entrepreneurship and economic development, identified entrepreneurs as innovators who implemented "new combinations" of the means of production – using different inputs or methods to produce goods and services, finding new markets, producing entirely new products and services, organizing production in new ways, and so on. The idea behind "new combinations" is that people innovate by shuffling a basic set of elements and possibilities in a manner that departs from conventional practice and leads to new results.

Music demonstrates that the potential for innovation through new combinations is virtually unlimited. Terrance Simien and his Mallet Playboys offer one modest example of "fusion music" which combines different musical styles:

> Simien marries Creole zydeco with Cajun music and Delta blues, spiced with touches of rock, reggae, fund and gospel....His energized zydeco sound effectively blends

accordion, rub-board, guitar and a throbbing rhythm section of bass guitar and drums. (Fulmer 1997b, p.5-B)

Given pieces of music can be played with widely different combinations of instruments, and adapted to many different styles. The same piece can be upsized for large ensembles and downsized for smaller ones. Tempos can be changed and rhythms and harmonies can be altered in uncountable ways. Classical pieces can be diluted into elevator music or adapted to jazz motifs, and Beatles music can be elaborated for symphony orchestras. Melody can be moved to the bass line and harmonies can be carried in upper registers. Tubas can solo and cornets can harmonize, and so on. Experience with the trombone offers an interesting illustration:

> In the early years of jazz in New Orleans, musicians like Edward (Kid) Ory...developed "tailgate" style in which the trombone serves as a hinge between melody and rhythm, improving a sort of ground bass behind the trumpet lead and clarinet obbligato. In the 1920s, the trombone evolved as a soloing instrument in the hands of the New York musicians Jimmy Harrison and Miffy Mole, and it contributed to the subsequent stylistic developments in the music, from be-bop...to the avant-garde in the 1960s.....[In] the 1970s, Albert Mangelsdorff and George Lewis were elaborating startlingly innovative, polyphonic solo vocabularies on the trombone, defying naysayers who had dismissed the instrument as unwieldy and lumbering. (Edwards, 2001, p.23)

Intentional innovation does not normally occur through the haphazard trial of random possibilities; certain combinations work better than others. The art of orchestration consists of following established principles in order to specify the instrumental combinations that best project a given piece. But within these principles there is room for imagination and creative departure from norms. The idea of "new combinations" leaves open the possibility that one can constantly reconsider the old formulas and every once in a while find a new mix that works well and strikes out in a fresh new direction. Indeed, Nelson and Winter explain that "Innovations in organizational routine ... consist, in large part, of new combinations of existing routines" (1982, p.130). Donald Tovey applies this idea to Beethoven:

> The technical resource by which he extended his art amounts to little more than a combination of the habits of Mozart and Haydn, stimulated in later years by an intensive study of Handel and ...Bach. But in art, as in chemistry and mathematics, such combinations are no mere arithmetical additions. They are integrations that produce results often incalculable and sometimes explosive. (Tovey, 1949, pp.346-347)

One way of seeking new combinations is to imitate a previous form in a new context. Innovations that result from this strategy may be trivial (adapting Beatles' tunes is unlikely to set off a revolution in symphonic music) but sometimes this imitative strategy can lead to much more significant results. For example, as Tovey illustrates, in Bach's time the organ was employed to play "...a fugue imitating the behaviors of a four-part or five-part chorus discussing a subject in dialogue, but usually taking advantage of your instrument to propound a florid proposition beyond the range of the most athletic singer" (1949, p.341).

Another application of new combinations is the intentional blending of substantially different approaches. A good example is the work of Bright Cheng, a modern composer who seeks to combine western and Chinese systems of musical expression:

> Cheng creates a convincing bridge between the differing instruments and scales....the piece begins with a thin-sounding, vibratoless folk-like sound from the cellist, accompanied by harps and gentle drums. Gradually, almost imperceptibly, the cello's richer tone quality takes over in a melody that maintains the wide-leaping, angular flavor of Chinese scales in a fuller, more harmonically rich Western context. (Stearns, 1997, p.8D)

Sometimes innovation comes about by accident, even by mistake, but organizations must be receptive to new possibilities and be prepared to exploit them. Better yet, they need to improve on serendipity to bring innovation about. Tovey's recounting of the story of the "lost chord" is interesting in this regard:

> ....That which trains the imagination is good; that which starves or dulls the imagination is bad. Sitting at the keyboard and fumbling for lost chords is bad for the imagination. The poetess [Adelaide Proctor] herself clearly tells us that the lost chord was struck by accident. Samuel Butler has already pointed out that it must have been two chords if it sounded like a great Amen, and my own theory is that the organist had stumbled into a plagal cadence, and probably often afterwards struck one or other of the chords without recognizing them...Obviously a little knowledge of theory would have given the organist's imagination the freedom of all the Amens in Berlioz's *Requiem*....This Charles Halle tells us, Berlioz actually discovered by letting his fingers wander idly over the keyboard. (Tovey, 1949, p.377)

The story of the lost chord suggests that searching for new combinations can be usefully guided by thorough knowledge and understanding of existing combinations and by an imperative to find a solution to some outstanding problem. Berlioz let his fingers wander idly over the keyboard for a reason; he was looking for an idea that fit into the piece he was working on. More broadly, innovation is often the result of a directed search for new solutions to problems not satisfactorily resolved by conventional means. In this way, managers seek to solve problems or exploit opportunities, and innovations are the results – sometimes even incidental but important by-products of the search:

> One way in which the routine functioning of an organization can contribute to the emergence of innovation is that useful questions arise in the form of puzzles or anomalies relating to prevailing routines.....the problem-solving responses routinely evoked by difficulties with existing routines may yield results that lead to major change. (Nelson and Winter, 1982, pp. 129-130)

Consider the band called the Derailers from Austin, Texas:

> How does a country band come up with something new? It's not easy and the problem is especially acute if it wants listeners to know it's country music rather than just music stuck with a 'country' label".... "It's very exciting trying to look for that new twist," rhythm guitarist/vocalist/songwriter Tony Villanueva said... "To me, you have to really nail down what you're doing so people know where the music comes from while at the same time drawing on a broad enough pallet so we can develop our own thing."...What the band developed ....is a style squarely based on the California sound of Buck Owens and Merle Haggard melded with Texas honky-tonk, Western swing and a throbbing rockabilly beat... "We basically took a lot of elements from the music we listened to but we were basically thinking about the twosomes," Villanueva said. "People like the Everlys, the Louvins, Buck (Owens) and Don (Rich), as well as Keith and Mick and John and Paul. We wanted the interaction between two strong identities that would jell into something that works." (Fulmer 1997a, p.17)

Carse argues that the entire evolution of the modern orchestra, essentially a story of experimenting with new combinations of instruments to solve various problems over time, can be understood as a quest for better expression of the musical art form:

> However much the growth of the orchestra has been the toy of circumstances, conditions, or the mechanical or technical development of instruments, the real driving force behind such evolution is after all the insistently growing demand of musical art for fit means of expression. The impelling power of a constantly advancing art has always carried with it the realization of better and more worthy means of expressing itself, and with the demand, the man, the instrument, and the opportunity have always been forthcoming. (Carse, 1964, p.7)

Viewing innovation through this lens of problem-solving suggests that innovation is a reactive and pragmatic process, stimulated by difficulties in current operations. However, long term planning, anticipation of trends or elaborate theorizing about new possibilities also play into this picture. Where the environment, especially technology, is changing rapidly, problem solving may call for a more coherent and sustained approach to innovation. In these circumstances, Baumol points out the seemingly paradoxical result that: "...the innovation process has veered toward becoming yet another humdrum activity of the firm, with corporate R&D taking over a substantial portion of the field and transforming it into preprogrammed activity" (1993, p.115). And, Nelson and Winter observe: "...organizations have [developed] well-defined routines for the support and direction of their innovative efforts" (1982, p.134).

Whether formally organized through a research and development enterprise, or pragmatically based in a problem-solving philosophy that is open to systematic consideration of new combinations, a problem-solving focus remains an important strategy for organizational innovation that allows for improvement in current ways of doing things and adaptation to new environmental circumstances over the long term.

Serendipity and directed change through research and development are two ends of a spectrum of ways in which new combinations can be produced and innovations manifested. A middle ground, well illustrated in the realm of music, yields innovation by allowing for intuitive and semi-systematic variation and experimentation within the framework of existing norms. Musicians call it improvisation: "...improvisation refers to composing and performing in the same moment, i.e. realizing a musical performance without the benefit of deliberate planning about how each note will be executed, the order and flavour of each solo, the direction the performance will take, how long it will last, etc." (Kamoche, Cunha and Cunha, 2002, pp.2-3).

Improvisation is not random. It requires structure to be in place, and it requires a set of rules and conventions within which variations may be tried. But these rules are also flexible, and pushing their limits is one way in which significant innovations may occur. Indeed, Weick (1998) points out that improvisation lies along a continuum of practices, or departures from convention, that range from "interpretation" to "embellishment" to "variation" of a melody, to full "improvisation" which radically transforms the melody in some significant way. As Tovey observes, improvisation may even lead to bad habits which can undermine effective operation, but it can nonetheless be critically important:

> Extemporization is a pastime which may lead to all manner of bad habits, but at least half the aesthetic resources of classical music have originated in it, and the wise teacher will neither close the playground nor supervise the games until they become a worse tyranny than the lessons. (Tovey, 1961, p. 378)

Clearly improvisation is best known in the world of jazz. Indeed Max DuPree (1992), John Kao (1996) and others have used jazz as their principal metaphor for leadership and creativity in dynamic business environments where adaptability and inventiveness are seen as prerequisites of success. John Coltrane provides a vivid illustration of how innovation can occur through improvisation in jazz:

> *My Favorite Things* was originally a bright, bouncy waltz in *aabb* form... Coltrane kept it in triple meter, but used its 16-measure sections to frame scale-based improvisations of indefinite lengths. A performance consisted of three solos – one by Coltrane, one by Tyner, and another by Coltrane – bounded by an introduction and coda of varying lengths. Because of the open-ended interpolations, different recorded performances vary in length from ten to fifty-six minutes....Coltrane weaves a fascinating tapestry of melodic threads, unfettered by any predetermined structural boundaries. In these performances the group clearly is redefining the traditional roles and relationships of jazz-group members. Garrison avoids playing walking bass lines, and instead concentrates on rhythmically more varied melodic lines. Tyner supplies an almost constant chordal barrage during Coltrane's lengthy solos. And Jones aggressively interacts with the soloists, creating energetic and dense textures with them. He seems to play drum solos during the sax and piano solos, but he is actually entering into a lively dialogue with them. The result is the musical equivalent of animated and excitable old friends conversing, interrupting one another, yet interacting and exchanging thoughts. It is a fascinating and brilliantly executed musical experience, one far removed from

earlier bebop. (Owens, 1995, pp.227-228)

The Elements of Innovation

Fostering innovation involves many of the same elements of management strategy that were considered in our discussions of coordination, motivation and niche-finding. Revisiting these elements further illuminates how innovation comes about and how managers can influence and exploit it.

Formal Rules and Procedures

Organizational routine is in some sense the antithesis of innovation. As Tovey notes, following the rules in mechanical fashion leads to uninspired results:

> Nobody is ever in doubt about the sound of a passage that keeps the rules. If it has not been imagined, it will be dull, though clearer than ditch-water. It if has been imagined, it may be vivid as the opening of Beethoven's Violin Concerto, even if it is as unoriginal as Handel's Hallelujah Chorus. (Tovey, 1961, p.392)

However, rules and standard procedures are also essential to innovation. Without standard ways of doing things there would be nothing nonstandard to be called an innovation. As Nelson and Winter put it: "...innovation involves change in routine." (1982, p.128). Routines serve as the foundations from which innovation takes place. Variations from routines may happen by accident or by changes in circumstances that require the same operations to take place under different conditions. For example, as Nelson and Winter point out, organizational routines can "mutate" when the personnel who carry them out change:

> ...because the new role occupant may himself be different in significant and durable ways from his predecessor, and also as the result of other contingencies affecting the role-learning process, it is highly unlikely that a near replica of the predecessor's role performance will result. In short, organizational routine will mutate. (Nelson and Winter, 1982, p.116)

An example of a routine in music that generates such mutation is ornamentation in baroque music:

> Ornamenting baroque music is something like trimming of the Christmas tree. Composers of the 17th and 18th centuries created musical structures as strong and beautiful as evergreens. Performers were expected to add expressive embellishments that gave the music sparkle and personality. (Salisbury, 1998a, p.3-E)

As the term "personality" suggests then, variations through the routine of ornamentation came about when personnel changed and musicians with different ideas offered new ornaments to the standard pieces played by their ensembles.

One could argue that ornamental variation is not true innovation because it is generated by fixed rules that constitute part of the essential (routine) core of Baroque music. (Weick would probably call it "embellishment".) This mode of "structured variation" nonetheless encourages exploration of new combinations. Hence, innovation can be a matter of degree – paradoxically, some of these variations may be "routine" while others can depart, sometimes radically, from the usual fare.

Again, innovation depends on a foundation of existing rules and procedures. In an interesting study, Bastien and Hostager (2002) observed a jazz quartet that had previously not played or rehearsed together but whose members were all accomplished musicians with a strong knowledge of the rules and customs of jazz. With no preparation they were able to immediately play and improvise around some simple well known songs and, as the performance progressed, were able to improvise more daringly around more complex melodies to a point where they eventually invented a new song. They were able to do this because they had knowledge of the initial song, the musical rules (chord progressions, rhythmic patterns) through which variations in the song could be constructed, as well as the social practices or protocols through which each player was expected to interact with fellow players and the group leader. Using the rules, the players were able to minimize uncertainty over what was coming next, and the risk of chaos, while exploring new possibilities. A similar experience is described by Peplowski (1998).

Many different musical ensembles may play the "same music" but each is likely to engage that music in its own way, and in some cases, significant innovation may occur. Traditional American folk songs were played in a standard, old-fashioned way by the Weavers in the early 1950s and their popularization of this genre of music was itself noteworthy. But when the Kingston Trio and Peter, Paul and Mary got hold of this music in the late 1950s and early 1960s, they created a whole new folk music style and audience.

In classical music, the basic routines and repertoires apply to all orchestras and chamber groups. Still, people are drawn to particular sounds and styles of ensembles that have managed to distinguish themselves from the crowd through some variation in those routines – perhaps a subtle but effective nuance in rhythm or dynamics, or an imaginative new combination of instruments. For example, such an innovation arose from the need to solve a unique problem that arose in putting the program together to celebrate the ninetieth birthday of distinguished harp teacher Alice Chalifoux: an unusual ensemble of 58 harpists was assembled for this occasion to play a unique program of rarely performed pieces on this normally singular instrument, in a progression from solo harp to the full ensemble:

> The program will grow from a sonata ...to a suite for two harps...to a concerto for harp and seven wind instruments to ensemble works for six harps, then 22 harps and then – imagine! – 58 harps. (Rosenberg, 1998a, p. 2-E)

Another way in which routines support innovation is through experimentation with the circumstances under which different sets of rules or routines are applied. Bringing a popular piece (a Beatles song) to a classical context, or a classical piece to a popular context (jazzing up Beethoven's *Ode to Joy*), are examples of innovating by changing from one set of rules to another. Mixing two or more sets of rules is yet another way. Gilbert and Sullivan innovated by mixing the rules for opera with those of popular music. Gershwin innovated by bringing classical structure to a jazz motif.

Rules also establish the basis for "planned innovation" through improvisation. While the results of improvisation vary from one application to another, and sometimes leads to unusual outcomes that strike out in substantially new directions, improvisation, as we have noted, is not a completely random process. The rules of improvisation guide and confine the possibilities but also permit surprises to occur. In jazz, there are scales that may be explored, particular intervals that are known to sound better than others, key changes that fit and others that do not, incidental notes and phrases (riffs) that may be inserted in various kinds of circumstances. The possibilities are many, but most are predefined. However, the number of combinations is enormous and never fully explored, leaving open the chance for important innovations to occur in the process of improvising by the rules. Moreover, there remain many yet to be imagined possibilities for variations in the rules themselves – incrementally different, but nonetheless new kinds of incidental notes and phrases, rhythmic and harmonic variations and so on, which potentially increase the number of "standard" combinations and which raise the prospect of introducing wholly new kinds of possibilities. This zone of bending the rules at the margins is where significant innovation often occurs:

In jazz, improvisation doesn't just have to consist of variations on the theme at hand. A few jazz musicians, ranging from Louis Armstrong to Stan Getz, have excelled at subtly altering the melody and the chords of standard tunes. Others, Dizzy Gillespie for example, are at their best developing ingenious new melodies on familiar chord structures. Ornette Coleman showed musicians how to improvise on the sound, the mood, the feeling of a tune, and many followed his example.

But all of these improvisers are fundamentally alike and each one has developed a distinctive musical syntax, a personal dialect of the language we call jazz. (Palmer, 1987, p.28)

Communication

Communication among members of an organization can be a critical element in achieving innovation. While inventiveness and creativity may be vested largely in the capacities of individuals, communication is essential to moving from the conception of ideas to their implementation. Moreover, the generation of new ideas per se is certainly stimulated by the interplay among individual organizational members.

Nowhere is the importance of communication to innovation more evident than in the process of improvisation. In jazz, improvisation requires that organizational members take turns trying to invent new phrases on the fly when their musical parts come around to them; group members set the context and provide the stimuli for individual solos. Improvisational sessions may be understood as conversations among ensemble members in which the musical response and inventiveness of one player inspires that of the next.

The quality of the communication and hence innovational success will depend on a number of factors, including how well the players know each other and can understand and anticipate each others' thoughts and ideas. Members of a tightly knit ensemble that have played together for a long time can lead each other about – – even into uncharted territory – more easily than a group of strangers. So too, even relative strangers who have common backgrounds of education and experience, will know "where each other are coming from" as they improvise, better than a group of players used to different styles and genres of music. This was the case for the jazz quartet observed by Bastien and Hostager (2002). The more the four musical strangers played together, the more capable they became in moving from routine to innovation, moving from minor variations on a simple theme in their first number, to the invention of a new song by the third. A similar rapport seems to have been achieved by Bobby McFerrin as he led the Cleveland Orchestra in accompanying jazz pianist Chick Corea:

> When Corea came onstage, he introduced Mozart's Piano Concerto No.20 in D minor, K.466, by improvising a simple harmonized melody that segued into the orchestral exposition. Then, he played along, almost inaudibly, and he also added extra notes to the solo part.
>
> Except for the cadenzas, most of his additions were well within the boundaries of the classical style. But in the cadenzas, he forged into a different world of free improvisation and chromatic harmonies.
>
> Although McFerrin sometimes let the ensemble overpower the soloist, he was an attentive partner who encouraged the pianist to take the lead...McFerrin set the pace, and Corea came along for the ride. At times, the musicians needed a few phrases to get into the same groove. But once they were on their way, their synchronized performances took flight. (Salisbury, 1997, p.5-B)

Education

The importance of understanding rules and having clear communications as prerequisites to successful innovation, suggests that the education of ensemble members also plays an important supportive role, though education is also a potential hindrance. Highly educated ensemble players will know the rules and have a deep understanding of both the existing routines and the ways in which they can be varied. Moreover, educated players are more likely to share common understandings of musical language, heuristics and routines for variation and hence will be able to communicate with each other more effectively on an extemporaneous basis than those not as well trained, even if they are from different musical venues.

However, education can also be a stumbling block to innovation where training blinds individuals to the possibilities that may lie outside their areas of expertise. Here is where less highly trained creative geniuses sometimes intrude on the world of professionals to introduce new forms that would never have been conceived by their most highly educated contemporaries. George Gershwin was an amateur in the world of classical writing and orchestration. Paul McCartney didn't read music. They broke rules because they didn't know all the rules. These innovators were in some sense aided by their ignorance because they were unconstrained by standard ways of thinking that might have restricted their imaginations. The role of education in fostering organizational innovation is therefore, paradoxical. The most erudite practitioners may foster innovation because they have not only mastered their disciplines but understand the limits of those disciplines as well, and hence are receptive to new possibilities. Less well educated practitioners may also be innovative if they have innate talent and genius and are not constrained by standard notions. Those occupying a middle ground of substantial education and limited imagination will be most likely to ignore and even eschew possible new combinations that could lead to important innovations.

Finally, there is another interesting twist to the relationship between education and innovation. Sophisticated improvisation requires deep musical knowledge by each of the players in an ensemble. The more knowledgeable each of the players, the more easily members of the ensemble can interact and follow each others' leads and cues. Hence, the group as a whole may be held back by its less sophisticated members. Bastien and Hostager thus speculate that "...groups that include musicians of very different knowledge bases will either produce jazz that is not well integrated or will perform at a level roughly equivalent to that of the least competent member" (2002, p.23).

Rehearsing

The role of rehearsing and repetition in innovation is similarly paradoxical. Certainly at the level of the individual, practice is a key ingredient in preparing players for innovation. Citing Berliner (1994, p.494), Weick emphasizes this point:

> ...Berliner is worried lest, in our fascination with the label "spontaneous", we overlook the major investment in practice, listening, and study that precedes a stunning performance. A jazz musician is more accurately described as a highly disciplined "practicer"....than as a practitioner. (Weick, 1998, p.544)

At the ensemble level, practice plays a very important role in innovation as well. An ensemble's playing of a given piece proceeds through successive stages of development. Initially, the group works out the operational problems and reaches a point where the performance is technically correct. From that point, the ensemble can fine tune its playing, working out nuances so that it achieves a high level of technical perfection. Subsequently, the ensemble may begin to put its own stamp on the piece, setting the tempo and dynamics according to its own taste and playing certain phrases in its own way, giving it an interpretation that can be associated with the ensemble's own special style. At this level, the ensemble may go further, actually making changes in the sequences, orchestration, or even melody, harmony and rhythm, possibly leading to significant innovation. While not going quite that far, the Cleveland Orchestra sometimes borders on innovation, even with standard Beethoven pieces:

> The Beethoven performances in Cleveland should in no way be viewed as rehearsals for Tokyo, if last night's program of the "Leonore" Overture No.1 and Symphonies No.4 and 5 was any indication. These weren't run-throughs of music we've heard on numerous occasions, but newly conceived interpretations by a conductor who never stops probing and an orchestra that abhors anything resembling routine. (Rosenberg, 1993, p.30)

This nominal sequence of development makes clear that continued practice and repetition can support innovation. The more a group masters a particular kind of work, the better position it is in to see where improvements or new approaches may apply. However, practice can be enervating as well. If the stage of technical mastery is not followed by creative interpretation and experimentation it can lead just as easily to a loss of enthusiasm and a deterioration in performance, and the opportunity for innovation may be lost.

The dangers of repetition coupled with the benefits of practice appear to call for an approach to innovation that emphasizes variety and experimentation. Ensembles can expand their repertoires so that they become expert in a reasonable number of different pieces, yet are able to avoid boredom with any specific piece. Practiced and revisited with reasonable frequency, individual pieces can remain both fresh and well-mastered, and each revisiting can become an opportunity to take a new look and consider additional variations in performance.

Practice and repetition are particularly useful components of success in improvisation. By definition, improvisational performance should never be the same from one performance to the next. No matter how many times the Preservation Hall dixieland band in New Orleans plays "The Saints Go Marching In", someone's solo will be slightly different and some variation will occur in the overall fabric of the piece. Thus, practice and repetition becomes an increasing challenge within an improvisational regime. The obvious variations will be dispensed with early on and new variations will be searched out with increasing urgency. A "surprise" that comes after many improvisational repetitions may represent a significant innovation. But if surprises cease to occur after a long while, it will be time to move on to other challenges before the creative juices dry up.

Personnel Practices

Earlier we observed that changing personnel inevitably introduces variation into the way an organization carries out its work, potentially leading to innovation. There are at least two ways to introduce change in the personnel mix of an ensemble. The first is to change individual members of the group and the second is to rearrange the roles of incumbent members.

It is the rare organization that maintains a completely stable mix of personnel over long periods of time. Such stability can be extremely important to successful innovation in ensembles where the combination of skills and personalities is unique and group members find themselves reinforcing and stimulating each others' creative energies. The Beatles, for example, were able to stay together for a long time and progress through several successive stages of creative, groundbreaking achievement. Introducing new personnel into such an ensemble when it is "on a roll" is likely to be counterproductive; it would forego the advantages associated with the fact that group members had achieved a high level of mutual understanding which enabled them to work together towards new horizons of creativity. At best, a new member would require a substantial learning period that would interrupt progress and slow the group's momentum.

Eventually, however, the personnel mix of any organization changes, either by natural causes or because the ensemble no longer senses that it can maintain the chemistry responsible for past success. In some cases, especially small groups like Simon and Garfunkel or the Supremes, the ensemble will simply dissolve. Larger organizations are more likely to survive key personnel changes, and their innovative potential may even benefit from them. For such organizations, the question of replacing old members and recruiting new ones is critical. New members will have different styles and personalities, so it will be important for them to be compatible with whomever remains. At the same time, new members are a source of fresh creative energy and ideas and they may introduce changes in style and expertise that can amplify the potential number of "new combinations" available to the ensemble as a whole. Recruitment, therefore, creates special opportunities for an organization to reconsider its current ways of doing things and to explore new possibilities that ultimately may prove to be innovative. Changes in organizational leadership provide the clearest illustrations. Consider Leonard Slatkin's experiences with different orchestras:

> I am delighted with the sound we have achieved here and I try to take a little bit of St. Louis with me wherever I conduct. But you can't do that with every orchestra you work with; if you're just visiting, you don't want to rearrange the furniture too much...I try to come in with a clear conception of the way a piece should be played and then I make adjustments for the personalities of the different orchestras I work with." (Page, 1992, p.138)

In smaller organizations, it is more likely that new people will come from the outside rather than rising through the ranks or entering through lateral personnel changes.   This increases the likelihood that new personnel will introduce substantial change, since they are not yet indoctrinated with the organization's culture and particular ways of doing things.   This is a mixed blessing for innovation.   New recruits must gain a common understanding with existing organizational members before new and old members can work productively together towards successful innovation.   Once they have done so, however, new recruits are likely to stimulate fresh approaches.   One way this can happen is by introducing new skills, just as new members of a musical ensemble can bring different instrumental capacities.   For example, jazz sextets can substitute banjos or trombones for guitars, if personnel with the capacities for playing those instruments are introduced and brass sextets can utilize different combinations of cornets, horns, trombones and tubas (Osterberg, 1996).

In larger organizations, there is a greater likelihood of changing the personnel mix internally, through changes in work assignments.   Individuals can move from one department to another, introducing new ideas, styles and perspectives while maintaining a consistency borne of experience in the same overall organizational environment.   To a large extent, such mobility is impeded by specialization, however.   Production workers rarely move into the accounting department, and human resources personnel are unlikely to shift to corporate finance.   A more likely scenario is the shift of personnel assignments within departments.

Orchestras illustrate both the possibilities and limitations of such shifting.   In a symphony orchestra, it would be the rare talent that could move from the string section to the woodwinds; these instrument sections are too specialized for most individuals to be accomplished in both.   Such individuals could potentially increase the likelihood for innovation by bringing the benefits of "woodwind thinking" to the strings or vice versa.   It is more likely, however, that individuals could move within such departments, for example, from the violas to violins, and certainly from second violins to first violins, or if not from clarinet to oboe, then from flute to piccolo.   Such shifting at opportune times within these subgroups – for example as practiced by the 15 member Concerto Soloists of Philadelphia chamber ensemble (Goodman, 1985a) – can enhance the potential for innovation by introducing different styles and perspectives on which to build new combinations.

However, the simple shifting of personnel among departments and roles within departments may not be sufficient to exploit the full creative potential of talented players.   Second violins and low brass simply may not have interesting enough parts.   Thus, another personnel approach that can enhance innovative potential is to juggle work assignments among roles.   Second violins and low brass can be given the melody line on occasion and first violins and trumpets can play accompaniment.   This approach, rather than shifting people around, effectively addresses the same goal.   The same set of first violin players, having grown a bit stale playing the melody lines together, may find wholly new perspectives in occasionally addressing (or revisiting) the challenges of harmony and counterpoint. Certainly, the tuba players will thrill to the possibilities of being in the melodic limelight and this too may introduce new creativity into the low brass section.

Overall, of course, changing work assignments in this manner, simply offers the chance for experimentation with new combinations for how the ensemble gets its work done; indeed it may find that some unusual combinations actually do work better for certain kinds of pieces or performances. Certainly the notion of rotating solos is implicit in the jazz motif where players in all sections normally get their chances, on a rotating basis, to display their ideas through improvisational solos – percussion, low brass and basses included.

The potential for innovation may be even further enhanced if hierarchical and status barriers between departments are broken down and members of each can deal with one another on a more egalitarian basis. This perspective is common in chamber music. Composer Ellen Taffe Zwilich illustrates the idea in her Double Quartet:

> This simply isn't an octet. I wanted the audience to realize that this was not just a piece for two cellos, two violas and four violins, but two separate string quartets, simultaneously competitive and cooperative. Chamber music demands a continual trade-off in musical hierarchy. Now the first violin has the melody, now it's taken by the cello; now the one quartet leads the way, now the other. (Page, 1992, p.149)

De-emphasis of hierarchy may encourage innovation for three reasons. First, greater equality will encourage greater mobility among work groups; first violinists will be more willing to play with the second violins if no loss in status is associated with such a move. In turn, the increased interdepartmental mobility will enhance the possibilities for mixing personnel from different groups and hence introducing new elements of creativity into various contexts from time to time. Second, greater equality will increase the likelihood that new combinations resulting from role reversals and exchanges will be considered. If first violins do not consider it an insult to play harmony or counterpoint, they will be open to doing it more often. Third, if greater equality prevails, better communication is likely among departments and a more robust exchange of ideas may result. Tuba players may be less reluctant to offer suggestions to the clarinets, and so on.

Leadership

The issue of how status affects innovation carries over into the question of what role leadership plays in innovation. Inspired leadership can be an important source of innovation. However, autocratic leadership can discourage innovation by suppressing the potential contributions of organizational members, especially those in low status departments.

The world of music is filled with names of strong leaders whose innovative ideas formed the foundation for the ensembles they led. Great composers such as Beethoven, Berlioz and Wagner conducted orchestras playing their own original works, and jazz bands under the leadership of Duke Ellington, Count Basie, Glen Miller, Benny Goodman and many others, have been vehicles for playing the path breaking works of those creative geniuses. As music directors of their own ensembles, these individuals assumed the role of Schumpeter's entrepreneurs, not only inventing new combinations but putting them into practice through bands or orchestras either created for the express purpose of playing their works or adapted over time to serve as vehicles for their particular musical contributions. This situation is referred to by Fischer and Jackson as "...the double metaphor of the conductor as performer; the orchestra as instrument" (1997, p.72).

The "orchestra as instrument" concept puts an enormous burden on the leader to be the sustaining source of inspiration and new ideas. While this entrepreneurial style of central leadership is an important source of innovation it is also limited because it depends on sustainable individual creative genius not only to continually invent new concepts but also to put them into practice. Most organizations seeking to innovate, especially larger ones, must exploit other means less critically dependent on enormous central leadership talent.

Even if they are not creative geniuses, leaders can play a central role in organizational innovation. In music, for example, conductors can be the critical link between composers of new or less-well known music and the playing of that music for a public audience. Leonard Bernstein was well known for championing the works of Gustav Mahler, for example, at a time when Mahler was not widely appreciated. In this sense, leaders perform a "boundary-spanning" function, scanning the environment for new ideas and possibilities and bringing them inside the organization to expand the repertoire. This can be a very important role, particularly in the case of highly experimental works. A conductor with a strong personal reputation who can afford to take risks, and with the personal acumen to understand the significance of a new idea, may be instrumental in promoting an important innovation on which others are unwilling to gamble. This appears to be the case with Elliot Carter and the Cleveland Orchestra:

> The Cleveland performance was eloquent testimony to a splendid orchestra operating in peak form, under a conductor, Dohnanyi, who is committed to playing new music and getting it right. There remains only the sadness and even the anger, that this was not all happening in New York. Since Pierre Boulez left the music directorship of the Philharmonic two decades ago, the orchestra has not played any new piece by either of the two venerable composers who have spent their working lives in or near New York: Carter or Milton Babbit. (Griffiths, 1997, p.8-E)

While leadership can be extraordinarily important as a source and support for innovation, it can also be problematic if it suppresses or ignores creative energies that reside within the rest of the organization's work force. A self-centered, autocratic leader may be unreceptive to the ideas of other organizational members, and hence may discourage their contributions. A leader that assumes the entire burden of responsibility for programming and repertoire, and fails to consult organizational members or cultivate their interests, runs the risk of lulling the organization into a sense of (possibly false) security that the boss is "taking care of these matters". Worse yet, an autocratic leader may have to overcome indifference with intimidation. Of course, a brilliant autocratic leader may also inspire organization members, thereby effectively engaging the organization as a vehicle for innovation.   However, a more open style of leadership which encourages participation, values suggestions, and removes risks associated with offering unorthodox ideas,   has perhaps the greater potential to unleash imaginative thinking that can lead to significant new possibilities. Over time, decentralized leadership can be far more effective in stimulating innovation than autocratic, central leadership unless the latter is unusually brilliant and enduring.

Here again is where the process of improvisation comes into play. Indeed, Bastien and Hostager argue that jazz is the antithesis of central leader-led innovation: "Jazz is ... a truly collective approach to the entire process of innovation, for it requires that the invention, adoption, and implementation of new musical ideas by individual musicians occurs within the context of a shared awareness of the group performance as it unfolds over time" (2002, p.14). While a leader may establish a procedural framework and supportive environment, improvisation is usually a bottom-up process that depends on individual initiative and creativity. The ensemble becomes an incubator, perhaps under the benevolent oversight of a conductor-coach-manager, within which section leaders and others with virtuoso leanings can explore their ideas, share them with others, and insert new combinations into the ensemble's overall repertoire. Such decentralized leadership arrangements foster innovation in a mode that is complementary to the entrepreneurial mode of the creative central leader, and perhaps is even better suited for that role in circumstances where towering geniuses are rare, work has become too complex for single individuals to exert complete mastery, and work forces abound with talent and proficiency.

The Circumstances of Innovation

Not all organizational contexts support or encourage innovation. Larger and smaller, more or less diverse, professional and amateur, and stable and transient, organizational settings present different challenges to generating and implementing new ways of doing things.

Size

With respect to innovation, smaller is generally better. All else constant, smaller organizations provide for greater ease of communication, less rigid adherence to standard procedures, and generally greater flexibility for making changes and trying new approaches. Moreover, smaller organizations accommodate both entrepreneurial leaders who may use the organization as a vehicle to implement their creative ideas, and egalitarian groups that prefer to share in the creative process. Thus, we can equally expect democratic chamber groups such as the Canadian Brass or Guarneri Quartet to be innovative as we can pop groups such as the Supremes or Huey Lewis and the News which revolve tightly around charismatic, creative leaders.

Innovation becomes a more difficult challenge in larger organizations where bureaucratic procedures and strong centralized administration may be more deeply entrenched. In this context, a conscious strategy of innovation is more critical, whether that be the creation of a central research and development program that explicitly generates new proposals for systematic testing and experimentation, or the establishment of a decentralized regime in which experimentation, improvisation and creativity are specifically encouraged, rewarded and systematically exploited throughout the organization.

In classical music, observers have argued that many of the larger organizations (orchestras) have begun to ossify and some have fallen by the wayside, victims of their inability to change. They have not had a systematic program for seeking innovation nor have they decentralized in a way that could exploit the benefits of small size. For example, in making recommendations for orchestras in the twenty-first century, Orleans suggests:

> A "think tank" for musicians...By beginning to address organizational problems at the artistic level ourselves, without the intrusion of managements, conductors, or marketing influences, we can define for ourselves our own mission, and present to management, in the most constructive way possible, very specific suggestions regarding, but not limited to, repertoire (symphony, pops, and youth concerts), program planning, and even areas that have been heretofore seen as the express responsibility of the music director, such as rehearsal time management and stage decorum. (Orleans, 1997, p.4)

Such a think tank would be akin to a central research and development process for orchestras. Alternatively, a decentralized approach would entail having orchestras exploit the advantages of smallness by breaking themselves down into smaller ensembles for different performance opportunities – chamber groups, sectional and chamber orchestras of various compositions, and so on. Within these subgroups, ideas can be more easily generated and cultivated on a continual basis than is easily done in the larger ensemble. In this way, an internal process of creativity is maintained that can invigorate the entire organization. Spich and Sylvester elaborate upon this idea as a model for orchestras of the future:

> The 21st century orchestra could consist of a string ensemble, two or three woodwind quintets, two or three brass quintets, an early music ensemble, a multitude of keyboards, a percussion ensemble, a jazz big band, a battery of synthesizers and digital acoustic recreative equipment, a host of electronic instruments...and a multitude of world-music ensembles. (Spich and Sylvester, 1999, p.36)

The value of such decentralization lies not only in the increased number of possibilities for innovation at the subgroup level, but also the ability of the overall organization to respond creatively to external opportunities. Spich and Sylvester offer the example of the Columbia Symphony:

> It worked as follows: Columbia Records wished to record major artists, soloists, and composers... In many cases, their time frame was much shorter than is typical of

program planning by a symphony orchestra. The traditional symphony orchestra is not terribly flexible in terms of available time for recording or isolated concert dates....The Columbia Symphony was a responsive and flexible organization, a virtual-type organization that could be created over and over again, each time including only the actual musicians needed, and each time dispersing after a particular project. (Spich and Sylvester, 1999, pp.36-37)

Such a "cut and paste" ensemble raises other issues regarding performance quality, similar to those experienced by pick-up bands as discussed earlier, but it does promise a new level of innovation and adaptation to a complex and changing environment.

Diversity

Other factors (such as size) held the same, an organization of diverse parts maintains a fundamental advantage for innovation that more homogeneous organizations forego: they intrinsically have more combinations with which they can potentially experiment. There are simply more possibilities to exploit in an orchestra of diverse instruments than in a homogeneous ensemble of tubas or accordions, or even human voices, no matter how flexible the instrument in question. Moreover, the number of combinations increases geometrically with the number of different types of participants. If there are two basic functions to be performed (melody and harmony), two instruments can combine to do this in two different ways (one plays melody, the other harmony or vice versa). If three instruments are available, the number of combinations rises to twelve (three choices for melody; then two for harmony; then the third can choose one or the other: $3 \times 2 \times 2 = 12$). Four instruments allows for 48 such combinations! And so on.

Of course the sheer number of possibilities is not the only determinant of innovative potential. While seemingly random mixing of radically different elements (e.g., Chinese and American musical systems; banjos and oboes) can sometimes be the basis for important innovations, there must also be a rationale for bringing such elements together; purely random experimentation rarely works – innovators usually have some idea of what they are looking for within a defined domain of possibilities. Moreover, there must be some common basis of communication so that diverse elements can be brought together in new, but sensible ways. Rap singers won't mix well with flutes unless some creative genius sees a connection and finds a way to meld these elements together. Nonetheless, such mixes are not necessarily to be dismissed out of hand. Indeed, the history of jazz features various instances where very different traditions have been mixed, including bebop with traditional Japanese music, and jazz with European concert music:

In the 1950s a few jazz and non-jazz composers wrote some works that attempted to blend jazz and European concert music and create a new music....Most of it joined a jazz group with a chamber ensemble or orchestra. Often the jazz musicians had to deal with structures, harmonies, and melodies that were foreign to their idiom, while the European-oriented musicians had to cope with equally unfamiliar rhythms, phrasings, and articulations. The results sometimes made the listener wish that the jazz group would simply play a jazz tune alone, and then let the chamber group or orchestra play some Bartok. But occasionally efforts to fuse the two traditions have worked. (Owens, 1995, p.234)

Professionalism

We have already seen how education can both foster and inhibit innovation. Thus, the level of professionalism in the work force can be an important determinant of an organization's innovative potential.   Generally, a certain level of professionalism or mastery is necessary before innovation is meaningfully addressed. If organizational participants have only a rudimentary knowledge of their field and are not experts in what they do, they cannot perform at the frontiers of their art, much less push those boundaries outward or in a different direction. Thus, amateur folk singing groups, jazz bands or orchestras are unlikely to advance their respective musical genres or change them in a significant way. If they are challenged simply to play the scores accurately and to maintain ensemble, they are unlikely to introduce changes in the music that alter its character in some important way. This opportunity is essentially reserved for ensembles at the top of their games which can take a score, or part of the existing repertoire, as a point of departure for experimentation. As noted earlier, ensembles can be held back in their progress towards innovation by the limitations of their least competent players.

However, mastery should not be entirely conflated with professional training. It is possible for amateurs or outsiders to achieve outstanding levels of performance and to apply their creative geniuses in ways that might never occur to those highly trained in traditional ways. Thus, an organization composed of eccentric but highly proficient amateurs, who have learned their art in nontraditional ways, may be even more likely to introduce substantial innovation than an organization in which the workforce is professional and traditional. While The Grateful Dead was a professional ensemble it captured this element of amateurism:

> For some people, the flaw in the Dead utopia is the music. Along with their commitment to live performance, they're fine on such rock virtues as democracy, pride in roots and lack of pretense. But they don't do so well with concision (both songs and sets sprawl) or drive (the music is more likely to lilt) or charisma...[But] they insist that with a wink and a grin and a little ingenuity – and with homespun, spur-of-the-moment, hippie-tonk music – it's possible to make it through...The Grateful Dead, lapses and all, are the right band to carry that message...The Dead are professional amateurs, happy to stay that way. And even if their music weren't such a pleasure, they'd be something rock always needs: the exception to every rule. (Pareles, 1987b, p.H-24)

Mixing traditional professional and proficient nontraditional elements within an organization in a manner that is functional and supportive of innovation is a substantial challenge. The two cultures are likely to be incompatible in many respects. A group of musicians accustomed to improvising and eschewing written scores cannot easily be dropped into the middle of a symphony orchestra, no matter how talented and creative they may be or how liberal and accepting the orchestra members are. Nontraditional players are likely to chaff under the discipline required to adhere precisely to directives, while traditional players are likely to be uncomfortable departing from prescribed ways of doing things. However, each type of player can draw on the other, and each may gain by emulating aspects of the others' viewpoint. Nontraditional groups can benefit from the structured, systematic thinking and discipline that underlies professional training, as this framework can help put ad hoc experimentation and improvisation into perspective and suggest directions for future invention. So too, highly professional groups that adhere rigorously to the precepts of their disciplines may benefit from questioning their assumptions periodically and being open-minded to the possibilities articulated and explored by nontraditional groups.

Examples of this kind of mixing of genres and personnel are uncommon but certainly not unknown in music. They often yield interesting "cross-over" combinations. For example, Apollo's Fire has mixed folk and early music classical players in concert, who were able to explore, perhaps for the first time, the musical connections between these two musical traditions. So too, an experiment incorporating folk instruments and players into a classical genre seemed to have worked out well for the Lincoln Center's Chamber Music Society, successfully producing some new varieties of musical expression:

> Edgar Mayer, the regular bassist of Lincoln Center's Chamber Music Society and a musician with equal experience in classical and bluegrass, has teamed up with the banjoist Bela Fleck and the mandolin player Mike Marshall for a new classical-crossover album, "Uncommon Ritual"...The Chamber Music Society's opening concert this season came mostly from the recording.... "Uncommon Ritual" is not a classical album. But neither does it belong to bluegrass, traditional Irish music, jazz or any of the other traditions it lightly borrows from....It's sort of a chamberized health shake of music that's acceptable to a National Public Radio listenership....If the music wasn't classical, the presentation was. Mr. Fleck got to parade his considerable improvising skills for only a few lone choruses and otherwise delighted in playing the fish out of water throughout. (Ratliff, 1997, p.B20)

Instability

Within limits, turmoil is the ally of innovation. If environmental conditions are too chaotic, organizations may be destroyed before they can adapt. While this may manifest innovation through Schumpeter's (1934) process of creative destruction, this situation is certainly dysfunctional for individual organizations, even if managed by progressive leaders who seek change. At the other extreme, organizations that operate in contexts of extreme stability are also unlikely to innovate. As Albert Hirschman (1970) has observed, organizations normally undertake constructive change only when the environment sends clears signals that support is threatened if no change is forthcoming, but where there is sufficient slack to allow change to take place in time to prevent organizational collapse.

Unfortunately, some orchestras in the United States seem to have neglected to heed the signs of instability and loss of support in their environments and, as a result, have failed. A few, however, have taken advantage of crisis to reconstitute themselves in innovative ways that promise a better future. The Colorado Symphony is an important example (Freeman, 1996a). In this case, rigid procedures of collective bargaining and traditional modes of governance and programming gave way to flexible compensation arrangements for musicians, shared governance between musicians and community leaders, and flexible programming in public squares, shopping malls and other venues. It took a severe crisis, however, to accomplish these changes.

Environmental instability is often reflected in work force turnover. In an organization that cannot assure stable employment under satisfactory conditions or in an environment where multiple opportunities abound for talented people, organizational members may come and go with substantial frequency. As noted earlier, such turnover can sometimes be healthy for innovation. New people bring fresh ideas and possibilities for new ways of doing things. However, much depends on who leaves and who stays, and whether internal stability and energy can be sustained in the transition. An organization where turnover is due to exciting cross-currents in its field of endeavor, where people come and go as a result of changing opportunities and personal growth, is likely to reap innovation benefits from this instability. But an organization that is losing its best personnel because it is stagnating or deteriorating relative to other organizations in its field, will tend to retain its less imaginative personnel, who have fewer options for alternative employment, and replace its lost talent with less creative individuals.

In summary, the potential for innovation varies with organizational context. The challenges to innovation are more substantial in larger organizations; in these organizations specific strategies for research and development and for emulating the benefits of small size through decentralization are required to foster innovation. Both highly professional organizations and organizations driven by very talented amateurs can nurture innovation, and each of these types of settings can benefit from the perspectives of the other. Finally, environmental and workforce instability can stimulate innovation, but chaotic environments can be destructive and workforce instability derived from organizational deterioration can inhibit the potential for innovation.

Priorities and Trade-Offs

In summary, we have seen that a variety of organizational circumstances affect innovation: size, heterogeneity, professionalism, and instability and task complexity. The matrix in Table 4.1 signals the variety of innovation challenges faced by a number of interesting alternative ensemble stereotypes.

Table 4.1   Ensemble Attributes and Innovation

	size	heterogeneity	professional level	instability	nonmusical analog
Fusion group	low	high	low	high	multidisciplinary research center
Military band	high	moderate	moderate	moderate	restaurant
Early music ensemble	moderate	moderate	high	low	church
Ethnic folk ensemble	moderate	low	moderate	low	family business
Small jazz combo	low	moderate	high	moderate	boutique retailer

The five illustrative stereotype ensembles present a wide variety of innovation challenges. For example, a fusion group, which combines two very different musical genres such as Cajun and rock music, can undertake fresh experimentation with largely unexplored combinations of musical expression from very different traditions, while the jazz combo can pursue established avenues of musical experimentation within a musical venue with a strong internal tradition of innovation. While both of these types of ensembles are small and flexible, they are best suited to pursuing innovation in very different ways. They also face somewhat different logistical challenges in doing so. The players in the jazz combo are likely to be transient but also highly educated in a common tradition. The transience can help stimulate innovation through the introduction of new ideas as players come and go, while their high level of training allows those players to experiment relatively easily during the time that they can play together. Hence the jazz combo is like a small boutique retailer, generating unique products from time to time, as its current, highly talented personnel permit. The fusion group, on the other hand, is more like a multi-disciplinary research center, bringing together experimenters with very different methods and ideas to work in teams on a new problem or product. The challenges in doing this are manifold. The players must learn to use common terminology in order to understand each others' perspectives. Moreover, they may come to the organization with very different levels of professional development, some perhaps even without formal musical training. And the group is likely to be highly unstable because players will be constantly drawn back to the different musical genres from which they emerged, just as researchers are commonly drawn back to their home disciplines rather than remaining as part of interdisciplinary teams. Still, because the combinations of musical background brought to the fusion ensemble are so different, the potential for interesting experimentation and occasionally successful innovation remain high.

The early music group and the ethnic folk ensemble offer a different window on innovation. Both are likely to be moderately sized, fairly stable groups which innovate by preserving, rediscovering and enriching old musical traditions. In early music, ensembles have not only rediscovered old music, such as pieces from the Renaissance or early Baroque compositions, but they have reconstituted this music by resurrecting and refurbishing the original instruments on which this music was played. Similarly, ethnic folk ensembles try to preserve the ethnic music and dance of communities that may no longer be sufficiently viable to maintain those traditions. In some cases, ethnic folk ensembles have achieved high levels of popularity, such as has been the case with Irish music, klezmer ensembles, and groups like the Chieftains, though these are more the exceptions than the norm. These two types of ensembles also face different challenges in their pursuit of innovation, and use different strategies as well. Early music ensembles pursue a highly professional approach, trying to unearth the true nature of past music and recreating it through research and intensive examination and experimentation. In some sense they are in search of a truth, not unlike that which might characterize members of a church. Ethnic folk ensembles, in some contrast, have a more celebratory approach, wishing to have fun with the music and preserving it by playing it for themselves and exhibiting it others, without excessive attention to its veracity. While such ensembles may suffer from some transience associated with amateur participation, they operate as a kind of family business, each player hoping to have a part in keeping the tradition going. In the process, members may seek to occasionally refresh the repertoire with varying interpretations or new songs, that can appeal to new members and audiences.

The military band enjoys modest levels of professionalism and stability in its player composition but must cope with relatively large size and also a hierarchical organizational structure in its approach to innovation. While it features moderate internal diversity of instrumentation, and hence has the capacity for experimenting with a fairly rich array of combinations, the rigidity that stems from size and structure, and the norms of the environment in which it operates, limit the degree to which unusual combinations are likely to be explored. Like a Chinese takeout restaurant, the military band can offer a fairly wide number of combination plates but most are likely to be recognizable variants of the standard fare. Hence, innovation will require either strong direction from the top, or a fundamental loosening of the structure.

Again, none of these stereotypes is completely characteristic of their counterparts in the musical world, nor are the suggested nonmusical analogs exact. Still, they are useful for prioritizing innovation strategies best suited to organizations that resemble each stereotype. The matrix in Table 4.2 describes relative emphases for innovation strategies for each ensemble stereotype.

Table 4.2   **Innovation Strategies**

	improvisation	internal dialogue	personnel turnover	role rotation	technical mastery	visionary leadership
Fusion group	2	1	6	4	5	3
Military band	6	5	3	4	2	1
Early music Ensemble	4	2	6	5	1	3
Ethnic folk ensemble	3	1	6	5	4	2
Small jazz combo	1	3	5	4	2	6

Internal dialogue is an important element of innovation strategy for all but the larger military band ensemble. That is because most of these ensembles are reasonably small in size and depend on the diverse experiences of their players to devise new ideas and new ways of doing things. Beyond that, the innovation strategies of these various ensembles diverge considerably. On the one hand, the fusion and jazz groups are virtually mandated to emphasize improvisation – indeed, their music is identified with either systematic or ad hoc experimentation with different combinations of notes, instrumental pairings, or rhythmic and melodic styles. Innovation at this level is a part of the product around which they define themselves. On the other hand, the early music and ethnic ensembles must keep improvisation within bounds so that they can focus on combinations that are likely to have been characteristic of the past. Within those parameters, however, these groups can employ improvisation to explore combinations that players from earlier times might have embraced.

The military band is limited in its ability to use internal dialogue and improvisation as strategies for innovation. It depends more heavily on inspiration and direction from the top, and in honing technical skills so that innovation may flow simply from doing things better than they have been done before, both at the level of individual playing and in putting individual contributions together into a more exquisite collective product. To a certain extent this top down innovation strategy can be supported by policies to recruit and retain the finest players, and possibly even trying new combinations of instruments within standard repertoires – such as reversing the roles of flutes and trombones in Sousa marches.

For different reasons, visionary leadership is likely to be an important element in innovation strategy for the fusion, ethnic and early music ensembles as well. Each of these groups needs a concept to work with, and leadership that can point the group in a particular direction as far as the nature and quality of its prospective product is concerned. While such groups can employ a democratic style of interplay to grope towards new and successful combinations they each need to work within a defined envelope of practice, driven by an informed, inspired vision that is likely to come from one or a few individuals. Some one (leader) has to have a concept of how two different musical genres can fit together, or what early music is supposed to sound like, or how ethnic music can be preserved and enriched, before these ensembles can begin their experimentation. On the other hand, while jazz combos often benefit from inspired leadership as well, they are better suited to a more collegial approach to improvisation. With the jazz idiom fairly widely understood, small groups of masterful players can experiment among themselves without a single visionary leader to set direction or keep them inbounds. Hence, this type of ensemble is likely to be less dependent on visionary leadership for its inspiration and guidance to innovate, and more dependent on the interplay of technical mastery and ideas distributed throughout the group.

Again, as in the analyses in previous movements, the priorities identified for these various stereotype ensembles should not be taken as strict protocols for pursuing innovation in those contexts. Rather, this discussion is meant to emphasize three main points: (a) that different types of organizations are likely to pursue different combinations of innovation strategy, (b) that there will be substantial variation of these strategy combinations within any categorical stereotype, and (c) that thinking of a given organization in terms of a musical ensemble analog can be helpful for determining what kinds of innovation strategies are likely to be productive.

A Case Study

The Jewish Board of Family and Children's Services (JBFCS) is a merger of two social service organizations with very different traditions and repertoire (Young, 1985). The old Jewish Board of Guardians (JBG) was a highly sophisticated professional organization that specialized in providing mental health and custodial care for delinquent, neglected and dependent children, mostly in institutional settings. The Jewish Family Service (JFS) was a neighborhood based organization that specialized in counseling of troubled families so as to prevent more acute socially problematic behaviors. Both organizations were good at what they did, but times were changing in the 1970s and these organizations felt both economic and social pressures to respond in new ways. An opportunity came in 1978 when the CEO of JFS decided to retire and saw this as an opportunity to break new ground. Together with his counterpart at JBG, they conceived the notion of merging the two organizations so that a new comprehensive approach to social and mental health services could be developed – one which would combine, and find the appropriate balance of, preventive and treatment services to help troubled youth and families.

The vision for this innovation came from the top, with the leaders of JBG and JFS setting the boundaries and direction for actually working out and implementing this new idea. Finding the specific adaptations and changes that would appropriately combine preventive and treatment oriented approaches into a new genre of mental health service, however, relied on several other basic strategies. Viewing JBFCS as a "fusion ensemble," internal dialogue and improvisation were critical as work groups were set up at the staff and governing board levels to devise plans for changing and combining their former repertoires. Role rotation played a part as individuals from the partner organizations tried on each others' tasks and responsibilities for size, and in some cases even decided that rotation of individual appointments would be appropriate (including chairmanship of the board). Technical mastery of contributing skills was assumed, but less emphasized until a new genre of care could be developed. Meanwhile, players already accomplished in their own disciplines would be depended upon to continue to do good work while becoming more adaptable to coordinating their work with that of others. And ultimately, achieving innovation would also depend on personnel turnover, as new people would join the organization with fresh perspectives on how a holistic approach to mental health care could be pursued through greater balance and synthesis of prevention and treatment.

The JBFCS case is distinctive both in its ultimate success, in the challenges it faced and the long time it took to really achieve innovation through the synthesis of complementary but substantially different approaches, and probably in its rarity as well. Like fusion groups in music, this mode to innovation through radical new combinations does not often occur and succeeds less often still, but when it does, the outcome can be path-breaking. The success of JBFCS in achieving innovation resulted from a conscious and calculated management strategy to exploit the differences between JBG and JFS so as to allow a new genre of service to emerge, while minimizing the pitfalls that could lead to the disintegration of this ensemble. Internal dialogue, improvisation and visionary leadership were the key elements of that strategy.

Diagnosing An Organization

The experiences of musical ensembles suggest a number of areas that managers can examine as potential sources of innovation within their own settings. In this connection, managers can ask themselves:

- What variations in the standard rules and procedures of the organization might lead to new and interesting ways of getting the work done?
- What styles of products or service delivery used in other fields of activity might be usefully adapted to the context of this organization?
- How can the roles and responsibilities of different work groups within the organization be periodically exchanged to encourage new ways of carrying out the organization's tasks?
- How can the roles of various workgroups be differentiated and recombined new ways?

Managers can consider doing a number of different things to improve the environment for innovation within their organizations. Hence, they can ask themselves:

- Where can rules and procedures be eliminated so as to permit organizational participants more room to improvise and use their creativity and judgment? What protocols can be devised to guide such innovation?
- What arrangements can be made to encourage a free flow of communication among organizational participants so that they can exchange and comment on each others' ideas? What arrangements can be made to allow participants to get to know each other better in order to encourage collaboration and sharing of ideas?
- How can organizational participants be further educated to become aware of both the limitations of, and basis for, existing ways of doing things? How can the narrowing effects of existing modes of worker education be overcome?
- How can the fresh perspectives of amateurs as well as diverse professional disciplines be brought into the thinking of the organization? How can elements of professionalism and amateurism be combined in the organization to encourage new ways of thinking?
- What degree of practice and repetition of particular organizational tasks will achieve levels of mastery capable of inducing innovation, but avoid decline from enervation?
- What mix of personnel in work groups will encourage a high level of creative interaction and group learning?
- What level of transience in work groups encourages the flow of new ideas without disrupting the creative energies of these groups? How can intergroup mobility facilitate the flow of new ideas?
- How can the status of different work groups be modified so that status differences do not inhibit the exchange of ideas?
- In larger organizations, how can think tanks, or research and development groups, be organized to stimulate and encourage innovation throughout the organization?
- How can a large organization be broken down into smaller groups for purposes of experimenting with new ideas?

Finally, the cultivation of leadership within the organization can be critically important to its support of innovation. Managers can ask themselves:

- How can entrepreneurial leaders be recruited or developed within the organization?
- How can leadership expectations be distributed among participants throughout the organization and how can localized leadership be encouraged?

Finale: Attaining Excellence

We're the best in our school!

The danger chiefly lies in acting well;
No crime's so great as daring to excel.
Charles Churchill, 1731-1764 (Oxford Dictionary, 1979, p.148)

Dangers notwithstanding, outstanding organizations seek to excel. But how is excellence achieved?:

On Friday afternoon, the most celebrated conductor in America's history led the New York Philharmonic in works by America's greatest composer. It's as simple – and complicated – as that. (Tim Page referring to a 1989 concert of Aaron Copeland's work by Leonard Bernstein, Page, 1992, p.187)

Perhaps music doesn't get any better than in the situation Tim Page describes. But excellence is indeed enigmatic; simply having all the proper ingredients in place doesn't guarantee success. There seems to be more to it.

So far we have identified four key management challenges affecting organizational success: Operations must be coordinated to run smoothly, people must be highly motivated, and the organization must offer a distinguishable product or service (have a niche) that is well supported by its resource providers.

In addition, an organization must accommodate change, which in part requires managing innovation. But what accounts for an organization's successful performance overall? Must all of these requirements be fulfilled to an equal extent? And if all are fulfilled, will the organization necessarily become and remain outstanding? Does it achieve "excellence"? Or, is there a missing ingredient that differentiates between an organization that does all the right things – coordinates, motivates, innovates and finds its niche – and one that truly excels in some greater sense?

There is a large, somewhat inconclusive, literature on the meaning of "organizational effectiveness" (e.g., see Cameron, 1986; Herman and Renz, 1999). Effectiveness can simply be considered the ability of an organization to survive or to grow over some reasonable period of time, or its ability to meet stipulated or expressed goals. But these are questionable standards. Poor organizations can linger for long periods of time because of fortunate economic supports that are slow to dissipate. If they are lucky and encounter favorable circumstances, mediocre organizations can survive and even grow over reasonably long periods of time. Such organizations may do good work, meet goals and serve useful purposes – but are they necessarily outstanding? Organizational "excellence" appears to call for a higher standard. Organizational excellence is the ability of an organization not only to survive or meet goals but to distinguish itself from the general population of organizations by achieving some manner of special recognition. Our interest, therefore, is in what makes the Cleveland Orchestra one of the "best" symphony orchestras in the world, and what makes the Chieftains perhaps the most revered Irish music group? What distinguishes the Orpheus Chamber Orchestra, the Guarneri Quartet, or the Robert Shaw Chorale from their peer ensembles? What allows such ensembles to maintain their excellence over long periods of time?

The Ingredients of Excellence

Organizational excellence undoubtedly requires outstanding performance along our four management dimensions – coordination, motivation, niche-finding and innovation – but perhaps *not* along all of them simultaneously. After all, there is a variety of ways in which an organization can excel, and an excellent organization need not excel in all ways. Additionally, the four dimensions are interactive, so that excellence in one dimension is likely to influence (complement or compensate for) excellence in another.

Some organizations excel by being exquisitely coordinated, even if they are not especially distinguished in other respects. The ensemble that plays its renditions of Vivaldi, Handel and Pachabel standards technically more perfectly than any other ensemble may be recognized as outstanding, even if its repertoire is undistinguished, even if its players are not always the most passionate, and even if the organization fails to experiment with its repertoire or style from time to time. Some combination of autocratic leadership, heavy rehearsals and short term player rewards might even achieve such distinction, though it might not sustain itself or be the most enjoyable organization to work for very long. The Jazz Messengers under Art Blakely had a reputation for inspired leadership that achieved great distinction for the ensemble's music but was oppressive to its players:

> His sidemen played *his* way or suffered the consequences....Musicians who have played in his groups often compare the experience with going to school. (Owens, 1995, pp.219-220)

Similarly, an organization could be outstanding by virtue of its ability to inspire extraordinary worker dedication. Good intentions, strong morale and high energy can compensate for technical imperfections and even for falling short of a first rate product. People come to hear their community orchestras, fire department marching bands, and student orchestras not because these groups have achieved exquisite levels of musical ensemble playing or because they are innovative or play some special repertoire or in some unique style, but because they are admired for their efforts, for their enthusiasm, and for the pride and spirit their members bring to their families, friends and neighbors. Referring to reviews of "little events in a church basement", critic Tim Page observes:

> It is a genuinely good thing that such concerts exist: they are unpretentious, they are usually reasonably well played and they bring happiness to people in the neighborhood. (Page, 1992, p.xv)

It is also possible for an organization to be outstanding by choosing the right niche, even if its offerings are not particularly innovative or played with the greatest mastery or its workers overwrought with enthusiasm. For example, community orchestras are simply not in the same category as major symphony orchestras, but they can excel within their own league and become a source of pride and recognition as a result of that. So it is reasonable for violin soloist Nadja Salerno-Sonnenberg to say about the Canton Symphony Orchestra that:

> Actually, this is a damned good orchestra...Canton is right up there with Pasadena on my list of the best community groups. (Page, 1992, p.123)

To be outstanding, therefore, is a relative concept which needs to be put into the specific context in which it is applied. Consider Peter Schickele and his ensemble which performs the music of the fictive P.D.Q. Bach. Although Schickele is himself a superb musician, when people come to hear his orchestra, they don't expect to experience a perfect or extremely dedicated ensemble, although its members are highly skilled and energized by the fun of the experience. Audiences do expect the unusual and the innovative, however, and they expect to laugh. Schickele's ensemble is one whose unique niche is humor mixed with novelty, and this is the field against which its performance is judged to be outstanding:

> For many fans of classical music... the cleverest and most consistently inventive parodist is Peter Schickele...Mr. Schickele has been presenting these faux-musicological explorations of the life and music of the fictional P.D.Q. Bach, purportedly the last and least of J.S. Bach's offspring and the supposed composer of consummately inept works.
>
> After more than 30 years, one might expect a comedian's creative well to run dry. But Mr. Schickele's ability to spot peculiarities in today's musical world and represent them as if they were a part of P.D.Q.'s universe has kept his shows lively, surprising and up to date. (Kozinn, 1997 p.32)

Finally, it is conceivable for an organization to be outstanding by virtue of its innovativeness, originality or propensity to experiment, regardless of whether it is run with great precision, highly motivated, or offers an especially unique style or repertoire. In the sense that Schickele plays with unusual (surprising and humorous) combinations of instruments and musical pieces, his P.D.Q. Bach ensemble illustrates this case. Schickele, or other musician/comedians such as Victor Borge, have established their own niche by creating odd new combinations of known musical products that evoke humor as they turn conventional musical practices on their heads (sometimes literally!) The excellence comes from doing this so well, and constantly producing surprising results. Many other ensembles, especially in jazz, draw interest and support because people know that the presentations will be unusual, even unique, and experience-expanding. Performances may be uneven, possibly even unpleasant, but reliably provocative in exploring new musical territory. When the Cleveland Orchestra played "Light", a new atonal work by Phillip Glass, it was greeted by a mix of boos and cheers (Page, 1992, p.51), but part of the Cleveland Orchestra's greatness is connected with its willingness to explore new possibilities, stretch the repertoire and master new work.

It seems reasonable to assume that the very best in any field will not be terribly deficient along any of the important dimensions of management performance. However, being proficient on all four dimensions does not assure organizational excellence if there is no one dimension on which achievement is really exceptional. Moreover, the "best of the best" may be those organizations which are outstanding in multiple ways. Perhaps the Cleveland Orchestra is "so good" because it is simultaneously exquisitely coordinated, has a style of its own among high-end professional symphony orchestras, and tries to remain fresh by integrating new compositions into its repertoire on a regular basis. Holland attributes this combination for excellence to a chemistry that was achieved when the ensemble took on its new music director:

> Christoph von Dohnanyi was the missing ingredient when he took over a brilliant band of Cleveland players in 1984. Extraordinary ensemble virtuosity met deep and implacable seriousness, setting off some of the most significant orchestra playing of the generation. Mr. Dohnanyi may not be the best conductor in the world, nor Cleveland the best orchestra, but together they are hard to beat. (Holland, 1999b, p.21)

But there seems to be even more to excellence than achieving proficiency on key facets of organizational management and excelling on one or more of those dimensions. An ensemble only seems to achieve excellence when its members share a special sense of identity. "A great orchestra must have a unique personality..." in the words of music critic Tim Page (1992, p. 141). For the Orpheus Chamber Orchestra, for example, that identity appears to be connected with commitment to excellence itself:

> Because Orpheus players share a commitment to perform at the highest possible level, each of their concerts and recordings is for them highly consequential. (Hackman, 2002, p.71)

Theorists define "organizational identity" as that which is essential and enduring about an organization (Whetten and Godfrey, 1998). In the musical world, an organization's identity is what distinguishes an ensemble, in the eyes of its own members, from other such groups. The Cleveland Orchestra's players see themselves as part of a world class ensemble that performs serious music. The players of the Cleveland Suburban Orchestra may see their ensemble essentially as a venue for local musicians to congregate for the mutual pleasure of playing together. Peter Schickele's orchestra may see itself as a vehicle for light entertainment and poking fun at the pretentiousness of the "serious music" field. Apollo's Fire may see itself as a pioneering group, leading the charge to establish early music on period instruments as a staple of musical performance in Northern Ohio, or perhaps beyond. The common element is that excellence seems to require both clarity and consensus about identity on the part of those who do the organizations work, and commitment to that identity.

The concept of organizational identity connects with each of the dimensions of management performance. For example, towards what particular end are members of an ensemble precisely coordinated? As explained in the first movement, the whole idea of having an organization in the first place is to better achieve a common result through more efficient coordination. So the articulation of that common purpose, stemming from identity, serves as a guide-star for how coordination is to be carried out.

Similarly for motivation. While we have argued (in the second movement) that members of the ensemble must be recognized and rewarded as individuals, it remains the case that motivation of ensemble members is also substantially derived from participating in a joint endeavor, inspired by a common sense of identity and purpose. Indeed, given an adequate foundation of an individualized reward system, it may be the satisfaction derived from pursuing a common mission that attracts and truly engages ensemble members and distinguishes motivation in a great ensemble from that in a merely good one. Recall that for amateur ensembles this satisfaction of participating in a common musical experience can be the dominant source of motivation!

Success in niche-finding is obviously related to a sense of identity and common purpose. A niche can only be defined in purposeful terms (this is what we do; this is what business we are in), and a niche can only be supported by consensus among those that provide an ensemble's resource base. Without an identity and a common purpose for which enthusiasm is demonstrated, adequate resource support is unlikely to be forthcoming.

Finally, successful management of innovation depends on a sense of identity in a number of important ways that affect the achievement of excellence. If innovativeness per se is the source of an ensemble's excellence then this will be reflected in its sense of identity directly. If proposed innovations promise to change or improve what the organization does or how it does it, a sense of mission and common purpose will be needed to assess if the innovation is indeed appropriate for doing that, or to the contrary, whether it might be diversionary or even destructive to the organization. A common understanding and identity will also help an organization to undertake possibly painful innovations that in the long run promise to allow it to more fully achieve its purpose. Alternatively, change in the environment (e.g., new technologies or product concepts entering the field in which the organization works) may signal to an organization that its current sense of purpose is outdated, or that its identity needs to be reinterpreted or revisited in light of new conditions. This in turn will require soul-searching among organization members to determine if they can innovate by coalescing around a new or adjusted mission. For example, if many members of a community orchestra or chorus have died or moved away, the ensemble may need to rethink what it means by "community" in order to achieve or maintain a sense of excellence.

In short, a clear sense of identity and enthusiasm for organizational purpose is a common factor that underlies success along each of the four dimensions of management challenge discussed in the previous movements. Overall, this sense of identity requires members of an ensemble to have a clear idea of what they are about as an organization, and to draw inspiration and direction from that concept. It is, in short, what the members of the organization feel, believe and take pride in as a group. Possibilities for that identity are as numerous as the number of organizations themselves. The group Harmonia identifies itself as the very best in playing and preserving ethnic central European music because they have a special "feel" for that music (Drexler, 1997). Alternatively, the Scottish folk band, the Tannahill Weavers, sees itself as bringing alive Celtic music through its special expertise with traditional tunes and instruments (Sangiacomo, 1997). The St. Petersburg String Quartet sees itself as a precision ensemble specializing in the clarity and crispness of its classical performances (Rosenberg, 1997b).

What one hears in the testimonials of excellent music groups is both a sense of identity and clarity of purpose and a joint enthusiasm borne of excitement with that purpose. Obviously this may be easier to achieve in smaller groups which often define themselves around singular concepts at the outset, but the same principle applies to larger ensembles: a common identity, dedication and enthusiasm for that identity, appears to drive the ensemble to be outstanding on those dimensions of management that matter most in achieving the aspirations implicit in that identity.

Maintaining Excellence Over Time

It is one thing to achieve a fleeting level of excellence and quite another to maintain excellence and improve upon it over long periods of time. It is notable, for example, that the original business corporations identified by Peters and Waterman (1982) in their book *In Search of Excellence* did not all maintain their positions of excellence over more than a decade. The same occurs in music. For example, Holland observed that somehow the Cleveland Orchestra was able to maintain the excellence built in the era of George Szell over a long period of time, while the New York Philharmonic was not able to sustain its earlier success (Holland, 1999b). To understand how organizations maintain their excellence requires the consideration of some additional ideas.

Maintaining excellence requires that the organization engage in an ongoing process by which it evaluates itself, makes adjustments to correct problems, and makes improvements over time. This is a simple but powerful idea that has been put forth in various forms by organizational scholars. It lies at the heart of Albert Hirschman's (1970) "exit and voice" theory which stipulates that successful organizations correct themselves from slackening or errant behavior by having to respond to direct and indirect feedback from its constituencies. It is reflected in Nelson's and Winter's (1982) idea of "problem-solving" through which organizations are prompted by symptoms of distress to invoke, implement and sometimes modify their internal diagnostic routines. It is incorporated in the idea of continuous improvement in the quality management literature (see Early, 1994) and in the concept of "learning organizations" (see Senge, 1990) wherein organizations continually examine their experiences in order to find improved ways of carrying out their work. There are basically two reasons why an organization which may be excellent at one point in time may retreat from that level as time goes on. First, as Hirschman argues, organizations have a natural tendency to lose their edge if there are no compensating forces to keep them sharp. Systems theorists (drawing on physics) call this "entropy". Vigilance is required to guard against this tendency even in stable circumstances. Second, organizations exist in a changing environment. What might have been best at one point in time, may no longer be best later on. For both reasons, organizations whose excellence endures constantly ask and respond to the question which former New York City Mayor Ed Koch made famous: "How'm I doing?" Indeed, even with such feedback, the best organizations probably go further – maintaining a degree of skepticism for excessive praise:

> Otto Klemperer was not known to be overly generous with praise. About the most exuberant he ever got was the time he shouted, "Good!" at the end of one difficult piece. The happy orchestra burst into applause. Klemperer scowled. "Not that good," he sneered. (Carlinsky and Goodgold, 1991, p.29)

Generically, the "evaluation and adjustment" process has two parts: First, organizations must continually generate or receive relevant information about their operations and performance. Second, they must be poised to respond to that information in timely and constructive ways. This process applies whether the organization exists in a stable or in a changing environment. If the environment is dynamic, as it usually is, an organization must monitor its position within the context of its field of activity and keep tabs on relevant trends that may affect its performance. It must also react to this information by considering what innovations may best enable it to respond to, or anticipate, new conditions. As noted earlier, this "evaluation and adjustment" process complements the management of innovation *per se*, in a comprehensive approach to the successful management of change.

The evaluation and adjustment process centers on information. Without good information, the intent to correct problems and make improvements will be aimless and haphazard. But even the best information is worthless if not taken seriously. Without that attention, the achievement of currently outstanding organizations may be fleeting, especially if success has come suddenly:

> ...something was seriously amiss at Alice Tully Hall on Saturday night. Much of the playing was sloppy and thoughtless. Most crucially, instead of meeting different aesthetics on their own terms, the Kronos musicians tended to streamline and homogenize whatever they played into an all-purpose modernism. It may be that the group is simply trying to do too much – too many composers, too many styles, too many performances throughout the country, throughout the world. Success came suddenly, with furious intensity, to the Kronos Quartet, and I suspect that the players may be in a period of transition. (Page, 1992, p.183)

This is a particularly interesting example because the Kronos seemed temporarily to have lost its keen sense of identity, and needed to both to recapture and to monitor itself relative to that identity over time.

The Elements of Evaluation and Adjustment

Many of the basic tools at management's disposal – including plans, communication, education, practice, incentives and rewards, and leadership in articulating a vision built on identity and common purpose – all come into play in addressing the dynamic challenge of maintaining excellence over the long term.

Plans

Gauging performance requires reference to standards. In formal music-making, much of the basis for gauging the nature and quality of performance is contained in the musical score. The score is the basic referent for how the music is to be played. Are the trumpets playing too loudly or is the ensemble speeding up too much? Is the intent to be serious and foreboding or should the projected atmosphere be more sarcastic and contemptuous? The answers to such questions may or may not be found in the score. Where the composer has indicated his or her intent, current playing can be compared to that intention, though the interpretation may be arguable. Pitch and tempo can be precisely specified in writing (though also subject to modification), but mood and feeling are more illusory:

> The authority of the score...knows various levels, and there is a whole rainbow of shades between fidelity and alteration. We would be surprised if a conductor were to change the harmony of a Beethoven passage; we are not too shocked to find a diversity of opinions about speed, accentuation or dynamic shape. The instructions in a score are not all equally dogmatic. (Griffiths, 1997, p.11)

Whatever ambiguity remains between the composer's instructions and implementation will require discussion and interpretation by the musicians and the conductor, implicit comparison with previous performances and those of other ensembles, and perhaps even with other pieces by the same composer. The important point, however, is not that a precise solution be found, but that the score be consulted as a plan, so that evaluations are made, deviations detected between the current performance and that which is intended, and appropriate adjustments implemented.

Scores can also serve the purpose of establishing the standard from which a performance is *intended to deviate*. If the score describes the standard way of performing a piece but the ensemble seeks to enhance the standard version or provide some new variation of it, then it can signal its intent to change by utilizing the original score as the baseline from which systematic departures are to be made. Hence, the score is not necessarily the holy grail from which excellence derives directly. Rather it is a referent from which unintended deviations are identified and corrected, as well as a baseline from which desired variations in performance can be systematically specified:

> ....The conductor Sir Colin Davis relates a story about performing Stravinsky's "Oedipus Rex" for an audience including the composer. After the concert, Stravinsky asked Sir Colin, "Young man, why did you take Jocasta's aria so slow?" Sir Colin answered that he was following the metronome mark. The composer replied, "My boy, the metronome mark is just a beginning." (Tommasini, 1999a, p.26)

Communication

In musical ensembles, several different channels of communication can be important to the evaluation and adjustment process. The channel between musicians and their leaders, e.g., the conductor, is often of primary importance. One major responsibility of the conductor is to detect and correct deficient aspects of the ensemble's operations. Part of the conductor's job is to listen carefully to each of the players, perhaps especially to the section leaders, to identify notes or phrases that need improvement, and to offer instructions on how the corrections can be best accomplished. The most talented conductors know the music so well, and have such keen hearing and discernment of pitch and rhythm, that they can pick out small individual nuances even in a large ensemble. And what they cannot pick up themselves will hopefully be detected by section leaders and corrected directly or relayed to the conductor for attention:

> Mr. Maazel, who is said to have perfect pitch and a photographic memory, had an earlier experience with a resentful orchestra – at the age of 11. Asked by Toscanini to conduct two summer concerts of the NBC Symphony Orchestra, the child prodigy arrived at a rehearsal to find the players sucking lollipops. His quick detection of a wrong note is said to have dispelled their disdain. Mr. Maazel...usually conducts without a score and is known for precision with his baton and an attention to details. (Blau, 1982, p.50)

However, perhaps the best, most enduring ensembles are those which feature not only clear communication from leaders to individual musicians, but also effective communication in the reverse direction, and laterally among musicians as well. Indeed, mutual patterns of communication may even offset the need to rely heavily on central leadership by assuring that unsatisfactory playing is detected and adjustments made through mutual, collaborative deliberations at the subgroup level. Section leaders, especially the concertmaster, are important in this process:

> "I try to make the job easier for the musicians and the conductor," said Ms. Ingraham. "As concertmaster you are in a sense, the assistant conductor. You have to know what the rest of the orchestra is doing. And if you hear something within the section that you feel the conductor is not asking for, you must say something." (Kraus, 1982, p.17)

Leonard Slatkin's experience with the St. Louis Symphony reveals a pattern of mutual understanding (around a common purpose) and good communication between players and conductor during rehearsal:

> Orchestra and conductor seem fellow pilgrims on a quest for the *Sibelius Second*...The orchestra responds reflexively to Slatkin's demands – the tympani right on time for a clap of Sibelian thunder, the flutes wild as Northern birds. A perfectly contoured crescendo sweeps from near inaudibility to an explosion of sound that fills the entire hall. As the last chord dies away, so clean and unanimous that it seems to have been produced by a seraphic organ, the musicians break into startled laughter. Are they *really* playing this well?

> They are indeed. Slatkin, red in the face and drenched with sweat looks out at his spent forces and grins. "O.K.," he says, with calculated understatement. "I think I can live with that." (Page, 1992, p. 133-134)

In many famous ensembles, a one-way pattern of communications from conductor to players is legendary. Arturo Toscanini serves as one example:

> Many tales are told about his explosiveness. Indeed, his treatment of the players – who nonetheless rarely questioned his musical genius – was so abusive that when his young granddaughter visited a rehearsal one day she asked, logically: "Why don't the musicians yell back at Grandfather?" (Carlinsky and Goodgold, 1991, p.69)

In the long run such oppressive behavior may be dysfunctional. Brilliant conductors with inspired concepts and plans for playing the music, the ability to communicate those intentions to talented players, and to detect and scold those making errors, is certainly one way of creating at least temporary improvement in an ensemble. Examples of this are not uncommon, but it is not a formula for continued greatness because it relies unduly on the talents of one individual leader and it contains the potential for deterioration if talented players are alienated or strong central direction cannot be sustained, as the experience of the Cleveland Orchestra after George Szell appears to reflect (Page, 1992, p.48).

A more stable approach is to cultivate two-way communications between leaders and players. The strategy of the Orpheus Chamber Orchestra, for example, is to deliberate as a group over needed changes and corrections, and to rotate leadership for different pieces. In other more conventional but successful ensembles, the authority of the conductor is preserved, but the players can also voice their judgements so that conductors may hear their constructive feedback or new ideas and maintain some range of flexibility to act on their own:

> For Dohnanyi, the ideal conductor is one who doesn't conduct at all. "The question is, how do you get to that point where you can lay down your baton, where the orchestra becomes a large chamber group?" he asked. "You have to give them a little help, especially in the transitions from one tempo to another. I think music-making is more important than any baton technique. When I was studying one summer in Tanglewood, it was Lenny Bernstein who told me, 'As long as it works, do whatever you want.' If you overconduct, you risk losing the spirit." (Rockwell, 1988, pp.64, 66)

Ensembles obviously also receive important feedback from external sources including audiences and critics. These sources provide different kinds of information. The critic or reviewer is sometimes like a shadow conductor, usually with some capacity to make expert judgments on the quality of play, the appropriateness of program selections, and various individual and collective lapses in the performance of the ensemble. Seiji Ozawa's experiences with critics during his tenure with the Boston Symphony Orchestra are illustrative:

> The 1998-99 season-long celebration of Mr. Ozawa's 25th anniversary with the symphony drew varying critical assessments. Writing in The New York Times in November, James R. Oestreich praised his conducting of the biting, driving "Miraculous Mandarin" by Bartok....But in February at Carnegie Hall, another Times critic, Bernard Holland, detected "a certain weariness" and said that Mr. Ozawa made the Beethoven Violin Concerto "sound almost vulgar."

> In an article in the Wall Street Journal last December, Greg Sandow likened the Boston Symphony under Mr. Ozawa to "a painting that badly needs to be restored." (Blumenthal, 1999, pp.A1, A15)

Critic qualifications vary widely and their evaluations can be off base, but ensembles do well to consider their views seriously. Although they have some incentive to be provocative in order to sell newspapers or make names for themselves, reviewers offer a relatively objective, knowledgeable source of evaluative information mostly devoid of the personal agendas or political factors that can affect judgments inside the organization. On the other hand, the actual content of the review may not always matter that much. As composer Philip Glass argues, it may be better to be reviewed than not reviewed, no matter what the review itself says (Page, 1992, p.77).

Indeed, filling the seats by bringing attention to performances is perhaps a principal contribution of reviewers. After that, audience reactions become another source of feedback, albeit more diffuse in character and harder to interpret than reviewer assessments. If attendance wanes the ensemble knows something is wrong, but precisely what is wrong may be difficult to discern. It could be the quality of the playing, the repertoire, the cost of attending, the convenience or comfort of the venue, or other factors. If there is a change in attendance, the ensemble needs to ask itself what else has changed that may account for the loss. If there is an increase in popularity it should try to understand that too. For example, in San Francisco, recent success has been attributed to the new music director Michael Tilson Thomas whose vitality, compared to the previous director, attracted the attention of a younger generation of music lovers (Tommasini, 1999b).

The reactions of audiences during performances also provides relevant feedback information. Cool or hostile receptions signal either that the performance was not done well or that the selected piece was unappealing. The latter in turn may raise questions about what the appropriate repertoire should be, or whether the ensemble should try to appeal to a different audience segment. Enthusiastic receptions can reinforce confidence in, and encourage maintenance of, current repertoire, but they can also be misleading. Standing ovations by diminishing, narrowly constituted or aging audiences can deceive ensembles into thinking they are on the path to continued success. Ensembles must seek to ask, through surveys or other means, what kinds of people are attending and why they are satisfied or dissatisfied, and they must question other groups who represent potential future audience segments or may have already dropped from attendance. And sometimes ensembles may simply be stretching their audiences too far and may have to wait for them to catch up if their objective is to plow new ground by educating to new musical ideas. Composer Steve Reich recalls a concert that included his modern piece "Four Organs":

> I remember when Michael Tilson Thomas and I played "Four Organs" on an otherwise typical Boston Symphony Orchestra program at Carnegie Hall in 1973. The subscribers came to hear the other music – C.P.E. Bach, Mozart, the Bartok "Music for Strings, Percussion and Celesta" and the Liszt "Hexameron". There was a pretty full house and, at times during my piece, I would say that well over three-quarters of the people were not just booing but *really* enraged – shaking umbrellas, you know, so loudly during that piece that, on stage, we began to lose count...There was so much active feedback from the audience that we got lost, and Michael had to shout out the numbers so that we could know what bar we were in. When the piece was over, a small crowd was bravoing and a

much larger crowd booing just as strongly as possible. And the reactions of the press! "Primitive" was one of the kinder epithets. (Page, 1992, p.70)

Such experiences notwithstanding, multiple communications channels are needed for effective evaluation and adjustment in musical ensembles, both for the purpose of monitoring short term performance and for ensuring continuing adjustment and improvement in the long run. And information through these multiple channels must be carefully interpreted. Even musicians hear only what they want to hear if they are not careful to structure and analyze their communications channels appropriately. On the other hand, sometimes good performance is acknowledged only by the professionals who are sensitive and schooled enough to recognize it. Speaking of his father's Hollywood String Quartet, Leonard Slatkin relates:

> This was a West Coast group and, as such, had to deal with Eastern chauvinism throughout its lifespan....I mean, after all, how could a New Yorker possibly take something called the Hollywood String Quartet seriously? But the group had quite a reputation among musicians. (Page, 1992, p.136)

Education

Education and training play important roles in supporting effective feedback within an organization. The higher the level of sophistication attained by players in an ensemble, the greater the potential for careful monitoring relative to complex standards and procedures, the more effective communications can be, and the more capacity there is for self-correction. The first two of these points are fairly obvious. Better musicians are more discerning in interpreting scores and more capable of implementing instructions given to them, either orally or in writing. Moreover, the level of player sophistication affects the extent of constructive discourse that can take place among players and leaders in efforts to diagnose problems and devise and implement effective solutions. Just as importantly, education and training gives ensemble players an enhanced ability to monitor and measure themselves. A professional musician is likely to have achieved an inner sense of quality, both in his or her own playing and in how well the ensemble plays together. At this level, individuals can make numerous small mutually accommodating adjustments, which cumulatively may lead to higher levels of ensemble performance. Interestingly, swing bands and modern jazz bands have taken different approaches to such adjustments in search of excellence, the former emphasizing coordination and the latter innovation:

> Where swing bands had made virtues of punch and precision, restricting solos in favor of orchestral unity, the small bands of modern jazz didn't mind an occasional misfire as they pushed towards frontiers. At times, the big bands had come within Lindying distance of the classical-music ideal of analyzing and practicing and rethinking and polishing a performance – perfecting it for a concert-hall recital.

But with modern jazz the notion of a perfect performance, always a dicey one in music that prizes improvisation, receded once again. Jazz musicians aren't searching for timeless perfection (although the best small groups, like the World Saxophone Quartet, deliver their ensemble arrangements with gorgeous unanimity) – they're acting and reacting in the moment of performance. Within a composition, innumerable details are the result of on-the-spot choices. (Pareles, 1987a, p.H22)

Practice

Rehearsals are a key means for ensembles to perfect their play in many respects – in coordinating their efforts, in detecting and correcting individual performance problems, in shaping their overall style of play, in testing new ideas for repertoire and experimenting with innovations of various kinds.   In evaluation and adjustment terms, rehearsals represent a major opportunity for ensembles to take stock of where they are, to facilitate constructive dialogue between leaders and players in order to work out issues, and to indulge in group thinking about selections for the repertoire and the image and style the ensemble wants to project.

Especially for highly skilled ensembles, the value of the rehearsal is not so much as a drill to ensure by repetition that everyone knows their parts or cues, but rather to provide the opportunity, in a relaxed atmosphere prior to the tension of the performance itself, to reflect on their performance as whole, and to detect and adjust for unanticipated problems associated with the current program. Often, highly skilled musicians can get by with minimal rehearsal or even none at all. However, this is usually a short term proposition at best. Long term excellence requires the feedback and adjustment that rehearsals can facilitate, even for professionals.   A contrast in approaches to rehearsal is found among jazz ensembles:

> Horace Silver's quintets, the Modern Jazz Quartet, and other great ensembles usually play well-rehearsed pieces and refine their ensemble playing over months or years of performances. But Miles Davis preferred to put together performances and recordings in the most casual way possible, letting things fall into place spontaneously. (Owens, 1995, p.224)

What Davis may have lost in preparation appears to have been gained in the excitement born of spontaneity that he sought.   Nonetheless, the excellence achieved through spontancity is still based on substantial prior preparation and improvement over time:

> A typical case is his 1956 recording of the old popular song, *Bye, Bye, Blackbird*...The preparation for this recording could have been no more than Davis announcing the title and key, and counting off the tempo. Yet because each player knew the piece, knew from previous experience what kinds of rhythms and textures to play, and knew each others' musical habits, the performance came together brilliantly. (Owens, 1995, p.225)

Incentives

Evaluative information and correctional advice will have little effect if the recipients of that information have no reason to heed it. Fortunately musicians, especially highly accomplished ones, normally have pride of craftsmanship, are concerned about their individual reputations, and usually wish to achieve what is expected of them. If they have a strong sense of common purpose, so much the better. Moreover, ensembles offer multiple incentives to respond constructively to feedback. For example, musicians play in peer groups in which there is substantial social pressure and where they are counting on one another to maintain quality and meet mutual expectations. Second, professional players are engaged in an employment relationship with their ensembles. They are therefore concerned with maintaining both the viability of their own positions and the prosperity of the ensemble from which they derive income.

But there are also situations in which incentives to ignore feedback can predominate. Itinerant ensemble leadership may offer advice but never be present to acknowledge its implementation. Indeed, such advice may even conflict with that provided by the next leader. Orchestras with a plethora of guest conductors may experience such problems. So too, itinerant players who go from one ensemble to another are unlikely to pay close attention to feedback intended to improve ensemble playing unless they plan to settle in for a while. Christoph von Dohnanyi provides an example:

> "I had tremendous difficulty in Hamburg....The thing I hate is when opera orchestras say: 'Today you'll have these players, tomorrow you'll have those, and we don't even know who is playing for the third rehearsal'. I had to fight. For one thing, intonation suffers. A first oboist who does not know his partner is always thinking: Is he high on that G or is he flat?" (Page, 1992, p.49)

Perhaps the best incentive that ensembles can provide for effectively implementing evaluative feedback is to ensure that follow-up behavior receives proper credit. Indiscriminate criticism or the issuing of commands to make this or that change will be ineffective if follow-up behavior is not monitored or acknowledged. Mutual acknowledgment of adjustments made and improvements resulting from those adjustments are the most elementary, but also among the most effective incentives that can be provided to ensure continuous improvement. Here is how Mark Stringer, an assistant conductor to Leonard Bernstein, describes Bernstein's approach to this process:

> "He was terribly supportive of his students' early progress...Just like a parent, you known – what a *nice* crayon drawing you made for me! Later on, if he thought you could handle it, he'd tell you ways that your performance might have been improved. But, at the time, he just gave you a kick in the pants to get you out there and then wrapped you in his arms when it was all over and you were safely backstage again." (Page, 1992, p. 252)

Leadership

Clearly leadership plays a key role in virtually all elements of the process of evaluation and adjustment. In musical ensembles, the conductor is usually the individual who chooses the score and then monitors performance according to that score. The ensemble leader also sets the protocol for communications. He or she provides evaluative and corrective information to the musicians, and also (hopefully) takes suggestive feedback from the players themselves. In addition, the leader is the "boundary spanner," translating the feedback received from audiences and reviewers into programmatic and operational adjustments intended to improve audience reactions. Musical directors play key roles in musician education as well, either engaging directly in teaching through a formal player development program, or otherwise ensuring that continuing education is a part of their musicians' regimen. Certainly the conductor controls the rehearsal process where a great deal of the coaching and correction in ensembles takes place, and he or she also dispenses at least some of the incentives and rewards associated with playing in the ensemble. Such leader-dispensed rewards may range from verbal compliments or chastisement to changes in role assignments within the ensemble, and even to the material terms of employment. Within institutional constraints (such as collective bargaining agreements), the ensemble leader can make the connections between the quality of performance and the dispensation of these rewards. Even verbal compliments can make a big difference:

> One of the most plaintively expressed sorrows of orchestra life is lack of individual recognition. "We did Stravinsky's 'Le Sacre du Printemps' not long ago," says Joseph Robinson, the [New York Philharmonic] orchestra's principal oboe. "We have a wonderful new bassoonist, Judith LeClair, and she played solos brilliantly. Not a word in the reviews about her. We feel our anonymity. When we play well, they write about the conductor but not about us." (Holland, 1981, p.36)

Perhaps the most important role of leadership in the evaluation and adjustment process comes in envisioning the ensemble's potential, setting expectations for the quality of its play, articulating its identity and common purpose, and guiding the ensemble towards achieving that vision. The standards to which an ensemble is held derive not only from composers' instructions in written scores, but more importantly from the guidance and expectations of its leadership. Leadership is instrumental in setting out a vision and set of standards, including choosing the repertoire, interpreting the scores, communicating expectations to ensemble members and holding them accountable for these expectations. Whether the leadership is singular or collective, it is what is in the head sof the leaders that ultimately frames what the ensemble can achieve. Like Beethoven, who composed many of his greatest works even after he lost his hearing, leadership must imagine what the ensemble should sound like, so that comparisons may be made with the actual performances and then coached, nurtured and corrected accordingly. Christoph Von Dohnanyi's leadership of a Cleveland Orchestra performance of

Schubert's C major symphony illustrates the process:

> Much has been written about the expansive nature of this work, which indeed can seem interminable if the conductor is in the mood for a leisurely stroll through a Viennese park. Not Dohnanyi. From the opening theme, he sent Schubert on a vigorous walk, avoiding the traps of ponderousness and invigorating every phrase...Orchestrally, it was a dumbfounding experience. The Cleveland musicians were so immersed in the narrative, aware of one another's place in the scheme of things and quick to heed Dohnanyi in terms of balance and energy that the score evinced the pristine, gleaming character it should possess, but only rarely does. (Rosenberg, 1999, p.7-B)

The Circumstances for Achieving and Maintaining Excellence

The challenges for attaining and maintaining excellence vary considerably with the character of the organization and the environment in which it operates. The size, complexity and professional sophistication of the organization all affect its quest for excellence, as do the stability of the organization's environment and the complexity of the work in which it is engaged.

Size

The larger the ensemble, the more difficult it will be for leadership to diagnose problems and pinpoint sources of difficulty. More reliance must be put on a reporting system through which section leaders monitor their own subgroups and either make corrections themselves or pass along relevant information to the ensemble's director. In smaller ensembles, deviations from desired performance parameters by individual players or by small clusters of players are easier to discern. Moreover, there are stronger incentives in small groups, because of social pressure, to maintain satisfactory performance levels and to respond to evaluative feedback. In large organizations, even after problems are diagnosed, change may be resisted more strongly and take longer to achieve.

Certainly, it is easier to achieve a common sense of identity and purpose in a smaller ensemble. The challenges of building and maintaining a large orchestra around a common purpose are substantial. As Rockwell notes, it requires imposing discipline and clear direction, as well as a gentle willingness to "prod underachievers and root out incompetents" (1988, p.56). Even the best music directors have trouble in this area. For example, Leonard Bernstein was noted for his vision, enthusiasm and vitality but an indifference to the hard, sometimes distasteful work of orchestra building (Rockwell, 1982).

There are also advantages to size in achieving and maintaining long term excellence. In a larger organization, there is more opportunity for individual advancement. Hence, the larger organization supports stronger incentives for individuals to excel in order to move up to higher status positions or into leadership roles. In addition, larger organizations can create special niches for achieving excellence which are unattainable by smaller organizations. There is really no substitute, for example, for the robust sound of a full symphony orchestra, a big jazz band, or a full chorus. Given its complexity, the simple achievement of a flawless performance by a large ensemble is remarkable in itself, and an avenue to a particular version of excellence:

> Otto Klemperer made a famous recording of Bach's *St. Matthew Passion* about twenty-five years ago. From a musicological point of view, we know his reading to be problematical – it is massive, heavy and semi-operatic, realized with a huge orchestra and chorus. But the terror, the pity, the grave power of this drama come across with unforgettable intensity. Compared to this monolith, most of the recordings for smaller, more stylistically appropriate ensembles seem cautious and scholarly, almost trivial. (Page, 1992, p.224)

Heterogeneity

For a given size, heterogeneous ensembles present different challenges to achieving excellence than homogeneous ensembles. In one sense, heterogeneity makes achieving excellence more difficult. Many different specialties must be mastered at once, and these must be coordinated successfully with one another. Leadership must be capable of evaluating many different types of contributions (inputs) to the ensemble's production, uniting different instrumental interests around a common idea, and providing feedback both on the individual efforts of ensemble players as well as their mutual adjustment to one another. A choral director must know the human voice in its various registers, but the orchestra conductor must understand strings, brass, woodwinds, and percussion playing of all types.

In another sense, however, the process of evaluation and adjustment is easier in heterogeneous ensembles. Organizing the ensemble into different instrument sections makes it simpler to pinpoint performance problems and to utilize local expertise (section leaders) and mutual feedback among section players to detect errors and make appropriate adjustments:

> The first clue that Dohnanyi's Beethoven wouldn't be stale came as the musicians took their places on-stage. In the style of orchestras of the classical period, the second violins sat at Dohnanyi's right, which heightened the separation of duties between first and second violins. (Rosenberg, 1993, p.30)

Sectioning logically falls along the lines of instrumentation – like instruments with like instruments – strings, woodwinds, brass, percussion, etc. However, there is no reason why such departmentalization cannot be implemented within more homogenous organizations as well. Within a chorus, for example, basses, tenors and soprano voices can be separated, and even within completely homogenous large ensembles such as a hundred tubas, sections can be set up either arbitrarily or according to different skill levels or part assignments (first tubas, second tubas, etc.) Going even further, even if all tubas are playing the same musical lines, one can still organize them into sections spatially, for purposes of evaluation and adjustment. Such sectioning is more natural in heterogeneous ensembles but this approach may also be applied to homogeneous ensembles. Indeed, this strategy even offers an advantage to homogeneous ensembles not available to heterogeneous ones – the ability to compare the performance of similar sections within the ensemble. If two or more homogenous sections play the same part then they can serve as benchmarks for one another, and to a certain extent the ensemble can take advantage of the implicit competition among these sections to improve the playing of each. Comparing violins with violins is certainly more effective than comparing violins and trumpets, if one is trying to offer one or another section an example of how it should be playing.

Finally, just as size offers a path towards uniqueness and hence a special way for an ensemble to excel, heterogeneity can do the same. Special excellence can be found not in being more or less homogeneous or heterogeneous per se, but rather in working with unusual combinations of instruments or using certain instruments in unusual ways. For example, reversing the roles of strings and low brass in playing melody versus harmony might provide a way for a heterogeneous ensemble to achieve unusual effects or a special style. Mixing conventional orchestra instruments with band instruments is potentially another way to exploit heterogeneity for achieving excellence. To this day, for example, it is still the rare orchestral piece or classical ensemble that includes saxophones or saxophone pieces in its instrumentation. Sir Thomas Beecham seemed to have something like this in mind in his performance of Handel's *Messiah* though it is unclear if he achieved excellence in this effort or could build a whole ensemble identity around this vision:

> ...he spiced up Handel's chaste Baroque instrumentation with a battery of tubas, trombones, cymbals, xylophones and other sore thumbs, engaged a giant chorus and equally sumptuous orchestra, and produced an exuberant, idiosyncratic (and loud) *Messiah* – a joyful noise, indeed! (Page, 1992, p.222)

Professionalism

Almost by definition, organizations whose work forces include professional employees can achieve higher levels of performance quality. They employ people with the training that prepares them for taking on more difficult tasks and performing those tasks more capably. Moreover, professionals are indoctrinated to standards of excellence as part of their educational and work experiences, and the best professionals routinely apply their own high standards to themselves in the course of their work. In addition, professionals often demonstrate by their career choice an intrinsic, long term dedication to their field of endeavor and an internal motivation to continually achieve higher levels of performance quality no matter what the organizational setting.

But there is an underside to professionalism as well, and lessons to be learned from the examples of amateurs. Professional musicians must depend on their playing to make a living and they can become dispirited by the circumstances they must sometimes endure in order to ensure an adequate income. They may burn themselves out and lose the original fervor they brought to their art, or the common sense of purpose with which they may have joined an ensemble.   Some professionals find solace and renewal in freelancing careers that provide a stream of fresh experiences to balance against the too frequent drudgery of professional ensemble playing:

> By its very nature, freelancing appears to prevent the burnout from which many members of permanent orchestras complain. "In St. Luke's and most of the groups that I play with," continues Mr. Lutzke [a cellist], "people still have a real sense of enjoyment in what they're doing, and it surfaces in the performances. Very often we're playing a piece for the first time. A permanent orchestra will play the same concert four times in a series and generally performs the same repertory over and over...For us, every concert is absolutely new and fresh, and we're on the edges of our chairs to make it right. It breeds vitality and freshness. It's what makes it exciting." (Elliot, 1988, pp.27, 30)

Amateurs are different. They play only for the love of playing. They may not have the same level of skill or understanding of the music that professionals may have, or the single-minded dedication that drives many professionals to reach their full potential or achieve distinction for their ensemble, but they often bring a fresh love to their musical work that can compensate for whatever they may lack in formal training and experience:

> "The insistence upon remaining by and of the community is not a bad thing", asserts Mark Arton, musical director of the Bay Area orchestra, which in its 14th year plays three concerts on its $12,000 budget. "Sure, we can't give a performance as polished as the New York Philharmonic....But I believe our audiences, even without the polish, get out of the music what the composer intended."

> "It takes careful programming, doing pieces we're capable of doing and also keeping away from well-known works so that if it isn't absolutely right the audience won't know it. But you know, we bring something to the music that the professionals who take their playing for granted can't. The struggle to excel creates a kind of excitement in the hall that's missing with routine perfection." (Delatiner, 1982, pp.9)

Amateurs and professionals also differ in the way they may react to evaluation of their work and guidance to change or improve it. Amateurs, in their enthusiasm, may embrace opportunities to learn more about the art and to become better players. They may also consider themselves privileged simply to be playing in an ensemble that gives them the opportunity to contribute to a musical performance and work with other musicians. But they are also volunteers, and if the demands on their playing become too severe they can become discouraged or even resentful.

All this is to say that the challenges to seeking excellence differ for ensembles that are primarily professional versus primarily amateur. Leaders of professional ensembles have more skill capacity with which to achieve a high quality of play or to undertake more challenging pieces. However, they must also be prepared to face resistance to their guidance from professionals who may they think they know better, or to deal with the indifference of professionals who are burned out, have become cynical or discouraged, or have reached plateaus in their careers.

There are also obviously different paths to excellence for professional versus amateur groups. Professional ensembles achieve excellence by playing at the top of their art or by pushing out the boundaries of standard repertoire. Amateur ensembles achieve excellence by the exuberance and the enthusiasm they excite among themselves and their fans. Amateurs can also prod professionals by reminding them of why they became musicians in the first place – love of the music. One of the challenges to professional ensembles is to constantly renew the spirit on which amateur ensembles regularly rely:

> "This sounds corny," said [Marlene] Krause 48 [flutist with the Suburban Symphony Orchestra], "but I think it's a privilege to be able to play some of this music. You sit in the middle of all these people making Beethoven's Fifth and you feel really lucky." (Sowd, 1990, p.31)

Task Complexity

One obvious way in which organizations excel is to take on tasks that are extremely difficult, perhaps never before accomplished, and carry them out successfully or better than others have previously achieved. Just as in physical exploration, there are mountains that can be climbed in music and other fields. The organization that gets to the top of the highest mountain, or most difficult mountain to climb, or the next frontier, achieves a certain kind of excellence.

Certain composers have been known to accommodate ensembles' appetites for difficult conquests! Beethoven's *Missa Solemnis* provides but one example:

> At last Thursday's performance of the *Missa Solemnis* at Avery Fisher Hall, Kurt Masur had all the virtuosity he needed. The New York Philharmonic gleamed; the New York Choral Artists and the American Boy-choir knocked down one scary passage after another. It was impressive and almost too easy. This is not easy music.
>
> Why did Beethoven make things so hard for the rest of us? Mozart and Liszt wrote music that likes to be played, though both are difficult in their separate ways. One explanation says that Beethoven was mad (which he must have been). Another is that he didn't care (he said as much, famously to a complaining violinist about another piece): Beethoven wanted an effect, and it was up to the performer to realize it. (Holland, 1999a, pp. B1,3)

While taking on challenging tasks (difficult music) is not the only path to excellence it is certainly a well recognized one in many fields. The risks associated with this route can be daunting. There is an obvious risk of failure. A poor performance of the *Missa Solemnis* achieves nothing but scorn. Audiences or critics, particularly for professional ensembles, are unlikely to applaud a "nice try". Another risk is that the mission will be achieved but not appreciated. A successful performance of the *Missa Solemnis* achieves an exquisite effect that audiences appreciate. A technically perfect performance of a piece by Schoenberg or Ives which might be equally as difficult, might still leave audiences cold and unappreciative. Excellence may require not only a wise choice of task difficulty but also selection of a task that is satisfying in other ways. Ensembles can indeed achieve excellence as players of Schoenberg or Ives but they must find a receptive context for such performances if they are to do so. Excellence requires that the difficulty of the task match external expectations as well as internal organizational capacity. Sometimes, as in a 1990 concert of the Los Angeles Philharmonic led by Andre Previn, these forces are not easy to reconcile:

> Andre Previn and the Los Angeles Philharmonic brought the best program I've heard from either of them to Avery Fisher Hall Friday night....The Shostakovich (Fourth Symphony) is not an easy work but amply repays any concentration that a listener may bring to it. After the long first movement, however, there was the usual noisy exodus by disgruntled patrons, apparently upset by the introduction of dread dissonance into their digestive meanderings.

> What followed was an aesthetic Boston Tea Party of sorts. As the escapees clacked righteously up the aisle, Previn, gently, effectively fought back. He turned and regarded the disruption with a gaze of weary amazement, shaking his head. The rest of the audience caught on and began to clap and stomp – at first facetiously, in honor of the departing guests (who wisely quickened their step) and then with genuine appreciation for Previn, the orchestra, and especially, Shostakovich. When the symphony ended...the listeners who stuck it out – about 90 percent of the hall....rose and provided an ovation of unusual intensity. (Page, 1992, p.200)

Environmental Instability

A dynamic environment creates special opportunities as well as risks for achieving organizational excellence. Organizations that can catch the wave and take advantage of changing conditions can carve out new niches for themselves and be the first and (at least temporarily) the best at what they do. Without Rock and Roll there would have been no Billy Halley and the Comets and ultimately no Beatles. In music, sea changes in popular taste (e.g., the advent of Rock and Roll), professional thinking (e.g., minimalism) or technological breakthroughs (e.g., electronic instruments) create new arenas of competition. But such changes also restrict opportunities for excellence when certain fields shrink at the expense of others. As exciting as Dixieland Jazz can be, the quest to be best in this arena will necessarily be confined to a handful of serious rivals. This constriction has an uncertain effect on the quality of performance achieved by the competitors that remain. The reduced set of opportunities will necessarily weed out all but the best among contemporary competitors. However, the best will ultimately be selected from a thinner field over the long run. A strategic decision for any organization is whether to try to excel in a smaller or contracting arena or to be relatively less outstanding in a larger or growing arena. Since alternative arenas are likely to be so different from one another when major environmental shifts take place, any particular ensemble may have little choice but to stick with what it knows how to do best. Lawrence Welk had his following among polka lovers, but he would no doubt have failed if he had tried to appeal to a wider audience by playing a more general selection of popular music. It is the rare organization that maintains its position of excellence in the face of major environmental changes by shifting genres. While not undertaken for reasons of environmental change, Duke Ellington's foray into orchestral music illustrates the dangers of entering new territory which may not match one's particular talents and which stray from the identity associated with success:

> In his symphonic works, Duke Ellington, one of the natural masters of jazz, writes like a tourist. It is as if he had somehow bought the old lie that American music should emulate European classical tradition, rather than striking out on its own path...It's a pity. A great popular song is much more useful, and "artistic," thing to have around than an uninteresting symphony, and a composition for jazz band is not necessarily improved by arranging it for orchestra. (Page, 1992, p.182)

Finally and paradoxically, stability itself may be a formula for excellence in a changing environment. Organizations that can provide safe harbors for people seeking to escape the whirlwind of change, can excel in that stability. There will always be some market for classics, in whatever genre they occur. Count on the Preservation Hall Jazz Band to be there forever, keeping the flame of Dixieland Jazz alive as long as people have any interest in it at all. And, there may always be a Guy Lombardo's band for New Year's Eve, as well.

Priorities and Trade-offs

Echoing the theme of previous movements, the matrix of Table 5.1 signals a variety challenges faced by different ensemble stereotypes in seeking excellence by evaluating and adjusting their operations and performance over time.

Both the professional symphony and the high school orchestra are relatively large organizations that require more formal approaches to the seeking of excellence. Both are also internally diverse in their instrumentation, further challenging their capacities for communication and achieving a common understanding and approach to issues. However, the symphony enjoys the advantages of greater professional training of its members, and lower turnover – suggesting a stronger role for players in developing and maintaining a strategy for achieving and maintaining excellence.

By contrast, the jazz combo and rock groups, though also internally diverse, are small and informal, giving them potentially greater flexibility in communication, reaching common understandings and coordinating responses to problems and evaluative judgments. Again the jazz combo may have certain advantages of advanced musical training although the amateur rock band, with its weaker orientation to convention, might have a more sensitive collective ear to the preferences of its audiences.

Table 5.1   Ensemble Attributes and Seeking Excellence

	size	professional level	heterogeneity	task complexity	instability	nonmusical analog
Symphony orchestra	high	high	high	high	low	hospital
High school orchestra	high	low	high	moderate	moderate	hotel
Jazz combo	low	high	moderate	high	high	boutique retailer
Rock band	low	low	moderate	moderate	moderate	small software company
Church choir	moderate	low	low	low	moderate	government license bureau

The church choir represents a middle ground, smaller and more homogeneous than the orchestras, and larger but also more homogenous than the rock group or jazz combo. Internal communications, common understandings and coordinated response are aided by this homogeneity but challenged by the size of this ensemble and the relatively low musical sophistication of its members.

The professional symphony orchestra can be compared to a hospital with many departments or specialties, each requiring high skill levels and professional training, all contributing to the complex overall task of healing patients with different kinds of illnesses. Like the hospital, the professional symphony takes on tasks (musical pieces/patient illnesses) at the highest level commensurate with its capacity. The high school orchestra, by contrast, is more like a hotel, responsible for carrying out in coordinated fashion the diverse tasks (housekeeping, check-in, food services, etc.) that make for a comfortable overnight stay. The overall challenge is not as severe or critical as it is for a hospital, and the skills required of the players not as technically complex. Still, achievement of excellence is certainly meaningful within the context of expectations for hotel performance.

The jazz combo may be compared to a boutique retailer, as noted in an earlier movement. Members of the combo are highly skilled in their moderately diverse instrumentation and they may seek to "push the envelope" of their music, both collectively and individually. Their products will therefore be unique and specialized, even one of a kind, hopefully appealing to audiences of like interests. In comparison, the amateur rock band may be compared to a small software company seeking to break into a large market with the best specialized product of its kind. This group also pushes the envelope, largely through collective experimentation, in the hope of finding a style or product that is new and widely appealing.

Finally, the church choir, as earlier noted, can be compared to a government license bureau, albeit one that hopefully takes great pride in its work. The skill set of its participants is relatively undemanding, most participants perform similar parts, and turnover is relatively low. Seeking of excellence requires guidance from experienced leaders and the creation of a supportive work environment that encourages willing and enthusiastic participation.

Again, none of these stereotypes is completely characteristic of their counterparts in the musical world, nor are the suggested nonmusical analogs exact. Still, they are useful for prioritizing excellence-seeking strategies best suited to organizations that resemble each stereotype. The matrix in Table 5.2 describes nominal priorities for innovation strategies for each ensemble stereotype. In a real sense each of the strategies across the top of the matrix may be thought of as mechanisms of evaluation and adjustment. However, some are better suited than others for different kinds of ensembles or organizations. For the professional symphony orchestra, for example, the score (plan) is a very important referent, because it represents the intent of the composer – hence the standard to which the ensemble as a whole aspires. And, since the orchestra conductor is the primary interpreter of that score, leadership represents a key ingredient in the evaluation and adjustment process. It is the responsibility of the leader to listen and correct, in rehearsal and in reviewing performances, so that the orchestra can come as close as possible to the standard of composer intent.

Incentives play a role in this context as well, since the ensemble is large enough so that players who excel can be rewarded with more prestigious positions and more prominent parts. This too is usually under the control of the music director. Communications obviously plays a role in evaluation and adjustment in this kind of ensemble, but the size of the group largely limits such communication to leader-player directives and responses as wells as some within-section discussion. Practice is also likely to be a limited strategy for seeking excellence in this kind of ensemble. While desirable and potentially effective, rehearsal time is constrained by resource budgets, labor union requirements and the demanding schedules of professional players. So too, promoting further education and training is probably not a productive option for already proficient players, whose own standards and motivations can usually be relied upon for self-improvement.

The high school orchestra requires a different strategic combination for evaluation and adjustment towards seeking excellence. Its players can benefit from all the additional education and practice that they can get. Investments in these areas are likely to yield substantial pay-offs, especially if designed within the context of improving weaknesses heard in ensemble play. Here, the role of the orchestra leader (conductor/teacher) is critical in leading the practices and providing advice and counsel as a teacher. The score remains a relatively important referent, not so much for achieving composer intent, as in providing concrete guideposts for the student musicians to check if they are playing the right notes in the right way at the right time. Incentives also play a part. Even players at the amateur level (and their parents!) appreciate recognition for achievement; hence incorporating opportunities for advancement within the ensemble in the evaluation and adjustment process can effectively contribute to seeking overall excellence. Finally, communications will also play an important role, again mostly between music director and players (and mostly from the former to the latter). For this type of ensemble, players are less likely to effectively evaluate one another or to contribute substantially to the thinking of the leader.

Table 5.2   **Strategies for Seeking Excellence**

	plans	communication	education	incentives	practice	leadership
Symphony orchestra	1	4	6	3	5	2
High school orchestra	4	6	1	5	2	3
Jazz combo	4	1	6	5	2	3
Rock band	5	1	3	6	2	4
Church choir	3	6	4	5	2	1

The jazz combo and the rock band, by contrast, depend heavily on internal communications and practice sessions (or just playing together over long periods of time) as primary mechanisms of evaluation and adjustment. These ensembles are small enough to support intense, egalitarian, internal player discussions focusing on continual experimentation, and review and adjustment of their individual and collective performances. Leadership plays a role in both groups if there are within them distinguished individual players ("equals among equals") who are mutually recognized as visionaries for their ensembles and can help guide the evaluation and adjustment process and provide a sense of direction and aspiration.

For the rock group, education is likely to be a relatively productive means for amateur players to hone their individual skills and understanding of music in order to elevate the playing of the ensemble as a whole, whereas the professional jazz combo, with its accomplished players, is less likely to emphasize this means to seeking excellence. Finally, these ensembles are too small for incentives to be effective and neither are sufficiently formal to use plans (scores) for basic guidance on how to improve themselves, although the jazz combo may be more likely to reflect on its performance relative to state of the art improvisational techniques.

The church choir depends more strongly than the other ensembles on central leadership to evaluate, adjust and improve its performance over time. Practice, teaching, and learning to follow the scores, as facilitated by the music director, are likely to be key strategies for seeking excellence. Internal communications among players are less likely to be productive in this way, and the ensemble embodies limited opportunities for internal advancement, although outstanding individual work can be rewarded with soloing opportunities.

Strategies for Excellence

Overall, excellence is a continuing quest – a process more than an outcome or a specific level of achievement. It is a relative phenomenon as well. There must be some reference criterion or peer group compared to which an organization is considered to be excellent or wanting. As such, managers seeking excellence must engage in evaluative processes that allow their organizations to understand how well they are doing, relative to some standard or benchmark, or other appropriate criterion, and then to make adjustments to improve their performance relative to that referent. In this discussion we have identified at least three such processes.

First, managers can make use of *design specifications* as standards. What is it that the creators of the music had in mind for performance? Operationalizing those design standards for the tempo, pitch, volume dynamics, and feelings to be transmitted by the music, and gauging actual performance by those standards, is one way that long term excellence can be sought through a process of evaluation and adjustment. Conductors can ask "From all the evidence we have, is this what Beethoven had in mind?" Better yet, when the opportunity presents itself, a conductor can ask a living composer to compare a performance to the intent represented by the composer's instructions and determine what adjustments are needed to meet that intent more closely.

Second, managers can make use of *environmental signals* to drive the quest for excellence. What are paying customers, donors and volunteers saying when they respond, or fail to respond well, to the programming that is offered? What are the audiences saying by their reactions to the ensemble's performances? What are the critics saying and what adjustments can be made in response to these various signals?

Third, managers can make use of *competition*, both within the organization and with other organizations, to promote excellence. How well are some groups within the ensemble or some individuals within particular groups, doing relative to others? What adjustments can be made in the performance of particular sections in order to improve overall playing? And how well is the ensemble doing relative to other ensembles? Is the ensemble's market share increasing or decreasing and what are critics and others saying about who is best at performing various pieces of the relevant repertoire? While there is no simple, singular standard by which ensembles can be rated against one another, the concept of standing relative to the competition, if properly taken in context, can serve as an incentive and guide for continual seeking of excellence:

The Cleveland Orchestra has received a rather nice New Year's present. In the Jan.10 issue of *Time Magazine*....Michael Walsh writes that under music director Christoph von Dohnanyi the orchestra "has become the best band in the land."...If the Times pronouncement increases the health of the Cleveland Orchestra at home and abroad by generating more financial support and sending more listeners to Severance Hall and record stores, the splash will serve a worthy purpose.

But...can we really pit orchestra against orchestra, like sports teams, and then rank them?...If Clevelanders want to indulge in the nutsy business of ranking orchestras along the lines of a Symphonic Superbowl, they need to hear lots of orchestras...before they begin waving the pompons. Severance Hall could help out by booking the Berlin and Vienna Philharmonics and the major orchestras of Boston, Chicago, Los Angeles, New York, Philadelphia, St. Louis, Amsterdam, Prague, London, St. Petersburg, Oslo, Stockholm, Paris, etc., etc.

Only after our ears become familiar with the artistic products from those cities will it be possible to make substantial statements about quality. For the time being, let's bask in our good fortune, thank the Cleveland Orchestra for its contribution to our artistic well being – and make a beeline for Severance Hall. (Rosenberg, 1994a, p.6-F)

Excellence can be fleeting and it does not take place in a vacuum. It is a relative concept, a moving target, but its quest is nonetheless a driving force in human achievement, both individually and collectively for organizations.

Case Studies

Citing organizations that are "excellent" in any absolute sense is a tenuous exercise, fraught with controversy about subjective judgments and appropriate criteria with which to measure performance. However, identifying organizations that aspire to excellence, and examining how they go about their quest to improve, is less difficult. The following cases offer alternative perspectives – each one best analyzed by comparing the organization to a different kind of musical ensemble.

The Association for Research on Nonprofit Organizations and Voluntary Action (ARNOVA)

ARNOVA is an association of researchers from various scholarly disciplines who share a common interest in studying voluntary and philanthropic activity, the behavior and performance of not-for-profit organizations, and policy issues affecting civil society and the not-for-profit sector of the economy. It was established in 1971 as the Association of Voluntary Action Scholars (AVAS) by a group of sociologists and political scientists who were primarily interested in voluntary behavior by individuals and groups. Until the late 1980s, ARNOVA (then known as AVAS) remained small and informal, publishing a low cost journal, holding its annual conference in inexpensive places, and attracting between a hundred and two hundred members. Over time, AVAS struggled to hold itself together with minimal resources and a part-time administrator to help its volunteer board of directors. However, as national interest in the nonprofit sector grew, beginning in the late 1970s and through the 1980s, AVAS began to attract a broader spectrum of scholars many of whom focused on economic, legal and policy issues of nonprofit organizations. While AVAS was the closest match they could find, these new members were really looking for a stronger organization that could bring together scholars from all of the various disciplines that were beginning to contribute to an understanding of the nonprofit sector, and they also wanted a stronger focus on sectoral, policy and organizational issues relative to voluntary action.

By the end of the 1980s one could think of AVAS as a large chorus of individuals singing somewhat different tunes but most of whom wanted to sing in unison. There were differences over whether the organization should become much larger or more formal, but there was also a general feeling that AVAS ought to become a more effective organization for serving its members needs and contributing to a wider understanding of voluntary activity and nonprofit organizations. Given its character as a large, loosely organized and undisciplined chorus, AVAS required strong leadership and a plan (a score) to move it forward towards excellence. That leadership came first from a small group of leaders from both the old and new guards who met in retreats to find a compelling common identity for the association, and a new structure and set of goals with which the organization could realize that identity. These leaders opted for a name change that would signal special emphasis on the nonprofit sector as well as voluntary action, and broad inclusion of all contributing disciplines. This was a slightly new niche for ARNOVA that would ensure a broader base of support into the future. The leaders recommended changing the name of the association's journal as well, from the *Journal of Voluntary Action Research* to the *Nonprofit and Voluntary Sector Quarterly*, and perhaps most importantly of all, they decided that ARNOVA would need a full time staff, a permanent central office, and a substantial budget with which to conduct its business. These changes in turn required that ARNOVA seek substantial foundation funding.

The plan was accepted by the membership in 1990 and new board leadership was elected that was committed to writing a strategic plan and grant proposals to implement that plan. Again, strong central leadership, in the form of co-presidents of the board during the transition, stepped in to point the way and to help bring the membership along. Within the next few years, a rigorous strategic plan was formulated and adopted, substantial external funding was secured, and the first full-time permanent executive director and supporting staff were hired. From that point forward, strong leadership was exercised by the executive director working in close partnership with successive board presidents (who served two year terms), and effective processes of evaluation and adjustment were manifested primarily by continual referral to goals set forth in the score (strategic plan and associated grant proposals). The goals focused on the quality of the organization's services, the diversity of its membership and the contribution of the association to society's understanding of the nonprofit sector.

The results were dramatic and self-reinforcing. Membership grew over the decade of the 1990s from approximately 100 to over 1000, and ARNOVA became known as the leading scholarly association in nonprofit studies worldwide. In the year 2000, a successful transition was achieved to a new executive director who has initiated another strategic planning effort to review and update the original goals and to continue the process of measuring progress towards those goals. ARNOVA is now a stable and well functioning chorus, still with a modest level of internal dissonance among its voices as is appropriate to that of a scholarly association, but with overall harmony relative to its general purpose and direction. Leadership and referencing of the score (plans), as well as internal dialogue (more in keeping with a professional than an amateur chorus) continue to be the mainstays of successful evaluation and adjustment in the quest for excellence.

Florida Sheriff Youth Fund

The Florida Sheriff Youth Fund (FSYF) was founded by the Florida Sheriffs Association in 1957 in the form of a Boys Ranch to help troubled boys before they got seriously involved with law breaking (Young, 1985). To a certain extent, this was a effort by the sheriffs to project a benevolent side to their public image as tough law enforcers. The Boys Ranch struggled in its early years, having only a small budget, serving just a few dozen boys, going through four different resident directors in four years, and floundering financially. Organizationally, it was like an amateur rock band, with a small cast of business leaders, local land owners, and leaders in the Sheriff's Association, who were generous with their resources and time commitments, united in their aspirations to make the organization work, but who were improvising as they went along without any real leadership, vision, basic procedures, or sense of direction.

Things changed in 1961 with the hiring of a professional administrator by the name of Harry Weaver. Weaver brought strong leadership and managerial skills to the organization and also a larger and more coherent vision. He helped the sheriffs and their associates see that the organization could become a much more substantial, visible and efficient operation, and indeed a show case for their cause, by drawing on the good name of the sheriffs to generate resources from contributions of major donors and ordinary citizens who believed in law and order and helping kids. Ultimately, the sheriffs bought into Weaver's vision, and the organization acquired a new identity and *modus operandi*. It was no longer a flailing rock band, but became more like a chamber orchestra, with Weaver conducting the ensemble so that the different parts worked in harmony according to his plan. Weaver's plan included expansion and upgrading of the physical plant, and the addition of new facilities including a Girls Villa, and a Youth Ranch for sibling groups. Weaver also had a plan to consolidate the administration of these separate programs under a single organizational structure, an option that was previously precluded by provisions in the legal documents that established the original Boys Ranch. Weaver's strategy was to build the organization through the awkward structure of separately incorporated organizations with distinct, though overlapping boards of directors and staffs, and then convince a court that it would be in the public's best interest to consolidate these organizations into a single administrative entity. It was as if FSYF was transformed from an opera with semi-autonomous musical and theatrical companies struggling to work together, into a single orchestra with distinct instrument sections under a unified command and support structure. Weaver conducted his orchestra in flawless fashion, growing FSYF into a multimillion dollar, multi-campus program under his unified administration by 1977. Strong leadership, which included boundary-spanning to ensure that support from the donor community was forthcoming, and reference to a plan were his primary instruments for evaluation and adjustment along the way and they continued to be so for sometime thereafter.

There is also a dimension in which the excellence of FSYF was limited by strategies that Weaver put into place. For all of the money that it raised and the marvelous facilities it constructed, FSYF really wasn't serving that many more children, nor was it serving a group of children with particularly challenging profiles. Weaver's evaluation and adjustment mechanisms were focused on his audience of donors who supported the sheriffs and who received recognition for their contributions to the organization. Partially because it avoided state funding, FSYF was not well attuned to outside voices more concerned with the problems of children. Until evaluation and adjustment was focused on this area as well, FSYF's quest for excellence would be limited in its scope. Just as orchestras need to constantly reassess their audience base in order to plan for the future, FSYF needed to expand its evaluation and adjustment process beyond the success it was having in the donor community.

Diagnosing An Organization

Given the ideas of organizational identity and the paradigm of evaluation and adjustment that lie at the heart of a search for excellence, it is especially appropriate to end here with a series of diagnostic questions that managers can ask themselves as they aspire for excellence in their organizations. First, and perhaps most fundamentally, managers may ask what is enduring and special about their organizations, and in what ways might their organizations potentially become excellent:

- How can my organization's identity be articulated in a manner that captures the consensus of its participants and illuminates the ways in which it seeks to excel?
- What is the common sense of purpose that can excite and inspire the organization's members to work together in achieving excellence?
- Can my organization distinguish itself through flawless (exquisitely coordinated) operations?
- Can my organization distinguish itself by virtue of an especially highly motivated work force?
- Can my organization distinguish itself by its ability to innovate and push the boundaries of conventional practice?
- How can the organization's products and services be selected to exploit the unique advantages associated with the organization's size and particular combination of skills and assets?
- What opportunities for excellence have been created by recent changes in the organization's environment? What opportunities have been restricted by

these changes? Are there new niches that the organization is well-positioned to exploit?
– When all is said and done, what makes my organization truly different and potentially better than others?

Next, managers may ask themselves questions about how they will gauge the level of performance of their organizations and make adjustments to improve performance:

– What criteria capture the organization's special sense of purpose and whether that purpose is being achieved?
– How well does my organization meet the standards set forth in its score (plans)? What corrections need to be made to improve performance relative to those specifications? Can the original planners and designers be consulted for their evaluative feedback?
– How can the organization constructively deviate from its score (existing plans) in order to improve its performance?
– How can two-way communications between organizational leaders and members (workers) be improved in order to facilitate constructive feedback?
– How can external evaluators (critics) be engaged to provide helpful feedback on organizational performance?
– How should changes in demand for the organization's services, and in customer evaluations of these services, be interpreted and translated into helpful adjustments of products and services?
– What information can be collected from current, former and potential consumers to guide the organization towards improving its products?
– With what other organizations can we compare ourselves? How well do we perform relative to those organizations?

Next, the manager can inquire about the various ways in which the organization's capacity for evaluation and adjustment can be increased:

– How can education and training be used to improve the ability of workers to discern and correct problems on their own and to communicate effectively with leaders?
– How can practice and simulated work sessions (rehearsals) be designed to effectively evaluate performance, ferret out problems, and make necessary adjustments in a relaxed and constructive atmosphere?
– How can turnover in the work force and in organizational leadership be minimized so that organizational participants maintain their incentives to take evaluative feedback seriously?
– How can changes made in response to constructive feedback be appropriately acknowledged and rewarded?
– How can the organization's size be exploited to create incentives for advancement connected to performance excellence?

- How can the organization be subdivided into sections that exploit the evaluation and adjustment flexibility of small groups, and the potential to compare one group with another?
- How can competition within the organization be used to promote evaluation and adjustment in pursuit of excellence?

Finally, the manager can ask questions about how the organization can invigorate itself with a renewed spirit for achieving excellence:

- How can the identity and common purpose of the organization be renewed or re-enforced and communicated in a way that inspires its members?
- How can inspired leadership be engaged to frame and articulate a vision and expectations for future excellence?
- What can be done to retain the spirit of amateurs in a professional work setting?
- What is the next logical challenge (task of greater difficulty) for the organization to address, one that will stretch its capacities but still be within reach?

Coda

To celebrate the conclusion of this volume and to summarize some of its ideas, I offer, with all due apologies to the composer, the following lyrics, set to the tune of Beethoven's *Ode to Joy* from his *Ninth Symphony*, including chords for accompaniment:

```
G    D7            G  D7 G    D7 G   D7
All ensembles must ensemble if they are to operate
G    D7            G  D7  G       D7 G    D7  G
But achieving more than that they must their members motivate
D7  G       D7   G     D7   G   D7  Em A   D7
Even then they need a niche to best support their special place
G           D7     G    D7 G      D7  G  D7  G
With luck, an innovative mind-set can help them achieve that grace
```

But what makes good does not make great, for best is more demanding still
Inspired by a common purpose helps to climb that daunting hill
Excellence comes many ways, different tacks for large and small
To be the top means that you've found your best combination of all

But excellence does not endure unless the vigil is maintained
Evaluating and adjusting is how the best on top remain
So be patient and determined, knowing that you can rely
On Mozart, Brahms and Ellington to be there as your special guides!

Bibliography

Albert, Stuart and Bell, Geoffrey G. (2002), 'Timing and Music', *Academy of Management Review*, Vol.27(4), pp.574-93.

Bamberger, Carl (ed.) (1965), *The Conductor's Art*, Columbia University Press, New York.

Barnard, Chester (1938), *The Functions of the Executive*, Harvard University Press, Cambridge.

Barrett, Frank J. (1998), 'Creativity and Improvisation in Jazz and Organizations: Implications for Organizational Learning', *Organization Science*, Vol.9(5), pp.605-22.

Barrett, Frank J. and Peplowski, Ken (1998), 'Minimal Structures Within a Song', *Organization Science*, Vol.9(5), pp. 558-60.

Bastien, David T. and Hostager, Todd J. (1988), 'Jazz as a Process of Organizational Innovation', *Communications Research*, Vol.15(5), pp.582-602.

Bastien, David T. and Hostager, Todd J. (2002), 'Jazz as a Process of Organizational Innovation', Chapter 2 in Kamoche, Cunha and Cunha, op.cit., pp.14-28.

Baumol, William J. (1993), *Entrepreneurship, Management, and the Structure of Payoffs*, M.I.T. Press, Cambridge.

Baumol, William J. and Bowen, William G. (1996), *Performing Arts: The Economic Dilemma*, Twentieth Century Fund, New York.

Berliner, Paul F. (1994), *Thinking in Jazz: The Infinite Art of Improvisation*, University of Chicago Press, Chicago.

Blau, Eleanor (1982), 'Maazel, Stepping Down, Calls Orchestra Flawless', *The New York Times*, May 23, p.50.

Blumenthal, Ralph (1999), 'Ozawa to Quit Boston Symphony, Adding to Void on U.S. Podiums', *The New York Times*, June 23, pp.A1,A15.

Bryson, John M. (1988), *Strategic Planning for Public and Nonprofit Organizations*, Jossey-Bass, San Francisco.

Cameron, Kim S. (1986), 'Effectiveness as Paradox: Consensus and Conflict in Conceptions of Organizational Effectiveness', *Management Science*, Vol.32, pp. 539-53.

Capozzoli, Jr., Michael A. (1999), 'Pop beat goes on for Alabama', *The Plain Dealer*, July 6, pp.1-E,4-E.

Carlinsky, Dan and Goodgold, Ed (1991), *The Armchair Conductor*, Dell Publishing, New York.

Carse, Adam (1964), *The History of Orchestration*, Dover Publications, New York.

Coase, Ronald H. (1988), *The Firm, the Market and the Law*, The University of Chicago Press, Chicago.

Cohn, Stuart (1996), 'Early Musicians Who Know the Score', *Early Music America*, Fall, pp.34-37.

Crutchfield, Will (1987a), 'Concert: Kronos Quartet at Weill Hall', *The New York Times*, January 18, p.49.

Crutchfield, Will (1987b), 'Why Our Greatest Composer Needs Serious Attention', *The New York Times*, May 10, pp.19,22.

Cyert, Richard M. and March, James G. (1972), *A Behavioral Theory of the Firm*, Prentice-Hall, Englewood Cliffs, New Jersey.

Davis, Francis (1999), '60's Free Jazz for the Sonic Youth Crowd', *The New York Times*, June 13, p.31.

Delatiner, Barbara (1982), 'Fewer Local Groups Play Without Pay,' *The New York Times*, January 31, pp.1,9.

Delatiner, Barbara (1985), '40 Years of Music, Unless It Rains', *The New York Times*, July 7, p.LI 11.

Delatiner, Barbara (1986), 'Philharmonic Spinoff: Chamber Players', *The New York Times*, September 14, p.LI 21.

DePree, Max (1992), *Leadership Jazz*, Dell Publishing, New York.

DiMaggio, Paul J. (1986), 'Cultural Entrepreneurship in Nineteenth Century Boston', Chapter 2 in DiMaggio, Paul J. (ed.), *Nonprofit Enterprise in the Arts*, Oxford University Press, New York, pp. 41-61.

Drexler, Michael (1997), 'Straight from the Heart of Europe', *The Plain Dealer*, December 30, pp.E1,E7.

Drucker, Peter F. (1980), *Managing in Turbulent Times*, Harper and Row, New York.

Early, John F. (1994), 'Quality Processes in Management', in Hampton, John J. (ed.), *AMA Management Handbook: Third Edition*, AMACOM, New York, pp.1-27.

Edwards, Brent Hayes (2001), 'An Essential Element in the Voice of Jazz', *The New York Times*, July 22, p.23AR.

Eisenberg, Eric M. (1990), 'Jamming: Transcendence Through Organizing', *Communication Research*, Vol.17(2), pp.139-64.

Elliott, Susan (1988), 'A Freelancer's Lot is Filled with Allegros', *The New York Times*, November 6, pp.27,30.

Faulkner, Robert R. (1973), 'Orchestra Interaction: Some Features of Communication and Authority in an Artistic Organization,' *The Sociological Quarterly*, Vol.14, Spring, pp.147-57.

Fischer, Marilyn and Jackson, Isaiah (1997), 'Toward a Vision of Mutual Responsiveness: Remythologizing the Symphony Orchestra', *Harmony*, No.4, April, pp.71-83.

Freeman, Everett J. (1996a), 'Research Issues in Orchestra Labor Relations', *Harmony*, No.2, April, pp.27-41.

Freeman, Robert (1996b), 'On the Future of America's Orchestras', *Harmony*, No.3, October, pp. 11-21.

Fulmer, Douglas (1997a), 'Derailers On Track With New Album', *The Plain Dealer, Friday* section, July 14, p.17.

Fulmer, Douglas (1997b), 'Zydeco Star's Return Hits Cain Park Show Like Delta Hurricane', *The Plain Dealer*, July 14, p.5-B.

Galkin, Elliot W. (1988), *A History of Orchestral Conducting*, Pendragon Press, New York.

Gammond, Peter (1995), *The Encyclopedia of Classical Music*, Revised Edition, Salamander Books Limited, London.

Goodman, Peter (1985a), 'Small group, ample pleasure', *Newsday*, February 18, p.II-19.

Goodman, Peter (1985b), 'The Philadelphia's Eugene Ormandy', *Newsday*, March 13, p.II-3.

Goodman, Peter (1987), 'A Big-Name Trio', *Newsday*, November 9, p.II-8.

Gould, Stephen J. (1996), *Full House*, Harmony Books, New York.

Griffiths, Paul (1997), 'Cleveland Orchestra Does Composer Proud', *The Plain Dealer*, July 1, p.8-E.

Griffiths, Paul (1997), Review of 'The Compleat Conductor' by Gunther Schuller, *The New York Times Book Review*, August 24, p.11.

Griffiths, Paul (1999), 'Making the Evolving Orchestra Fit to Survive', *The New York Times*, June 13, p.32.

Guthrie, Kevin M. (1996), *The New York Historical Society*, Jossey-Bass, San Francisco.

Hackman, Richard J. (2002), *Leading Teams*, Harvard Business School Press, Boston.

Handy, Charles (1990), *The Age of Unreason*, Arrow Books, London.

Hannan, Michael T. and Freeman, John (1989), *Organizational Ecology*, Harvard University Press, Cambridge.

Hatch, Mary Jo (1998), 'Jazz as a Metaphor for Organizing', *Organization Science*, Vol.9 (5), pp.565-68.

Heifetz, Ronald A. (1994), *Leadership Without Easy Answers*, Harvard University Press, Cambridge.

Herman, Robert D. and Renz, David O. (1999) 'Theses on Nonprofit Organizational Effectiveness', *Nonprofit and Voluntary Sector Quarterly*, Vol. 28(2), pp. 107-26.

Hirschman, Albert O. (1970), *Exit, Voice and Loyalty*, Harvard University Press, Cambridge.

Holland, Bernard (1981), 'Philharmonic Opens Its Rehearsals', *The New York Times*, November 29, pp.1, 36.

Holland, Bernard (1985), 'Music: Maurizio Pollini Conducts', *The New York Times*, March 17, p.52.

Holland, Bernard (1988), 'Flutes, and Only Flutes', *The New York Times*, May 18.

Holland, Bernard (1999a), 'When Composers Make It Hard, Fright and Strain Become Muses', *New York Times*, June 1, pp. B1,3.

Holland, Bernard (1999b),'Conducting a Chemical Experiment', *The New York Times*, June 20, p.21.

Judy, Paul R. (1996a), 'Life and Work in Symphony Orchestras: An Interview with J. Richard Hackman', *Harmony*, No.2, April, pp.1-13.

Judy, Paul R. (1996b), 'Pierre Boulez: Reflections on Symphony Orchestra Organizations', *Harmony*, No.3, October, pp.30-38.

Kamoche, Ken N., Cunha, Miguel Pina E and Cunha, Joao Vieira Da (eds.) (2002), *Organizational Improvisation*, Routledge, London.

Kanter, Rosabeth M. (1989), *When Giants Learn to Dance*, Simon & Schuster, New York.

Kao, John J. (1991), *The Entrepreneurial Organization*, Prentice Hall, Englewood Cliffs, New Jersey.

Kao, John (1996), *Jamming: The Art and Discipline of Business Creativity*, HarperBusiness, New York.

Kaplan, Max (1955), 'Teleopractice: A Symphony Orchestra As It Prepares for a Concert', *Social Forces*, May, pp.352-55.

Kaufman, Herbert (1967), *The Forest Ranger*, The Johns Hopkins University Press, Baltimore.

Kerres, Bernhard H. (1999), 'Orchestras in a Complex World', *Harmony*, No.8, April, pp.45-58.

Kimmelman, Michael (1987), 'Major Symphony Orchestras Are Narrowing Their Focus', *The New York Times*, May 31, pp.19, 24.

Kirkpatrick, David D. with Rutenberg, Jim (2002), 'A Search for Harmony Within a Feuding AOL', *The New York Times*, July 21, p. 19.

Kotler, Philip (1997), *Marketing Management*, Prentice Hall, Upper Saddle River, New Jersey.

Kozinn, Allan (1994), 'The Los Angeles Philharmonic Energized by the Spell of Salonen', *The New York Times*, November 30, pp.B1-B2.

Kozinn, Allan (1997), 'Still Snipping Buttons Off the Stuffed Shirts', *The New York Times*, December 21, p.32.

Kraus, Lucy (1982), 'Being Called 'Concertmaster' Is All Right With Her', *The New York Times*, August 1, pp.17, 20.

Lehman, Erin (1995), 'Recruitment Practices in American and British Symphony

Orchestras: Contrasts and Consequences', *The Journal of Arts Management, Law and Society*, Vol.24 (4), pp.325-43.

Lehman, Erin and Galinsky, Adam (1994), 'The London Symphony Orchestra', Case Study No. N9-494-034, March 9, Harvard Business School Publishing, Cambridge.

Levine, Seymour and Levine, Robert (1996), 'Why They're Not Smiling: Stress and Discontent in the Orchestral Workplace', *Harmony*, No.2, April, pp.15-25.

Lewin, Arie Y. (1998), 'Jazz Improvisation as a Metaphor for Organization Theory', *Organization Science*, Vol.9(5), pp.539-42.

Liebschutz, Sarah F. (1992), 'Coping by Nonprofit Organizations During the Reagan Years', *Nonprofit Management and Leadership*, Vol. 2(4), pp.363-80.

McKay, Bill (1996), 'Pete Wernick', *Banjo Newsletter*, Vol.23(11), pp.14-18.

Miller, Sarah Bryan (1994), 'Three Years After His Departure, Solti Remains a Hard Act to Follow', *The New York Times*, May 8, p.27.

Mintzberg, Henry (1994), *The Rise and Fall of Strategic Planning*, The Free Press, New York.

Mintzberg, Henry (1998), 'Covert Leadership: Note on Managing Professionals', *Harvard Business Review*, November-December, pp.140-47.

Monson, Jr., Charles C. (1967),'Metaphors for the University', *Educational Record*, pp.22-29.

Morgan, Gareth (1997), *Images of Organization*, Sage Publications, Thousand Oaks, California.

Mount, Timothy (1980), 'Section Rehearsals', *The Choral Journal*, October, pp.15-17.

Nelson, Richard R. and Winter, Sidney G. (1982), *An Evolutionary Theory of Economic Change*, Harvard University Press, Cambridge.

New York Times, The, 'For Aged Singers, Boys Will Be Boys' (1987), December 20, p.51.

New York Times, The, 'Ilya Musin, Russian Conductor and Mentor, Dies at 95' (1999), Obituaries, June 14, p.A21.

Olson, Mancur (1965), *The Logic of Collective Action*, Harvard University Press, Cambridge.

Orgill, Roxanne (1996), 'A Sideman's Life: Whichever Way the Horns Blow', *The New York Times*, September 1, pp. 24, 28.

Orleans, James (1997), 'Rebuilding the Repertoire for the 21st Century', *Harmony*, No.4, April, pp.57-69.

Osterberg, Anne-Marie (1996), *Ensembles in Sweden*, Musikmuseet, Stockholm.

Owens, Thomas (1995). *Bebop*, Oxford University Press, New York.

Oxford Companion to Music (1970), 10th Edition, Oxford University Press, London.

Oxford Dictionary of Quotations, The (1979), Third Edition, Oxford University Press, New York.

Page, Tim (1984), 'The Emerson Quartet - Attuned to the New and the Innovative', *The New York Times*, April 29, p.H21.

Page, Tim (1992), *Music from the Road*, Oxford University Press, New York.

Palmer, Robert (1987), 'Musicians in Quest of Language', *The New York Times*, October 4, p.28.

Pantsios, Anastasia (1999), 'Spinning the Same Songs, but without Spinning Guitars', *The Plain Dealer*, July 2, p.17.

Pareles, Jon (1987a), 'Hearing Jazz at Its Risky Best - in the Clubs', *The New York Times*, June 28, p.H22.

Pareles, Jon (1987b), 'The Grateful Dead, Most Alive on the Stage', *The New York Times*, July 26, p.H24.

Pasmore, William A. (1998), 'Organizing for Jazz', *Organization Science*, Vol.9 (5), pp.562-64.

Peplowski, Ken (1998), 'The Process of Improvisation', *Organization Science*, Vol.9 (5), pp.560-61.

Peters, Thomas J. and Waterman, Robert H. (1982), *In Search of Excellence*, Warner Books, New York.

Powers, Ann (1999), 'Winter Welcomes Summer, and Invites the Crowd to Sit Back and Listen', *The New York Times*, June 23, p.B5.

Pratt, John W. and Zeckhauser, Richard J. (1991), *Principals and Agents: The Structure of Business*, Harvard Business School Press, Boston.

Ratliff, Ben (1997), 'A Puzzle Whose Pieces Are Bass, Banjo and Mandolin', *The New York Times*, October 17, p.B20.

Rockwell, John (1982), 'Why Isn't the Philharmonic Better?', *The New York Times Magazine*, September 19, pp.46-64.

Rockwell, John (1988), 'Settling the Score', *The New York Times Magazine*, April 24, pp.54-68.

Rosenberg, Donald (1993), 'Dohnanyi Brings Out Bold Best of Beethoven', *The Plain Dealer*, September 17, p.30.

Rosenberg, Donald (1994a), '"Best Band" Crown is Fine, but We Need to Hear Others', *The Plain Dealer*, January 5, p.6-F.

Rosenberg, Donald (1994b), 'Choral Conductor Gives Voice to his Muse', *The Plain Dealer*, April 24, p.2-J.

Rosenberg, Donald (1994c), 'Strings Sing Despite Dry Acoustics', *The Plain Dealer*, October 6, p.10-E.

Rosenberg, Donald (1994d), 'Assertive Conductor Brings Musical Vigor', *The Plain Dealer*, November 14, p.4-E.

Rosenberg, Donald (1995), 'Mahler Awes New York', *The Plain Dealer*, May 6, p.12-E.

Rosenberg, Donald (1996), 'Special Treat for Music Lovers', *The Plain Dealer*, October 21, p.9-D.

Rosenberg, Donald (1997a), 'Comparing Notes', *The Plain Dealer*, February 3, p.5-B.

Rosenberg, Donald (1997b), 'Ensemble's Artistry Brings Excitement to Oberlin', *The Plain Dealer*, September 23, p.7-B.

Rosenberg, Donald (1998a), 'Harp, Harp, Hurrah!', *The Plain Dealer*, April 21, p.2-E.

Rosenberg, Donald (1998b), 'Conducting Cleveland Fills Absolute Dream', *The Plain Dealer*, July 23, p.6-E.

Rosenberg, Donald (1998c), 'Ingolfsson Brings Mozart to Life', *The Plain Dealer*, November 9, p.4-E.

Rosenberg, Donald (1998d), 'Ensemble Plays First in Series with Fresh Energy', *The Plain Dealer*, November 24, p.4-E.

Rosenberg, Donald (1998e), 'Personnel Changes Don't Alter Quartet's Distinguished Artistry', *The Plain Dealer*, December 14, p.3-E.

Rosenberg, Donald (1998f), 'Orchestra Soars with Premiere of Viola Concerto', *The Plain Dealer*, April 24, p.7-B.

Rosenberg, Donald (1998g), 'Orchestra has a Rough Weekend at Blossom', *The Plain Dealer*, August 17, p.4-E.

Rosenberg, Donald (1998h), 'Successes Surprise Busy Conductor', *The Plain Dealer*, August 27, pp.1-E, 4-E.

Rosenberg, Donald (1999), '"Prime Schubert;" Prime Dohnanyi; Prime Cleveland', *The Plain Dealer*, January 8, p.7-B.

Rosenberg, Donald (2000), *The Cleveland Orchestra*, Gray and Company, Cleveland.

Sachs, Harvey (1987), 'Italy: The Symphony Front', *The New York Times*, August 9, pp.21,26.

Salipante, Paul F. and Golden-Biddle, Karen (1995), 'Managing Traditionality and Strategic Change in Nonprofit Organizations', *Nonprofit Management and Leadership*, Vol.6(1), pp.3-20.

Salisbury, Wilma (1994), 'Nonprofessional Ensemble Has Fun', *The Plain Dealer*, May 4, p.8F.

Salisbury, Wilma (1997), 'McFerrin-Corea: Ever Inventive, Irrepressible', *The Plain Dealer*, August 25, p.5-B.

Salisbury, Wilma (1998a), 'All Ornaments Shine During Oberlin Baroque Concert', *The Plain Dealer*, July 8, p.3-E.

Salisbury, Wilma (1998b), 'Leaden Conducting Turns Ensemble's Rags into Drags', *The Plain Dealer*, September 21, p.3-E.

Salisbury, Wilma (1998c), 'Charming "Olde World" Christmas Concert Comes Early', *The Plain Dealer*, November 24, p.4-E.

Salisbury,Wilma (1999), 'Ensemble Turns Tango into High Art', *The Plain Dealer*, June 14, p.4-E.

Sangiacomo, Michael (1997), 'Weavers Bringing Scottish Tradition', *The Plain Dealer*, September 16, p.10-E.

Sangiacomo, Michael (1999), 'A Musical World Tour, with an Irish Accent', *The Plain Dealer*, July 20, p.5-B.

Sayles, L.R. (1964), *Managerial Behaviour: Administration in Complex Organizations*, McGraw Hill, New York.

Schiff, David (1995), 'An Older, Wiser, Humbler Wunderkind', *The New York Times Magazine*, August 20, pp.29-31.

Schonberg, Harold C. (1981), 'A Leader No Orchestra Can Resist', *The New York Times*, September 24, p. C19.

Schumpeter, Joseph A. (1934), *The Theory of Economic Development*, Harvard University Press, Cambridge.

Schwarz, Robert (1991), 'A Conductor Scales Down To Move Up', *The New York Times*, November 3, pp.25, 30.

Scott, Jane (1995), 'New Conductor Keeps Count', *The Plain Dealer*, September 14, p.9-B.

Senge, Peter (1990), *The Fifth Discipline*, Doubleday, New York.

Sowd, David (1990), 'For the Love of Music', *The Plain Dealer*, May 18, pp.30-31.

Spich, Robert S. and Sylvester, Robert M. (1999), 'The Jurassic Symphony: Part Two', *Harmony*, No.8, April, pp.14-43.

Stearns, David Patrick (1997), 'Composer Cheng Boldly Bridges Musical Traditions', *USA Today*, March 11, p.8D.

Steinberg, Michael (1999), 'Toward Fresh and Friendly Concerts', *The New York Times*, Section 2, June 13, pp.1,34.

Tommasini, Anthony (1999a), 'Conducting Stravinsky: His Own Reading vs. Others', *The New York Times*, June 6, p. 26.

Tommasini, Anthony (1999b), 'A Pied Piper Lures San Franciscans Into the Concert Hall', *The New York Times*, June 22, pp.B1,B3.

Tovey, Donald Francis (1961), *The Main Stream of Music and Other Essays*, World Publishing Company, Cleveland.

Traub, James (1996), 'Passing the Baton', *The New Yorker*, August 26 & September 2, pp.100-105.

Walker, Rob (2002), 'Creating Synergy Out of Thin Air', *New York Times*, July 28, wk-p.13.

Watson, Robert A. and Brown, Ben (2001), *The Most Effective Organization in the U.S.*,

Crown Business, New York.

Weick Karl E., Gilfillan, David P. and Keith, Thomas A. (1973), 'The Effect of Composer Credibility on Orchestra Performance', *Sociometry*, September, pp.435-62.

Weick, Karl W. (1998), 'Improvisation as a Mindset for Organizational Analysis', *Organization Science*, Vol.9(5), pp.543-55.

Whetten, David A. and Godfrey, Paul C. (1998), *Identity in Organizations*, Sage Publications, Thousand Oaks, California.

Williamson, Oliver E. (1975), *Markets and Hierarchies*, The Free Press, New York.

Wilson, John S. (1986), 'Jazz: At the Blue Not, Basie and Byard Bands', *The New York Times*, November 29, p.14.

Wolfe, Thomas (1992), 'The Financial Condition of Symphony Orchestras', American Symphony Orchestra League, Washington, D.C.

Wolff, Carlo (1999), 'Quintet Works Jazz, World-beat Magic', *The Plain Dealer*, February 27, p.4-E.

Young, Dennis R. (1983), *If Not for Profit, For What?*, Lexington Books, Lexington, Massachusetts.

Young, Dennis R. (1985), *Casebook of Management for Nonprofit Organizations*, Haworth Press, New York.

Young, Dennis R. (2001), 'Organizational Identity and the Structure of Nonprofit Umbrella Associations', *Nonprofit Management and Leadership*, Vol.11(3), pp.289-304.

Young, Vivienne and Colman, Andrew M. (1979), 'Some Psychological Processes in String Quartets', *Psychology of Music*, Vol.7 (1), pp.12-18.

Index

Note: bold page numbers indicate tables

Akiyoshi, Toshiko 72
Albert, Stuart 3, 12
Alsop, Marin 43-4, 78
amateurs 42-3, 55, 68, 84, **84**, 86, 114, 127
  excellence among 142-3, 147-8
AOL Time Warner 33
Apollo's Fire 74-5, 115, 127
Association for Research on Nonprofit Organizations and Voluntary Action (ARNOVA) 150-2
Association of Voluntary Action Scholars (AVAS) 150-1
audiences 134-5, 138, 143, 153
auditions 47

Bach, P.D.Q. 125-6
barbershop quartets **58**, 59
Barnard, Chester 2-3
Baroque music 101, 102, 117-18
Barrett, Frank J. 12
Basie, Count 28
  Orchestra 48, 76
Bastien, David T. 95, 102, 104, 105, 111
Bay Area Orchestra 142
Beatles, The 107, 144
bebop 94
Beecham, Sir Thomas 141
Beethoven, Ludwig van 13, 138, 143-4
Bell, Geoffrey G. 3, 12
benchmarking 149
Bernstein, Leonard 53, 110, 123, 133, 137, 139
big band orchestras 48, 57, **58**, 59
  strategies for excellence in 135-6
Blakey, Art 125
Blau, Eleanor 132
Blumenthal, Ralph 133
Borge, Victor 126
Boston Pops 84
Boston Symphony Orchestra 80, 133, 134-5

Boulez, Pierre 55
branding 83, 90
Brendel, Alfred 54
Brown, Clifford 94
bureaucracy 61-2

Canton Symphony Orchestra 125
Carlinsky, Dan 13, 16-17, 129, 132
Carse, Adam 99
Carter, Elliot 110
Cerone, David 6
chair system 49-50, 56
Chalifoux, Alice 102
chamber orchestras **84**, 85, **87**, 88
change management 93-4
  evaluation/adjustment process 94
  innovation process *see* innovation
Cheng, Bright 98
Chieftains, The 124
choirs **58**, 59, 69
  children's **84**, 86-7, **87**
  church 146-7, **146**, 148, **148**
Cleveland Orchestra 18, 22, 23, 52, 54, 67, 75, 129, 133, 149-50
  innovation in 106, 110, 126, 138-9
  organizational identity of 127
Coase, Ronald 9-10, 11
Cohn, Stuart 28-9
collective good 38, 39
Colman, Andrew M. 4, 21
Colorado Symphony Orchestra (CSO) 55, 82, 116
Coltrane, John 100-1
Columbia Symphony Orchestra 112-13
communication 5, 23, 31, **31**, 148, **148**
  case studies 32
  as element of ensemble 11, 12-14, 25
  evaluation/adjustment process for 131-5
  and innovation 103-4
  and niche-finding 71-2, **87**
community orchestras 125, 128

community organizations 85-6, 120-1
competition 149
    see also markets
Concordia Chamber Symphony 78
conductors 13, 16-20, 21, 53-4, 132-3
    development of role 17
    function of 18-20, 147
    orchestras without 17-18, 26, 54
continuous improvement 129
coordination 4, 5, 9-36, 68
    case studies 32-4
    circumstances of 21-4
    diagnosis of, in organizations 34-6
    elements of 11-20
        communication 12-14
        education/training 14-15
        leadership 10, 16-20
        plans/procedures 11-12, 27-9
        rehearsals 15-16
    and excellence 124-5, 127
    and innovation 95
    and market transactions 9-10
    priorities/trade-offs 29-32
    strategies 29-32, 34-6
copy-cat behavior 83
Corea, Chick 104
critics 133-4, 143
Crutchfield, Will 24
Cunha, Joao Vieira Da 100
Cunha, Miguel Pina 100
customers 5
    see also markets

Darwinism 68-9, 81
Davis, Francis 81, 96
Davis, Miles 136
Davis, Sir Colin 131
Delatiner, Barbara 43, 47, 142
Detroit Symphony Orchestra 83
Dixieland Jazz 144-5
Dohnanyi, Christoph von 126, 133, 137,
    138-9
"double loop" learning 94
Drucker, Peter F. 3
DuPree, Max 3, 100

early music group, analysis of 117-20,
    117, 119
ecology metaphor 68-9, 81
education *see* training

Edwards, Brent Hayes 97
effectiveness 124
Eisenberg, Eric M. 15
Ellington, Duke 71, 145
Elliott, Susan 142
Emerson Quartet 21
Emilia-Romagna orchestra 45
ensembles *see* orchestras; rock groups;
    string quartets
entrepreneurship 16, 82
    and innovation 96, 109-10
entropy 129
environment, organizational 75, 81, 149
    instability in 116, 129, 144-5
evaluation/adjustment process 94, 129-
    39, 147-8, 154-5
    elements of 130-9
        communication 131-5
        environment 153
        incentives 137
        leadership 138-9, 153
        planning 130-1
        training/rehearsal 135-6
excellence 123-55
    case studies 150-3
        ARNOVA 150-2
        Florida Sherrif Youth Fund 152-3
    circumstances for 139-45
        heterogeneity 140-1
        instability 144-5
        organization size 139-40, **146**
        professionalism 141-3
        task complexity 143-4
    defined 124
    diagnosis of, in organizations 153-5
    evaluating *see* evaluation/adjustment
        process
    ingredients of 124-8
        coordination 124-5, 127
        innovation 125-6, 128
        motivation 125, 127
        niche-finding 125, 127-8
        organizational identity 126-8
    maintaining *see*
        evaluation/adjustment process
    priorities/trade-offs for 145-8
    strategies for 149-50
"exit and voice" theory 129

Faulkner, Robert R. 3

feedback 129, 133-4, 137, 138, 149
Fiedler, Arthur 84
Fischer, Marilyn 110
Fleck, Bela 79
Florida Sherrif Youth Fund (FSYF) 152-3
folk music 72, 79, 83, 102, 115, 128
  ensembles, analysis of 117-20, **117, 119**
formality 45
Foster, Frank 76
free-riders *see* under-performers
freelancing 142
Freeman, John 79
Freeman, Robert 48, 49-50
Fulmer, Douglas 97, 99
fusion music 77, 78, 96-7, 98, 113-14
  matrix analysis of 117-20, **117, 119**

Galinsky, Adam 74
Gammond, Peter 17, 18
Girls Incorporated 89-90
Glass, Philip 126, 134
Godfrey, Paul C. 127
Goodgold, Ed 13, 16-17, 129, 132
Goodman, Peter 42
government support 68
Grateful Dead, The 73, 75, 114
Griffiths, Paul 70, 131
Grisman, David 14
Guarneri String Quartet 23, 48, 79, 111

Hackman, Richard 3, 17, 18, 19, 127
Handy, Charles 10
Hannan, Michael T. 79
Harmonia 128
Hatch, Mary Jo 13
Heifetz, Ron 7
heterogeneity/homogeneity 6, 21-2, 24, 27, **30**, 70, 90
  and excellence 140-1, 146, **146**
  and motivation 41, 57, **58**
  and niche-finding 77, 84
  and stability 29
hierarchies 2, 49-51, 53-5, 109
Hirschman, Albert 115-16, 129
Holland, Bernard 45, 126, 129, 138, 143
Hollywood String Quartet 135
homogeneity *see* heterogeneity
Hostager, Todd J. 95, 102, 104, 105, 111

humor in music 125-6

identity, organizational 126-7, 139, 141, 153
improvisation 9-10, 12, 100-4, 105, 106, 111
  excellence in 136
incentives 37-9, 57, 73-4, 137-8, 147-8, **148**
  selective 6, 38, 52
infrastructure 10
innovation 5, 94-122
  accidental 98, 100
  case study 120-1
  circumstances of 111-16
    diversity 113-14
    instability 115-16
    size of organization 111-13
  and coordination 95
  defined 94
  diagnosis of, in organizations 121-2
  elements of 101-11
    communication 103-4
    education 104-5
    leadership 109-11
    personnel practices 107-9
    rehearsal 105-6
    rules/procedures 101-3
  and entrepreneurship 96
  and excellence 125-6, 128
  and improvisation 100-1
  and motivation 95
  and niche-finding 95-6
  priorities/trade-offs 116-20
  and problem-solving 98-9
  strategies 103, 119-20, **119**, 147, **148**
instability 43-4, 79-82, 115-16, 129, 144-5, **146**
Ives, Charles 24

Jackson, Isiah 110
jam sessions 9-10
  see also improvisation
jazz 3, 45, 71, 73
  bebop 94
  combo, analysis of 117-20, **117, 119**, 145-8, **146, 148**
  coordination in 13-14, 15, 30, **30**, 31, **31**
  Dixieland 144-5

education in 72-3
fusion 77, 78
improvisation in *see* improvisation
leadership in 125
and musical scores 27-8
rehearsal in 136
see also big band orchestras
Jazz Messengers, The 125
Jewish Board of Family & Children's
    Services (JBFCS) 120-1
Johann Strauss Orchestra 72
Jones, Thad 76
Judy, Paul R. 55
Juilliard String Quartet 14

Kamoche, Ken N. 100
Kanter, Rosabeth M. 3
Kao, John 3, 100
Kaplan, Max 3
Kaufman, Herbert 32
Kaye, Danny 17
Kerres, Bernard H. 83
Kimmelman, Michael 80-1
Kingston Trio 72, 83, 102
Klemperer, Otto 129, 140
Koch, Ed 129
Kozinn, Allan 126
Kraus, Lucy 132
Kronos Quartet 49, 130

leadership 5, 10, 11, 16-20, 22-3, **31**, 36
    authoritarian 73-4, 110, 124
    case studies 32, 33, 152
    changes in 107
    evaluation/adjustment process for
        132-3, 138-9, 153
    and excellence 124-5, 148, **148**, 152-3
    and innovation 109-11, 122
    and motivation 40, 51-2, 53-5, 59, 60-
        1, **60**
    and niche-finding/maintaining 70, 74-
        6, 82, 84-5, 87-90, **87**
    roles of 25-7, 45, 139, 140
    shared 57, 62, 63, 148
learning organizations 94, 129
Lehman, Erin 74
Liebschutz, Sarah 73
London Symphony Orchestra 55, 74
Long Island Philharmonic Orchestra 43-
    4, 46-7

Los Angeles Philharmonic Orchestra 144
"lost chord" 98

Maazel, Lorin 132
McFerrin, Bobby 104
McKay, Bill 14
Mahler, Gustav 45, 110
Majeske, Daniel 52
management, challenges 4-5
managers, as musicians 3
markets 4-5, 9, 69, 75, 144-5
    see also niches
matrix analysis 6, 29-32, 57-61, 83-9,
    116-20, 145-8
Melville House project 61-2
metaphors, value of 3-4, 7, 34
military bands 117-20, **117**, **119**
Miller, Sarah Bryan 50-1
Mintzberg, Henry 3
Missa Solemnis (Beethoven) 143-4
Mitchell, Grover 28, 48
monitoring 6, 39, 40, 45, 52-3, 57, 129-
    30, 154
    lack of 59, 62
Monson, Charles C. 3
Morgan, Gareth 4
motivation 4, 5, 37-65, 68
    circumstances of 40-5
    diagnosis of, in organizations 63-5
    and excellence 125, 127
    and formality 45
    and innovation 95
    and instability 43-4
    and leadership 40, 45, 51-2, 53-5
    priorities/trade-offs 57-61
    and professionalism 41-3, 57, **58**
    and recruitment 45, 46-7
    and status/responsibility 49-52
    strategies 45-61, **60**
        case studies 61-3
        collaboration 56, 62
        competition 53, 56-7
    and task assignment 47-9, 53
    and task complexity 44-5, 57, **58**
Mount, Timothy 16, 18
music metaphor 1-4, 6, 7
    risk of overstretching 4
musical scores 11-12, 24, 70-1, 130-1
    adaptations of 97
    development of 12

interpretation of 19, 20, 131, 147
Musin, Ilya 19

natural task leaders 4
Nelson, Richard R. 98, 99, 101, 129
New York Philharmonic Orchestra 129, 138
niche-finding 5, 67-91
  case study 89-90
  circumstances of 75-82
  communicating 71-2
  diagnosis of, in organizations 90-1
  and excellence 125, 127-8
  incentives/rewards for 73-4
  and innovation 95-6
  and instability 79-82, 144-5
  planning for 70-1
  priorities/trade-offs in 83-9
  rehearsing for 73
  role of leaders in 70, 74-5
  strategies 75, 82-3
  training for 72-3
Nixon, Richard 93

Olson, Mancur 38, 39, 52
orchestras
  chamber **84**, 85, **87**, 88
  communication in 12-14, 71-2, 131-2
  community 125, 128
  competition within 49-51, 53, 56-7
  coordination in 10-11, **30**, 31, **31**, 34
  excellence in 145, 146, **146**, 147, **148**, 149-50
  funding for 67-8
  heterogeneity in 41, 76-7
  hierarchies in 53-5
  high school 145-8, **146**, **148**
  homogenization of 70
  innovation in 97, 107-9
  instability in 80-2
  leadership in 16-20, 53-5, 75, 139, 140
  motivation in 39-40
  organization in 1-3
  pops 84, **84**, **87**, 88
  professionalism in 41-3, 78
  recruitment in 46-7, 76, 108
  rehearsals in 15-16, 20, 73, 105-6
  relationship with conductors 26-7
  repertoires of 69-71, 76-7, 80-1

sections 18, 47-9, 59-60, 132, 140-1
  sub-groups of 49-51
  self-governing 55
  see also Orpheus Chamber Orchestra
  stability/instability in 23, 43-4
  task assignment in 47-9, 53
  task complexity in 44-5, 78-9
  see also individual orchestras
organization studies 2
organizational effectiveness 124
organizational identity 126-7
organizational learning 94, 129
organizational teams 11
organizations
  competition within 49-51, 53, 57
  coordination strategies of 24-6, 29-32
  see also coordination
  diagnosis of 34-6, 63-5, 90-1, 153-5
  diversity within 5
  heterogeneity in *see* heterogeneity
  improvisation in 3
  individuals within 38-9
  see also personnel
  instability in 79-82, 115-16
  interdepartmental mobility in 108-9
  internal diversity of 76-7
  leadership issues 26-7, 55, 107-8
  learning 94, 129
  and music, literature on 2-3
  personnel in *see* personnel
  range of structures in 2
  "single-celled" 3
  size 6, 21, 40-1, 57, **58**, 62, 76, 81, 139-40
  success in *see* excellence
  task assignment in 49, 53
  task complexity in 23-4
Orleans, James 112
Ormandy, Eugene 53, 75
ornamentation 101-2
Orpheus Chamber Orchestra 17-18, 19, 23, 25-6, 127
  communication within 72, 133
  hierarchy within 51
  responsibility within 54, 55, 72
Ory, Kid 97
Owens, Thomas 76, 94, 100-1, 113-14, 125, 136
Oxford Companion to Music 18-19

Ozawa, Seiji 133

Page, Tim 18, 21, 44, 109, 123, 125,
    127, 130, 132, 134-5, 137, 140, 141,
    144, 145
Palmer, Robert 15, 103
Pareles, Jon 114, 135-6
Pasmore, Bill 72-3
Peplowski, Ken 12, 102
performance
    monitoring 6, 39, 40, 45, 52-3, 57, 59,
        60-1, **60**, 129-30, 154
    pay related to 38, 39
personnel
    amateur *see* amateurs
    changes in 14, 23, 107-9, 116
    competition amongst 49-51, 53, 56-7
    and innovation 107-9
    loyalty/comradery in 32-3
    motivation of *see* motivation
    pride amongst 60, **60**, 61
    professionalism in *see*
        professionalism
    recruitment of *see* recruitment
    under-performers 38, 40-1, 51, 52,
        139
Peter, Paul & Mary 72, 83, 102
Peters, Thomas J. 129
Philadelphia Orchestra 75
planning 6, 22, 29, 36, 68, 147, **148**
    degree of formality in 45
    as element of ensemble 11-12, 20
    evaluation/adjustment process for
        130-1, 151-2
    and niche-finding 70-1
    role of 27-8
Pollini, Maurizio 53
pop music 75, 83, 95-6, 144
Powers, Ann 13
Pratt, John W. 41, 47
Previn, Andre 144
principal-agent theory 38-9
problem-solving 98-9, 129
product differentiation 82
professionalism 22-3, 41-3, 78, 84, 114-
    15, 141-3
    and excellence 141-3, 146, **146**, 148

quality management 129

Ratliff, Ben 115
recruitment 45, 46-7, 57, 59, **60**, 61, 62-3
rehearsals 15-16, 20, 24, 25-6, 28, **31**,
    36, **148**
    evaluation/adjustment process for 135
    and innovation 105-6
    and niche-finding 73
Reich, Steve 69, 134-5
repertoires 69-71, 73-4, 80-1, 85, 87,
    106, 112
    and excellence 124
research & development (R&D) 19, 100,
    112
resources 67-9
    coordination of 4, 9
reward *see* incentives
Roach, Max 94
Robert Shaw Chorale 16
rock groups 46, 84-5, **84**, **87**, 145-6, **146**,
    148, **148**
rock and roll 75, 81, 95, 144
Rockwell, John 133, 139
Romulo Larrea Tango Ensemble 77
Ronald, Sir Landon 16-17
Rosenberg, Donald 11, 20, 22, 102, 140,
    149-50

Sachs, Harvey 44-5
St. Lous Symphony Orchestra 132
St. Petersburg String Quartet 128
sales 68
    see also markets
Salisbury, Wilma 16, 42, 101, 104
Salvation Army 62-3
Sayles, L.R. 3
Schickele, Peter 125-6, 127
Schiff, David 47
Schonberg, Harold C. 17
Schumpeter, Joseph 96, 110, 115
Schwarz, Robert 71
selective incentives 6, 38, 52
serendipity 98, 100
services 68
Shaw, Robert 22
Simien, Terrance 96-7
"single-celled" organizations 3
Slatkin, Leonard 107, 132, 135
soloists 38, 49-50, 53, 56, 148
Sorrell, Jeanette 74-5
Sowd, David 143

Spich, Robert S. 112-13
spontaneity *see* improvisation
Stearns, David Patrick 98
Steinberg, Michael 69, 78-9
strategy formation 5
string quartets 14, 30, **30**, 77, 128
  conflict in 21
  stability in 23
  task assignment in 49
  see also individual groups
Stringer, Mark 137
Sylvester, Robert M. 112-13
symphony metaphor 6
systems theory 129
Szell, George 52, 54, 75, 129, 133

Tanahill Weavers, The 128
task assignment 47-9, 53, 108
task complexity 23-4, 44-5, 57, **58**, 78-9,
  84, 143-4, **146**
tempo 19
think tanks 112
Thompson, Virgil 69
Tilson Thomas, Michael 47, 134
Tommasini, Anthony 131
Toscanini, Arturo 132
Tovey, Donald 97-8, 100, 101
training/education 5, 24, 29, 31-2, **31**,
  36, 138
  as element of ensemble 11, 14-15, 20
  evaluation/adjustment process for
    135-6
  and excellence 145-6, 148, **148**
  and innovation 104-5, 117
  and motivation 55, 57, 63

and niche-finding 72-3
transactions cost theory 9
Traub, James 18, 19, 25-6, 51
trios 42
tubafests 41, 58, **58**, 59-60, **60**

uncertainty 10
under-performers 38, 40-1, 51, 52, 139
US Forest Service study 32-3

Vienna Philharmonic Orchestra 55
volunteers *see* amateurs

Walker, Rob 33
Waterman, Robert H. 129
Weaver, Harry 152-3
Weavers, The 72, 83, 102
Weick, Karl E. 3, 100, 105
Weisbrod, Burton 69
Welk, Lawrence 145
Wernick, Pete 14
Whetten, David A. 127
Williamson, Oliver 10
Winter, Paul 13, 129
Winter, Sidney G. 98, 99, 101
World Saxophone Quartet 136

Young, Vivienne 4, 21

Zeckhauser, Richard J. 41, 46
Zwilich, Ellen Taffe 109